UNIVERSITY OF WESTMINSTER

HUMAN-COMPUTER INTERACTION SERIES

VOLUME 3

Funology

From Usability to Enjoyment

Edited by

Mark A. Blythe
Department of Psychology,
University of York, UK

Kees Overbeeke
Industrial Design,
Eindhoven University of Technology
Eindhoven, The Netherlands

Andrew F. Monk
Department of Psychology,
University of York, UK

and

Peter C. Wright
Department of Computer Science,
University of York, UK

KLUWER ACADEMIC PUBLISHERS

DORDRECHT / BOSTON / LONDON

A C.I.P. Catalogue record for this book is available from the Library of Congress

ISBN 1-4020-2966-7 (PB)
ISBN 1-4020-1252-7 (HB)
ISBN 1-4020-2967-5 (e-book)

Published by Kluwer Academic Publishers,
P.O. Box 17, 3300 AA Dordrecht, The Netherlands.

Sold and distributed in North, Central and South America
by Kluwer Academic Publishers,
101 Philip Drive, Norwell, MA 02061, U.S.A.

In all other countries, sold and distributed
by Kluwer Academic Publishers,
P.O. Box 322, 3300 AH Dordrecht, The Netherlands.

Printed on acid-free paper

Printed in the Netherlands.

Contents

PREFACE - HOW TO USE THIS BOOK

Mark:	Ah, someone is reading our book.
Andrew:	So they are, quick, say something interesting!
Mark:	What?
Andrew:	Tell them what a great book this is! We need to get their attention and keep them reading! Quick!
Mark:	Oh … uhm, I can't think of anything to say now. Can't Pete do it; he'd put it much better than I could.
Peter:	What's going on?
Andrew:	We've got a reader and we're introducing the Funology book.
Mark:	Snappy title! I thought of that.
Andrew:	That's as may be, but it doesn't really say what it's about does it?
Peter:	Well, the book is about the move in Human Computer Interaction studies from standard usability concerns towards a wider set of problems to do with fun, enjoyment, aesthetics and the experience of use. Traditionally HCI has been concerned with work and task based applications but as digital technologies proliferate in the home -
Andrew:	Gah! Shut up! That sounds really dull! This book is supposed to be about enjoyment! Can't you say something that makes it sound like fun? Where's Kees?
Kees:	I'm just relaxing over here. It's very hard work editing a book you know. Andrew, you need to take things easier.
Andrew:	But the reader –
Kees:	Yes, yes, but the reader can see from the contents page that we have an interesting collection here. For a long time now people in the field have been talking about expanding the concept of usability, even people like Jakob Nielsen -
Andrew:	He's in the book!
Kees:	Yeah, sure the web guru is here, and even Nielsen, who has been associated with a "no frills" straight usability approach, has been thinking about *engaging* the user.
Peter:	The community has been asking questions about enjoyment for some time and we're now at the stage where we have a critical mass of work providing answers. We've seen quite a lot of ideas in this area coming through at the Computers and Fun workshops at York over the last four years –
Andrew:	My idea, those, you know.
Peter:	And then the Funology workshop at CHI last year which this collection is based on.
Kees:	Yeah, I think the collection maps the field pretty well… but it isn't fun.
Andrew:	Gah!

Mark:	Well no-one expects an analysis of humour to make them laugh do they? We should be telling them "how to use the book" and skip the boring bits.
Andrew	There aren't any boring bits! Each sentence is a glittering jewel!
Mark:	Well that's as may be, but nobody has to read all of it, that's why it's in sections.
Andrew:	Three very *exciting* sections! The first is ***theories and concepts***. HCI has always been a magpie discipline and here we have a range of positions borrowed from a number of fields: anthropology, sociology, psychology, literary and cultural studies.
Peter:	This section will be of most interest to people who want answers to questions like, what's wrong with standard usability approaches, what is "user experience", what do we mean by enjoyment, play, fun and is it possible to design user experience at all? This kind of theoretical -
Kees:	Bullsh-
Andrew:	Challenging and stimulating discussion! With each chapter more interesting than the last will appeal to -
Kees:	People with too much time on their hands? No, I'm kidding. It will appeal to … uhm …
Mark:	People with an interest in understanding the psychological, social and philosophical problems inherent in the study of enjoyment and the design of enjoyable experiences…. Did that sound alright? I think I might go and lie down now.
Peter:	And then more practically we have the ***methods and techniques*** section.
Kees:	Yeah, not so many of those though.
Peter:	No there aren't and I think this might reflect the field. As a relatively new area of interest there aren't that many HCI techniques for looking at enjoyment that have proven to be useful. So this section begins with adaptations of fairly standard usability approaches and moves towards more innovative methods.
Andrew:	And then in the final section we have a series of case studies -
Kees:	A collection of neat ideas.
Andrew:	Oh, it's much more than that! Each of the ***case studies*** reflects on the problems raised in the previous two sections and tells the story of how the theoretical problems were addressed in practice, what methods were used, what they produc-
Kees:	Yeah, it's a collection of neat ideas. If you are a designer and you want to be inspired – go there straight away.
Mark:	Well I think that's the preface taken care of don't you?
Peter:	Yeah, what's next?
Kees:	Lunch?
Mark:	No it's the foreword isn't it?
Andrew	Yes! The famous Patrick Jordan is up next. That should be *very* interesting indeed!
Mark:	And then it's the introduction.
Kees:	What's the difference between a foreword, a preface and an introduction?

Peter   The introduction is longer. It talks to the ontological problems that the
           publisher wanted us to address doesn't it?
Andrew   Bastards.
Mark: What?
Andrew   Publishers. Bastards. "You do all the copy editing, proof reading and
           work, and we'll take any and all of the money made. Oh and by the way
           can you address the "ontological" problems too". Bastards.
Kees: Well this was fun, let's do it again some time.
Andrew: Are you taking the piss?
Peter: How's that reader doing? Are they looking engaged?
Mark: I'm not sure, it's difficult to see from here.

DESIGNING GREAT STUFF THAT PEOPLE LOVE

FOREWORD BY PATRICK W. JORDAN

For a product or service offer to be really compelling it has to engage with the people for whom it is designed at three different levels. In the first instance it has to be able to perform the task for which it was designed. A car has to be able to get you from A to B, a TV has to show TV shows, you have to be able to make a call using a telephone. The product's functionality should work well and it should be easy to use. The second level is to do with the emotions associated with the product or service. These should be appropriate in the context of the associated tasks. For example, if you are using an electronic banking system, then feelings of trust and security might be appropriate, whereas using a stereo should be fun and exciting, driving a sports car should be exciting too, but there should also be a feeling of safety and security.

The third level reflects the aspirational qualities associated with the product or service. What does owning the product or using the service say about you? If you own the latest, smallest mobile phone, then you must be a pretty cool person. If you own a Bang and Olufsen stereo, then you've got really refined taste. If you buy your groceries over the internet, then you're up to date, with it, and an all round smart person. Well, at least these are some of the stereotypes! The point is that our consumer choices say something about us to others and to ourselves. It is important that the customer feels his or her choices are 'lifestyle affirming'. In other words owning the product or using the service should make people feel the way they want to feel about themselves, not embarrass them or make them feel lousy in some other way.

Traditionally, when human-factors and human-computer interaction (HF/HCI) approaches have been used to evaluate the fit between people and products or services, it is the first of these levels that is emphasized. The suggestion is that provided the product or service helps a person to achieve what they want to do and that this can be done comfortably within their physical and cognitive capabilities then the product or service can be said to 'fit' the person.

These kinds of approaches tend to see the person as a 'user' and the product or service as a 'tool' - the idea being that the user uses the tool to complete a task. Another metaphor that is often used is that of a system comprising user, tool and task. Here the user tends to be characterized as a physical and cognitive component of a system. If the 'tool' facilitates the 'task' without exceeding the capabilities of the 'component' then, again, the product or service is declared to be 'usable' and to be a good fit to the user.

While these usability-based approaches certainly tackle some very important issues, they tend to take a view of people that is somewhat limited - perhaps even dehumanising. The problem is that they tend to ignore or de-emphasize wider aspects of our humanness. What about our hopes, our fears, our dreams, our feelings, our self-image, the way that we want others to see us? All these things that are associated with the emotional and aspirational levels of a person's experience with a product or service.

More recent HF/HCI approaches have started to take these factors into account. These approaches - variously known as 'pleasure-based', 'affective' or simply 'new' human factors approaches - look at the user holistically. In addition to fitting the design of a product or service to the cognitive and physical characteristics of the person using it, they also look at how the design fits with the person's values, tastes and image. The emphasis here is to look at the relationship between the product and person in all its facets. Certainly, the issue of completing tasks with the product or service may be important - depending on what the product/service is - however there are many other aspects of the design which will influence how enjoyable it is to interact with.

This book makes a very important contribution to this emerging area. The list of contributors includes many of the world's leading HF/HCI practitioners and the contributions cover a range of important issues core to both the theory and practice of creating pleasurable designs.

The chapters contained in this book offer inspiration and guidance as we work to design better and more enjoyable products and services. The authors look at those whom we design for as human-beings rather than just 'users'. This work can help us to create products and services, which promise an enhanced quality of life and a better society for us all.

I wish the book every success.

Pat W. Jordan
Pittsburgh 12-13-02

FROM USABILITY TO ENJOYMENT

INTRODUCTION BY MARK BLYTHE
AND PETER WRIGHT

All I want to do is have a little fun before I die
Says this man next to me out of nowhere
It's apropos of nothing
All I Wanna Do: Sheryl Crow.

This book is about enjoyment and Human Computer Interaction (HCI). This may seem like a relatively straightforward topic but humans enjoy so many things that it very quickly becomes tangled and messy. Are we talking about entertainment and play? There's a clear link to technology but games aren't the only applications we enjoy. What about work? People can enjoy that too and a good interface can make a task more enjoyable, but isn't that just usability? Are we talking about cute interfaces or that awful winking paperclip in windows? Is this all about aesthetics? It's possible to enjoy a beautiful web page so long as it doesn't take half an hour to download. Or are we talking about pornography, isn't this the main way an awful lot of people enjoy interacting with their computers?

And what is enjoyment anyway? Is it an experience, is it an emotion, a sensation, a perception, is it a state of mind, is it a state of being? There is an ontological problem inherent in addressing enjoyment and its associated terms. These terms can be organised fairly simplistically by degrees of intensity: satisfaction, gratification, pleasure, joy, euphoria and so on. The settings in which these states commonly occur can also be organised: work and play, games and entertainment, and so on. But this does not answer the question – to what do these states refer - sensations, emotions, perceptions?

These ontological questions are thousands of years old and many literatures address them. This introduction will provide a very broad sketch of some of the areas of literature relevant to these questions, briefly outline previous work in HCI relevant to the project of extending the concept of usability and finally indicate the differing approaches taken by some of the contributing authors in this book.

Ontological Problems and Relevant Literatures

Almost every philosopher who ever philosophised has speculated on how and why we enjoy, or take pleasure, in certain things. For Plato pleasure was the absence of pain; in the *Phaedo* a chain is removed from Socrates' ankle and he remarks on the pleasure of relief. For Aristotle, pleasure was caused by the stimulation of the senses through action, in the *Nicomachean Ethics* he is able to explain pleasures that involve no absence of pain such as novelty: when something is new the mind is active and stimulated, the next time it is encountered the mind is less aroused so there is less pleasure in the novelty. In the Confessions of St Augustine pleasures are largely "unlawful" or "awful" unless they are pleasures in the contemplation of God. Historians of Philosophy argue that Aristotelian and Christian views of pleasure set the parameters of thought on the subject up until the time of Descartes (Honderich, 1995). The Cartesian distinction between self and world, observer and observed paved the way for the measurement of pleasure and Enlightenment philosophers argued that it was possible to do just that. Jeremy Bentham claimed that pleasures could be judged by intensity and duration and that these could be meaningfully represented on a scale and so measured in a "hedonic calculus" (Honderich, 1995). However, Wittgenstein (1953) argued that when we measure some behavioural correlate of enjoyment, we are not getting at the thing itself - the experience; meaning cannot be measured it has to be grasped. Freud famously argued for the existence of a pleasure principle (and later a death principle) as a motivating force for human action that could not necessarily be known by the conscious mind. Questions on pleasure and enjoyment, then, have a long history. Western philosophy offers no coherent approach and nor should we expect it to. Nevertheless it is possible for these literatures to inspire work in HCI; although the current technological challenges are new the fundamental ontological questions are very old indeed.

Physical and social scientists have also created a large body of work that relates to enjoyment. Neurologists have discovered "pleasure centres" in the septal region of the brain which when electrically stimulated produced enjoyable feelings; when animals were wired up so that they could press a lever and administer this stimulation themselves they did so for hours ignoring food, sex and every other need. (Gregory, 1987). Pleasure then can be regarded as a physical response of the nervous system. But in the twentieth century the apparently simple question – what is an emotion - provoked vexed and contentions debates in psychology. The debate can be broadly characterised as between two schools: the physical and the cognitive. The physical model of emotion, first established by William James, held that "our feeling of (bodily) changes as they occur IS the emotion" (cited: Gregory, 1987). The cognitive model suggested that emotion was a decision-making and evaluative process. During grief, for example, we make evaluative decision about the loss, its severity, its permanence and so on. Later, other positions emerged which combined the physical and cognitive aspects of emotion. John Dewey and others suggested that discrepancies between our expectations and the state of the world produce visceral events and that evaluations of these discrepancies dictate whether the emotion is positive or negative. On a roller coaster for example our expectations about the direction and speed at which we move are disrupted producing a visceral response, this is evaluated in terms of how safe we feel and we love or hate the ride accordingly (Gregory, 1987). Dewey took the strong position that experience and sense making are relational processes, which, when decomposed into their constituent parts, simply disappear (Dewey, 1934). Although chronological accounts of competing theories can suggest a seamless development of coherent thought, it should be noted that there is still considerable debate in these areas.

There are other large bodies of social and anthropological literature on enjoyment. The sociology of leisure is almost as large as the sociology of work. Play has been seen as one of the most important and fundamentally human of activities. Perhaps the best-known study on the subject of play is *Homo Ludens* by Johan Huizinga. In it he argues that play is not only a defining characteristic of the human being but that it is also at the root of all human culture. He claimed that play (in both representation and contest) is the basis of all myth and ritual and therefore behind all the great "forces of civilised life" law, commerce, art, literature, and science (Huizinga, 1950). Although Huizinga and others make clear the importance of play to the development of civilisation, until recently, little was known about how and why we do it. Piaget argued that the child at play "repeats his behaviour not in any further effort to learn or investigate but for the mere joy of mastering it" (cited, Gross, 1996: 639). He divided play into three stages: mastery play (practice play involving repetitive behaviour) symbolic play (fantasy and role playing) and play with rules (structured games). Mastery and skill development form a point of connection to the work of Csikszentmihalyi who offers one of the few theories of intense or peak experiences in his account of "flow". After studying diverse groups engaged in self motivating activities like rock climbing Csikszentmihalyi identified the euphoric feeling of "flow" as a common characteristic of their experiences (Csikszentmihalyi, 1975). He was also able to identify the conditions necessary for this feeling to occur. Such models of experience suggest a great many implications for the design of enjoyable products and this work has been drawn on by several of the authors in this book.

There is a further body of literature relevant to the study of enjoyment to be found in the Arts and Humanities. Perhaps the most famous literary movement to focus on pleasure was that of the aesthetes in the late nineteenth century. The protagonist of Huysman's novel *A Rebours* pursues pleasure so exhaustively that he devotes weeks of study and an entire chapter of description to the subtle differences between scents as he attempts to create a new perfume. The development of enjoyable or pleasurable products and applications can form curious bedfellows. Computer Science departments and industrial developers alike are beginning to employ artists to work with programmers. The Surrealist and Situationist art movements of the nineteen sixties have been drawn on by HCI researchers. The work of literary and art critics is also proving, perhaps surprisingly, useful. Concepts such as dialogism drawn from the work of the Russian literary critic Bakhtin have been used to reason about on line shopping, Dewey's theories of aesthetics and the co-construction of meaning between the artist, contemplator and art object, have been adapted to consider the enchantments of such technologies as mobile phones. Insights have also been drawn from film criticism and other branches of cultural studies. There is, perhaps, a degree of similarity between HCI and literary and cultural criticism. The HCI specialist is not necessarily a programmer just as the critic is not necessarily a writer. HCI can be seen as a specialised form of reading, where an application or programme is the object of study rather than a static text. literary and cultural studies are, perhaps more than any other discipline, concerned with enjoyment and pleasures of a very profound kind; it may be for this reason that a number of the authors in this collection draw on these traditions.

The limits of Traditional Conceptions of Usability

In many respects then, the field of Human Computer Interaction is a late-comer to the study of enjoyment. Traditionally, HCI has been concerned with work and work systems, however enjoyment has become a major issue as information and communication technology have moved out of the office and into the living room. Understandings of user concerns derived from studies of the world of work are simply not adequate to the new design challenges. At work we are paid to interact with computers, in the home our motivations are different. Some domestic activities are task based and look very much like work, for example, cleaning and shopping. Clearly efficiency and effectiveness are equally important in the design of technologies to support, on-line shopping for instance, but even here these are not the only important considerations. It is increasingly acknowledged that work tasks are performed better if they are enjoyable. The distinctions between "work" and leisure" and "tool" and "toy" have been challenged by new approaches to design. Further, many activities in the home are not task related at all: they are leisure activities. Where is the task in listening to a piece of music or looking at a family photo album? Of course the activation and control of media can be thought of as tasks and it is even possible to argue that the task in a leisure activity is to relax; but an entirely task based focus is clearly inappropriate.

It is argued throughout this book that traditional usability approaches are too limited and must be extended to encompass enjoyment. Of course HCI has always been concerned with satisfaction. Indeed "usability" is defined as "the effectiveness, efficiency and satisfaction with which a product is used "(ISO 9241-11). But satisfaction is a relatively narrow term; it is an aspect of the question - does this work? In practice the satisfaction element of usability testing often amounts to investigating whether the product frustrates users or not. It is primarily concerned with the prevention of pain. Since the time of Aristotle this has been a limited view of pleasure. If we are attempting to design enjoyable applications there are further questions to be asked.

There have been many attempts in HCI to put enjoyment into focus (Monk et al, 2002). In the early nineteen eighties Malone published a heuristics for designing *enjoyable* user interfaces (Malone, 1984). Four years later Carroll and Thomas (1988) proposed game-like, metaphoric cover stories for standard process control jobs as a possible means of addressing boredom and vigilance problems inherent in routine tasks. In the early nineteen nineties Brenda Laurel's (1993) *Computers as Theatre* argued that engagement in computer mediated activity is as much about emotional and aesthetic relations as it is about rational and intellectual ones. It is worth noting that this book offered an important warning, Laurel argued that software cannot be made enjoyable with the introduction of gratuitous game-like features. If a student must solve a maths problem before they can play a game in a piece of educational software then either the game or the maths problem is superfluous: both most be shaped in a "causally related way" (Laurel, 1993: 74). Two years after Laurel's seminal work, Sherry Turkle explored the social meaning of computers, the culture of computing and its impact on our sense of self in the age of the Internet. Toward the end of the nineties Donald Norman challenged designers to follow three axioms: simplicity, versatility and pleasurability (Norman, 1998). A year later Patrick Jordan's ground breaking book *Designing Pleasurable Products* explored theoretical models of pleasure drawn from anthropology to make concrete recommendations to product designers in terms of aesthetics and ergonomics. Recently applications have emerged which attempt to make even serious work based activities more enjoyable. Dennis Chao's PSDoom, for example, is a Unix process manager that adapts the popular first person shoot 'em up DOOM as the user interface (Chao, 2001) and a good example of Laurel's causally related enjoyment.

The move from theories and concepts to design is never an easy one whether as a research activity or as a practical application. Bannon (1997) talks of HCI as dwelling in the "great divide" between the social and the technical sciences. This volume is concerned with theories of experience and enjoyment which originate not only from social sciences but also from the arts and humanities and in some senses we have created for ourselves an even larger, albeit more colourful divide. One of the concerns of many of the 'human scientists' (psychologists, sociologists etc.) who dwell in the great divide has been to develop theories and methods that make the 'important things' of human activity visible and to find ways of 'translating' such information into a form that is usable by designers. It is significant that HCI began as a partnership between computer scientists and cognitive psychologists; one of the main attractions of cognitive psychology was precisely its underlying metaphor of the human as an information processor. This greatly reduces the translation problem since at least in principle, both user and system are modelled in the same framework of concepts. The problem however, is the limitations on what such a theory of human activity makes visible. In this volume, several authors allude to the limitations of cognitive science when it comes to dealing with the affective, and many of the chapters represent attempts to understand what needs to be made visible and how we ought to theorise experience.

The Breadth of Approaches

Given the ontological uncertainties outlined above, this book provides an overview of where the HCI community, or a part of it, is in terms of theories and concepts, methods and techniques and case studies. The contributions in the theories and concepts section draw on a very wide literature: computer science, psychology, sociology, philosophy, history, literary and cultural studies. The methods and techniques section begins with adaptations of traditional usability approaches to satisfaction and moves on to more innovative methods. The case studies presented in the final section were chosen to provoke and inspire researchers, designers and product developers. Each section is preceded by a brief introduction which summaries the contributions and provides a road map to the section.

The "absence of pain" model of enjoyment can be thought of as a standard usability approach to pleasure; if an application does not frustrate the user then it is more likely that using it will be enjoyable. Contributions in this book from Pagulayan, Nielsen and also Karat and Karat show how standard usability tests can be adapted to focus on enjoyment. Psychological accounts of pleasure inform contributions by Brantdzaeg et al, Desmet and Hassenzahl. An emphasis on the physical rather than purely cognitive aspects of enjoyment can be found in chapters by Overbeeke et al, Hummels et al and Wensveen et al. Anthropological and social approaches to questions of enjoyment inform chapters by Sengers, Reed, and Blythe and Hassenzahl. The intricacies of social practices are analysed and deconstructed in chapters by Dix, Sykes, Rizzo and Falk in order to generate design implications for technological developments. The influence of art can be seen clearly in the chapter by Hull and Reid, which reflects on a collaborative project with artists, Anderson et al, in the use of techniques inspired by the surrealist movement to develop research methods and by Holmquist et al in the influence of the artist Mondrian on a particular application. Work drawing on literary and film studies can be found in the chapters by Wright and McCarthy on understanding user experience and also in Braun in the development of an interactive story engine. A concern with making serious or work-based activities more enjoyable can be found in many of the contributions and particularly in Hohl et al and Rosson and Carrol.

To return to the questions at the beginning of this introduction - are we talking about work, play, games, entertainment and aesthetics, or what? The answer is yes to all of the above, including the - or what. The subject of pornography however will have to wait for another book.

We have not, as editors, attempted to impose a particular theoretical perspective or engineer the appearance of a coherent approach amongst the authors. In fact many of the authors have radically different approaches, where one attempts to measure another tries to grasp. We believe that this breadth of approaches and subjects reflects the development of a relatively young discipline in a dynamic field of enquiry.

References

Aristotle. (2002). *Nicomachean Ethics* (Christopher Rowe, Trans.): Oxford University Press.

Augustine, S. (1960). *The Confessions of St Augustine*. (Sheed F H ed.). London & New York: Sheed & Ward.

Bannon, L. J. (1997). Dwelling in the great divide: The case of HCI and CSCW. In G. C. Bowker, Star, S.L., Turner, W. and Gasser, L (Ed.), *Social science, technical systems and cooperative work* : Lawrence Earlbaum Associates.

Caroll, J.M., & Thomas, J.C. (1988). Fun. *SIGCHI Bulletin, 19*, 21-24.

Chao, D. (2001). *Doom as an Interface for Process Management*. Paper presented at the CHI.

Csikszentmihalyi , M (1975). *Beyond Boredom and Anxiety: The Experience of Work and Play in Games*. San Fancisco: Jossey Bass Publishers.

Gregory, R. (Ed.). (1987). *The Oxford Companion to the Mind*. Oxford and New York. Oxford University Press.

Gross, R.D., (1996). *Psychology: The Science of Mind and Behaviour*. Third Edition. London. Hodder & Stoughton.

Honderich, T. (1995). The Oxford Companion to Philosophy. Oxford and New York. Oxford University Press.

Huizinga, J. (1950). *Homo Ludens: a study of the play element in culture*. Boston: The Beacon Press.

Huysmans, J. (1998). *A Rebours (Against Nature)* (Margaret Mauldon, Trans.).

Jordan, P. (2000). *Designing Pleasurable Products: An Introduction to the New Human Factors*: Taylor and Francis.

Laurel, B. (1993). *Computer as Theatre*. Reading, MA: Addison-Wesley.

Malone, T. W. (1984). Heuristics for designing enjoyable user interfaces: Lessons from computer games. In J. C. Thomas & M. L. Schneider (Eds.), *Human Factors in Computer Systems* (pp. 1-12). Norwood, NJ: Ablex.

Norman, D. A. (1998). *The invisible computer*. Cambridge MA: MIT Press.

Monk, A. F., Hassenzahl, M., Blythe, M., & Reed, D. (2002). *Funology: designing enjoyment*. CHI2002, *Changing the World, Changing Ourselves*. Extended Abstracts. pp 924-5.

Plato. (1993). *Phaedo* (C.J. Rowe, Trans.): Cambridge University Press.

Turkle, S. (1995). *Life on the Screen: Identity in the Age of the Internet*. London: Phoenix.

Wittgenstein, L. (1953). *Philosophical investigations*. Oxford: Blackwell.

SECTION ONE: THEORIES AND CONCEPTS

The introduction to this book questions the limited scope of traditional conceptions of usability. Conventionally, designers are mainly concerned with concepts such as ease-of-learning, low-level ease-of-use and task fit. This has arisen because HCI has been primarily concerned with developing methods and concepts for the design of products to support work. Now that the designers of information and communication technology are turning their attention to the home new concerns come to the fore. Aesthetic attractiveness and enjoyment have their place in the design of products for work but are not of primary importance. In the home, where people are not paid to use the technology, they suddenly become critical. But, as the introduction to this book also suggests, there is no well thought out theory of enjoyment. This first section of the book is to suggest some ways in which the concept of enjoyment may be developed in a way that facilitates the design of enjoyable products.

It is instructive to examine how early concepts in HCI, such as ease of learning were developed. HCI is a great borrower of ideas. It started as a collaboration between psychologists and computer scientists. Concepts and methodologies were borrowed from these disciplines and woven into theories and design methods. For example, psychologists contributed ways of measuring ease-of-learning. Computer scientists contributed abstract system properties such as "mode" and "reversibility" that govern ease-of-learning. In the process the concepts borrowed were subtly changed, to the point they are no longer be recognised by the parent discipline. Thus a psychologist would be very critical of the procedures commonly used to assess usability and many computer scientists would consider that these abstractions lack mathematical formality. They have however lead to the design of better, that is more usable, systems.

HCI continues to borrow from: ergonomics, human factors, sociology and anthropology. Further, as we shall see in the chapters in this section, the need identified above to develop the concept of enjoyment suggests a whole new range of borrowings. The first two chapters examine the problem of designing products that facilitate an enjoyable user experience and take from a classic design perspective. In **Let's Make Things Engaging** *Kees Overbeeke* calls for a less overtly cognitive approach to design. He argues that for a design to be engaging and hence enjoyable it should be physical showing us "the works" and providing clear affordances for action. The point is illustrated by a number of novel designs for digital artefacts with very physical forms and through some putative design principles. In **The Engineering of Experience** *Phoebe Sengers* goes further and questions whether the analytic approach inherent in engineering can be applied to the design of enjoyable products at all. She calls for a holistic approach to design. She rejects the task-based approach to design that can be traced back to Taylor and the deskilling of work and proposes instead a more culturally inspired multidisciplinary approach. She also presents examples of products that fulfil the characteristics she is calling for. By

Mark A. Blythe, Andrew F. Monk, Kees Overbeeke and Peter C. Wright *(eds.)*,
Funology: From Usability to Enjoyment, 3—5.

describing the process by which they were created she illustrates the interdisciplinary process she believes is necessary.

These two chapters by Overbeeke and Sengers with their emphasis on concrete examples of design and the process by which they were created could almost be thought of as being anti-theoretical but really they are not. They set a clear agenda for the remaining chapters in this section by illustrating how the problem of designing for enjoyment is radically different from the problem of designing for ease-of-use or task fit. The remaining chapters in this section present different frameworks for thinking about the design of user experience and enjoyment borrowed from a variety of sources.

In **The Thing and I: Understanding the Relationship between User and Product** *Marc Hassenzahl* makes a basic distinction between pragmatic and hedonic attributes of products. His framework is based around a model of user experience. Design features, including content and presentation, lead the user to perceive the product as having a certain character leading in turn to consequences such as appeal. In this way he is able to characterise the relationship between task oriented pragmatic concerns and the hedonic concern of enjoyment. In **Making Sense of Experience** *Peter Wright, John McCarthy and Lisa Meekison* develop a parallel framework. This can be seen as an extension of Sengers' manifesto for a holistic interdisciplinary approach. Four relational elements of experience are identified: emotional, sensual, compositional and spatio-temporal. The process by which a user experience arises is described in terms of sense making through the activities of anticipation, interpretation, reflection, assimilation and recounting.

In their chapters Hassenzahl, also Wright and McCarthy, have ambitious goals. They seek to provide an overarching framework for thinking about user experience as a whole. The next three chapters are more modest in their aims. In **Making it Fun: Lessons from Karasek** *Petter Brandtzæg, Asbjørn Følstad and Jan Heim* draw parallels between Karasek's model of what makes work a rewarding experience (e.g. varied demands and decision latitude) to the design of technology for fun. In **Having Fun on the Phone: the Situated Experience of Recreational Telephone Conferences** *Darren Reed* points out that enjoyment is often a social experience and as such can be described from the point of view of the group rather than the individual. He draws on Goffman and Bateson's idea about play and illustrates the approach by describing the roles for laughter in a conversational analysis. In **The Enchantments of Technology** *John McCarthy and Peter Wright* draw on Boorstin's account of how film enchants the viewer.

Finally, the chapter **The Semantics of Fun** *Mark Blythe and Marc Hassenzahl* examine the semantics of the word "fun" and other words such as "pleasure" and "enjoyment". As in any new field there is as yet no agreed set of terms and this chapter considers problems of definition. They find that "fun" has certain connotations of distraction and frivolity that distinguishes it from other forms of enjoyment.

In these chapters we can begin to see how ideas from various disciplines may be adapted to our purpose of designing for enjoyment. Ideas have been identified from psychology (Csikzentmilhalyi), literary theory (Bakhtin), art history (Dewey), sociology (Goffman), anthropology (Bateson), film (Boorstin) and work design

(Karasek). It will take time to adapt the original concepts into a coherent framework. The next step in this process is to refine the concepts by using them in practical guides for design. The second section of this book illustrates some attempts to do just that.

KEES OVERBEEKE, TOM DJAJADININGRAT, CAROLINE
HUMMELS, STEPHAN WENSVEEN AND JOEP FRENS

CHAPTER 1

LET'S MAKE THINGS ENGAGING

1. INTRODUCTION

Technology and electronics have given us many positive things. However, in recent years the appearance of and the way we interact with products have changed dramatically resulting in a less engaging relationship with products (Hummels, 2000). She makes the point that machinery withdrew to the background and control by means of buttons and icons became prevalent (Figure 1). The physicality of the machinery became an unnoticeable means to deliver the goods.

Figure 1. *Buttons and icons stand between the user and the machine's functionality.*

People all have senses and a body with which we can respond to what our environment affords (Gibson, 1986). Why, then, do human-product interaction designers not use these bodily skills more often and make electronic interaction more tangible (Figure 2)?

Mark A. Blythe, Andrew F. Monk, Kees Overbeeke and Peter C. Wright *(eds.),*
Funology: From Usability to Enjoyment, 7—17.
© 2003 *Kluwer Academic Publishers. Printed in the Netherlands.*

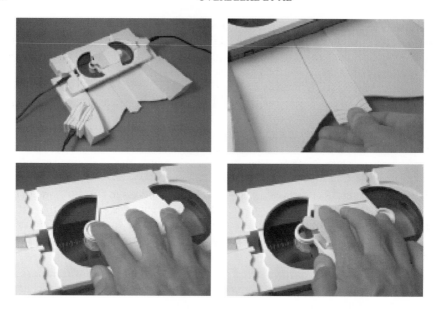

Figure 2. *The action of the user opens up the functionality. Starting top-left clockwise: the cassette remains visible whilst in the machine, pulling a ribbon triggers eject, and fast-forward/reverse becomes intuitively clear through a toggle placed between the tape reels.*

And, as humans are emotional beings, why not make interaction a more fun and beautiful experience? We believe that the physicality of the product should be reinstated, to restore engagement. Fun, as such is not the issue, engagement is. This contribution focuses on those neglected aspects of human-product interaction.

2.   WHAT IS WRONG?

Nowadays, too many products are designed by people not trained in product design.. The resulting products reflect their maker's training. Psychologists make products that are very "cognitive' (or instruct designers to do so). Software engineers design interfaces that resemble the logic of programming. Alan Cooper (1999) has made a convincing analysis of the latter phenomenon. As a solution, he proposes to get away from "technological artefacts whose interaction is expressed in terms in which they are constructed" (p. 27).

Furthermore, everybody claims to take man, not technology, as his starting point. The talk is all about user-centred design. But what does this mean? This faith is often professed but seldom applied. We think that user-centred design should be interpreted as design, which shows respect for people as a whole. For the sake of analysis, people's skills, which are used when interacting with products, may be considered on three levels: cognitive skills, perceptual-motor skills and emotional skills. In other words: knowing, doing and feeling; the wholly trinity of interaction

(Overbeeke et al, 2002). Until recently research on human-product interaction, however, has concentrated on cognitive skills. Products have become "intelligent", and intelligence has no form. Design research, quite naturally, turned to the intelligent part of humans and thus to the science of cognition to find answers. This has resulted in interface design placing a heavy burden on human intellect. For example, designers start grouping and colour-coding related functions, adding displays with an abundance of text and icons, and writing logically structured manuals. And many design methodologies also suffer from the "logical" disease. Emotions are narrowed down to fun and fun becomes a glued on quality. Products smile at you. I'm not dying to open a bottle of good white wine with a smiling corkscrew. When addressing emotions many designers take a Walt Disney approach and, by doing so, sidestep the real issue: addressing emotions in an adult way. In our opinion the design of electronic products has got stuck as a result of this rather cognitive approach, which neglects the user physically and emotionally. We think that an approach, which mainly addresses the rational and quantifiable human skills, simply does not cut it.

3. HOW DO WE SEE IT?

Users are not interested in products; they are in search of challenging experiences. Therefore the designer needs to create a context for experience, rather than just a product. He offers the user a context in which he may enjoy a film, a dinner, cleaning, playing, working, *with all his senses*. Current efforts on improving usability focus on making things easier. However, there is more to usability than ease of use. A user may choose to work with a product despite it being difficult to use, because it is challenging, seductive, playful, surprising, memorable or even moody, resulting in enjoyment of the experience. No musician learnt to play the violin because it was easy. Bringing together 'contexts for experience' and 'aesthetics of interaction' means that we do not strive for making a function as easy to access as possible, but for making the unlocking of the functionality contribute to the overall experience.

Usability is generally treated separately from aesthetics. Aesthetics in industrial design appears to be restricted to making products beautiful in appearance. As the ease of use strategies do not appear to pay off, this has left us in the curious situation that we have products, which look good at first sight, but frustrate us as soon as we start interacting with them. We think that the emphasis should shift from a beautiful appearance to beautiful interaction, to engaging interaction. And this should not be a glued on quality. Beauty in interaction is the core, the starting point of interaction design.

This calls for a re-think of product design from the ground up. Design should be given back to designers, as a part of a multi-disciplinary team. Products should elicit the user to engage with them through their physicality. Fun can result from engagement, but is not a goal as such. Design is not about the smile on the product, it is about the smile in the user's heart.

4.   HOW DO WE DO IT?

But what should designers do once design is given back to them? How can designers open up the products functionality while engaging the user in a beautiful way? The answer to this question is multi-layered and as yet incomplete. In several publications we touched upon parts of the answer. In the first part of this section we mention two, starting from the more general level of a context for experience to the level of design rules of thumb for augmenting fun and beauty. In the second section we give a few examples, as we believe actions speak louder than words.

4.1 Trying to answer the question

In her PhD thesis Hummels (2000) makes a strong case for engagement as a means to augment fun and beauty. She argues that the shift towards involvement during interaction means that the designer's emphasis should be placed on a beautiful, engaging interaction with a product. Consequently, the focus shifts towards the aesthetics of interaction. In general one could say that the aesthetics of interaction is the sense of beauty that arises during the interplay between a user and a product in their context. What creates this sense of beauty? Why do some products resonate with a user, while others do not? She believes that five aspects are essential to evoke this sense of beauty. She considers the following five aspects essential.

1.   Functional possibilities and performance of the product

A proper functioning product forms the basis of the aesthetics of interaction. A product that does not do what it is supposed to do, will never allow the user to get intimate and experience the beauty. Spiffy solutions that work well can smooth the way for intimate interactions.

2.   The user's desires, needs, interests and skills (perceptual-motor, cognitive and
       emotional)

A contextual design approach is based on the experience of the individual. A product may resonate with one person, whereas another person may be indifferent to it. The user's character, skills, needs (short-term and long-term), mood, etc. determine the value of the interaction for an individual.

3.   General context

Although a designer is not able to control the general context in which a person will use his product, this context can influence the experiences of the user when interacting with the product.

4.   Richness with respect to all the senses

Aesthetic interaction requires richness that covers all the senses. Not only does it refer to richness in visual aspects of the product, but the wealth and subtlety of auditory, olfactory, flavoury, tactile and kinaesthetic aspects during interaction, are at least as important to achieve a beautiful interaction and an engaging experience. This richness bears on feed-forward as well as feedback (see below). Moreover, designers need to exploit the range and diversity of design solutions to evoke or intensify the range of feelings (although they can never enforce a specific experience).

5.   Possibility to create one's own story and ritual

Each product tells a story about the user and the relationship between them as it evolves from the moment of purchase onwards (Djajadiningrat et al, 2002). Intimacy with a product can be enhanced when the product stimulates the user to create his story and rituals during usage. A product should be an open system, which is not an open book, rather a tempting means for exploration and interaction. Due to the advancing digital technology, intelligent products can even adapt to the user and actively help to create a never-ending story.

These are very general aspects: they do not tell the designer what exactly he has to do to realize them when designing. Therefore, a few years ago we published a pamphlet with 10 rules to augment fun and beauty in interaction design (Djajadiningrat, Overbeeke & Wensveen, 2000). These 10 rules do not constitute a guide to "good" design however, and we did not mean to provide one. A poster can be downloaded from

http://www.io.tudelft.nl/id-studiolab/djajadiningrat/publications.html

Here are the 10 rules:

1. Don't think products, think experiences.

The designer needs to offer the user a context in which he may enjoy a film, dinner, cleaning, playing, working with all his senses. We talk of creating a context for experience rather than just an experience, because we cannot impose a particular experience on a user, who is bound to explore the design in his manner. A design should offer the user the freedom for building his or her experiences.

2. Don't think beauty in appearance, think beauty in interaction.

Usability is generally treated separately from aesthetics. Aesthetics in product design appears to be restricted to making products beautiful in appearance. As the ease of use strategies do not appear to pay off, this has left us in the curious situation that we have products, which look good at first sight, but frustrate us as soon as we start interacting with them. We think that the emphasis should shift from a beautiful appearance to beautiful interaction, of which beautiful appearance is a part. Dunne (1999) too talks of 'aesthetics of use': an aesthetics which, through the interactivity made possible by computing, seeks a developing and more nuanced cooperation with the object - a cooperation which, it is hoped, might enhance social contact and everyday experience.

3. Don't think ease of use, think enjoyment of the experience.

Current efforts on improving usability focus on making things easier. However, there is more to usability than ease of use. A user may choose to work with a product despite it being difficult to use, because it is challenging, seductive, playful, surprising, memorable or rewarding, resulting in enjoyment of the experience. No musician learnt to play the violin because it was easy. Bringing together 'contexts for experience' and 'aesthetics of interaction' means that we do not strive for making a function as easy to access as possible, but for making the unlocking of the functionality contribute to the overall experience.

4. Don't think buttons, think rich actions.

The controls of the current generation of electronic products, whether physical or screen-based, require the same actions. By increasing the richness of actions, controls cannot only be perceptually differentiated, but also motorically. Here again the goal is not differentiation for differentiation's sake, but the design of actions, which are in accordance with the purpose of a control.

5. Don't think labels, think expressiveness and identity.

Not only do current electronic products themselves look highly similar, their controls, whether physical or screen-based, also are often hard to tell apart. This has made it necessary for controls to be labeled with explanatory texts and icons, which are either illegible or unintelligible, regardless of whether they are physical or screen-based. We think that instead designers should differentiate between controls to make them look, sound and feel different. More importantly though, this differentiation should not be arbitrary. The 'formgiving' should express what purpose a product or control serves. This would require a replacement for the current aesthetic with rows of identical controls which so heavily relies on repetition as a means to a achieve a unified and aesthetically pleasing whole, for which the expression of the individual controls are sacrificed.

6. Metaphor sucks.

The use of metaphor has become commonplace in both HCI and product design. 'We could use a such and such metaphor' is an often-heard statement. We think the usefulness of metaphor is overrated. When trying to describe a design in absence of the thing itself it may be necessary to rely on metaphor. But this does not necessarily mean that whilst interacting with the product the user understands the design through one single, consistent metaphor. Gentner and Nielsen (1996) and Gaver (1995) also point out the limits of perfect fitting metaphors. The challenge here is to avoid the temptation of relying on metaphor and to create products, which have an identity of their own.

7. Don't hide, don't represent. Show.

Current product design has a tendency to hide the physical components, even those that are highly informative to a product's operation. A choice is made in favour of an alternative representations rather than physical manifestation.

Figure 3. *First the tape is hidden completely inside the machine, to be then represented on a display.*

For example, a videotape becomes completely hidden inside a video recorder when inserted and is then represented on a display (Figure 3). In photocopiers paper is put inside drawers so that we need sophisticated displays to tell us which paper format lives where. It is the designer's task to make these last remaining physical hold-ons visible and make optimal use of them in the interaction process.

8.   Don't think affordances, think irresistibles.

Both the HCI and product design communities have borrowed the term affordances from perception-psychology and have hooked onto mainly its structural aspects whilst neglecting the affective aspects. We lament this clinical interpretation of affordance. People are not invited to act only because a design fits their physical measurements. They can also be attracted to act, even irresistibly so, through the expectation of beauty of interaction.

9.   Hit me, touch me, and I know how you feel.

We may slam doors in anger, chew a pen or write with it frantically, sip our coffee or gulp it down in haste. If we design products, which invite rich actions, we can get an idea about the user's emotions by looking at these actions (Wensveen et al, 2002).

10. Don't think thinking, just do doing.

HCI methodologies often separate the cognitive, verbal, diagrammatic and abstract 'thinking' design phase from the visual, concrete, 'doing' phase, and emphasize the former. In product design, 'doing' is seen as equally valid as thinking and as beneficial to the design process even in the very early stages. Handling physical objects and manipulating materials can allow one to be creative in ways that flow diagrams cannot. In the design of the physical, knowledge cannot replace skills. You can think and talk all you want, but in the end, the creation of contexts for experience, the enjoyment and the expressiveness require hands-on skills.

4.2 Examples

Keeping the last of the 10 rules in mind let's turn now our attention to the examples.

In his graduation project, Frens used new methods to explore aesthetics, interaction and role (Djajadiningrat, Gaver & Frens, 2000). One of these methods is designing for extreme characters. Designers create products for fictitious characters that are emotional exaggerations. This helps to expose character traits which otherwise remain hidden. For example, Frens used an hedonistic, polyandrous twenty-year old woman as an extreme character. This choice of character required Frens to come up with an appointment manager which allows the woman to maximize the fun in her life and which supports her in juggling appointments with multiple boyfriends who may not know of each other. In his final design, Frens aimed to achieve aesthetics of interaction by treating hardware and on-screen graphics as inseparable. The user navigates through time by means of a rotatable ring, which sits around the top screen (Figure 4).

The appointment manager of the polyandrous woman makes use of five circular screens, which fold up in a fan-like manner. To support the woman in her polyandrous behaviour, the fan is usable in two modes. In the first mode, which is called public mode, all the screens are folded in and only the top screen is visible. This is the mode, which she can use without worries while amongst other people. In the second mode, called private mode, the screens are folded out. In this mode the woman can check upon sensitive information.

Figure 4. Appointment manager(top-left). Public and private mode (top-right). With rotating ring around the top screen (bottom-right). Boyfriend profiles (bottom-left).

Through the playful positioning of the screens, the woman can rate and compare her boyfriends on a fun profile with issues such as dining, shopping, partying, sex etc. The appointment fan fits the twenty-year-old's attitudes. It helps her maintain her hedonistic lifestyle by remembering attributes of boyfriends and allowing her to adjust these through an uncomplicated, playful interface. The dual modes allow her to use the device in public without disclosing the details of her agenda, satisfying her special need for privacy.

The direct coupling between the rotation of the ring and the flow of characters over the screen makes for a beautiful interaction. Through the positioning of the multiple screens, the woman can rate her boyfriends on various issues such as shopping, dining, sex etc. in a playful manner. These aspects of the design show respect for the user's perceptual-motor skills, not only from a structural but also from a fun point of view.

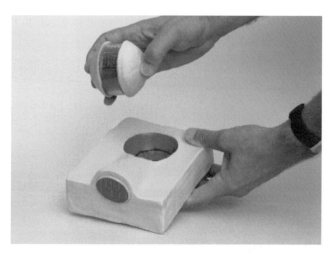

Figure 5. An alarm clock (design: De Groot and Van de Velden)

The next example (Figure 5) is an alarm clock from a student exercise. The alarm clock consists of two parts, a base station and an alarm ball. The alarm ball is used to set the wake up time and consists of a display strip flanked by two rotating semi-spheres. If the left hemisphere of the alarm ball is turned while holding the display strip, the hour of the waking time is adjusted. If the right hemisphere is rotated, the minutes are adjusted. The size of the ball and the way it matches the recess in the base station afford picking up and the two halves afford rotation. But more importantly, the positioning of the halves adjacent to the hour digits and the minute digits, informs the user of what he will adjust.

The alarm clock can sense the distance between the base station and the alarm ball. The further the user moves or throws the alarm ball from the base station, the louder, the more aggressive and the more insistent the waking sound may be in the morning. The closer the alarm ball is placed to the base station, the softer and more gentle the waking sound will be. Here it is both the appearance and the actions that are carriers of meaning. Throwing the ball to the other side of the room is a different action from placing it just to the side of the base station and can thus have different consequences. This is also consistent with the actions the user has to carry out to silence the alarm clock. The further the alarm ball is away from the base station, the more of an effort he has to make to find it, to pick it up and to place it over the speaker to muffle the sound. Here again the fit of the alarm ball to the recess and the idea of covering the loudspeaker inform the user of the consequences of his action. The user's actions thus become carriers of meaning and influence the alarm's behaviour.

Figure 6. *Turning of the hemispheres*

If the left hemisphere of the alarm ball is turned while holding the display strip, the hours of the waking time are adjusted (top Figure 6)). If the right hemisphere is rotated, the minutes are adjusted (bottom). The alarm clock can sense the distance between the base station and the alarm ball. The further the alarm ball is placed away, the more insistent the sound will be in the morning. The user's actions thus become carriers of meaning and influence the alarm clock's behaviour.

5.   CONCLUSIONS

This chapter summarises a position that has been developed over many years and a number of projects. Our work can be thought of as a manifesto for design. Our arguments are deliberately provocative. For too long psychologists have led designers to make overly cognitive designs. We repeat: design should be left to designers! Too often fun is a "glued on" property and interfaces smile. Enjoyment should not be an afterthought and fun does not have to be cute. In order to design enjoyable products we must design for engagement on every level and the physicality of products must be restored, Product design must address the user's action potential and capacity to appreciate sensory richness. Products must elicit rich interaction from the user. In this way, not only the functionality but beauty and fun in interaction are opened up. And there is more. Rich physical interaction offers even more possibilities. Products might 'read' the user's emotions and react to it in different ways. (See for example Wensveen and Overbeeke, Chapter 24 in this book).

We believe our approach frees products from clumsy interaction and opens ways to beauty and fun. From a product design perspective, the appearance of interactive products can no longer be considered as arbitrary. A tight coupling between action and appearance in interaction design is necessary. Appearance and interaction need to be designed concurrently.

6. ACKNOWLEDGEMENT

Part of this chapter was published earlier in Djajadiningrat et al, 2000. The Frens project was conducted in collaboration with Bill Gaver of RCA London. Most of the work reported was done when all authors were affiliated to the Delft University of Technology.

7. REFERENCES

Cooper, A. (1999) *The inmates are running the asylum*. Indianapolis: SAMS. McMillan, Sams.
Djajadiningrat, J.P, Overbeeke, C.J. & Wensveen, S.A.G. (2002). But how, Donald, tell us *how*? In: N. Macdonald (Ed.), *Proceedings of DIS2002*, London, 25-28 June 2002, pp. 285-291.
Djajadiningrat, J.P., Gaver, W.W. and Frens, J.W. (2000). Interaction Relabelling and extreme characters: Methods for exploring aesthetic interactions. *Proceedings of DIS'00, Designing Interactive Systems*. ACM, New York, pp. 66-71.
Djajadiningrat, J.P, Overbeeke, C.J. & Wensveen, S.A.G. (2000). Augmenting Fun and Beauty: A Pamphlet. In: W.E. Mackay (Ed.) *Proceedings of DARE'2000*. Helsingor, pp.131-134.F
Dunne, A. (1999). *Hertzian Tales: electronic products, aesthetic experience and critical design*. London: RCA CRD Research publications.
Gaver, W.W. (1995). Oh what a tangled web we weave: metaphor and mapping in graphical interfaces. Adjunct proceedings of CHI'95, 270-271.
Gentner, D., & Nielsen, J. (1996). The anti-Mac interface. *Communications of the ACM*, 39 (8), 70-82.
Gibson, J. J. (1986). *The ecological approach to visual perception*. Hillsdale, NJ: Lawrence Erlbaum.
Hummels, C.C.M. (2000). *An exploratory expedition to create engaging experiences through gestural jam sessions*. Doctoral dissertation. Delft University of Technology.
Overbeeke, C.J., Djajadiningrat, J.P., Hummels, C.C.M, and Wensveen S.A.G. (2002) Beauty in Usability: Forget about Ease of Use! In: W.S. Green & P.W. Jordan (Eds.) Pleasure with products: Beyond usability. Taylor & Francis, pp. 9-18.
Wensveen, S.A.G., Overbeeke, C.J., & Djajadiningrat, P.J. (2002). Push me, shove me and I know how you feel. Recognising mood from emotionally rich interaction. In: N. Macdonald (Ed.), Proceedings of DIS2002, London, 25-28 June 2002, pp. 335-340.

PHOEBE SENGERS

CHAPTER 2

THE ENGINEERING OF EXPERIENCE

A deep shift in Western culture has occurred in the last 200 years. We have moved from lifestyles in which work, play, and other forms of experience are inextricably intertwined, to one in which most people separate their work life from a private (and often less societally valued) life of fun and play. Engineering has played a central role in this bifurcation, fulfilling a cultural desire to engineer human experience for optimal functionality. The result has been a great increase in our material comforts, coupled with a harried, frenzied lifestyle for many. In this chapter, I will argue that designing systems to support rich, meaningful, and pleasurable human experiences requires moving away from the model of engineering experience and towards an interdisciplinary approach to computing, in which technology design is intertwined with philosophical and cultural analysis.

1.   FUN IS THE DREGS OF ENGINEERING EXPERIENCE

The history of the industrial revolution is a story of the gradual optimisation and rationalization of work. Over the last two centuries, work has gone from an integral part of daily life, to something which is bought and sold per hour and engaged in standardized ways. Craftspeople were collected into factories, their work was split into pieces along a production line, some steps of the production line were taken over by machines, and gradually craftspeople became tenders of rote machinery, engaged in soulless work.

This shift is epitomized by the work of the efficiency expert Frederick Winslow Taylor, who in the early 20th century developed the system of scientific management or 'Taylorism.' Taylorist engineers maximize the efficiency of human labour by observing workers, analysing their movements, and developing a script for the 'one best way' to achieve their work tasks, in the process eliminating all unnecessary or wasteful motions. After the development of the assembly line, which rationalized and optimised machine labour in the production process, the last source of inefficiency in factories was human labour. Businessmen were naturally eager to find ways to reduce this inefficiency, a task which Taylorism solved.

After Taylorist analysis, a worker is told not only the steps to take in order to fulfil a task, but also what order to do those steps in and exactly how to move in order to minimize waste in their work. Because of the mindless, rote nature of Taylorized work, the quality of experience of work is reduced. Rote labour causes both repetitive stress injuries and rebellious, unhappy workers. Offsetting this

19

Mark A. Blythe, Andrew F. Monk, Kees Overbeeke and Peter C. Wright *(eds.)*,
Funology: From Usability to Enjoyment, 19-29.
© 2003 *Kluwer Academic Publishers. Printed in the Netherlands.*

reduction in experience is a drastic increase in its efficiency and productivity. Because of these great increases in efficiency, Taylorism took the business world by storm. The impact of Taylorism on Western, especially American, culture can hardly be underestimated. It is still felt through later, less extreme manifestations such as ergonomics and time management. Despite the problems of Taylorism, many of us have remained with a model of work in which experience is engineered for maximum efficiency and minimum pleasure. We have also imported these models to the home: to-do lists, appointment calendars, and a clutter of chores regiment our home lives and attempt to ensure that we are as efficient at home as we are at work.

Engineering work leads to a bifurcation of experience. As Blythe and Hassenzahl argue in this volume, if work, on the one hand, maximizes efficiency at the cost of pleasure, we balance out in our free time by engaging in fun: maximizing pleasure and minimizing task achievement. Many of us spend 8-10 hour days working efficiently and unhappily, then race home for a mindless evening in front of the TV or Playstation.. In the post-industrial West, and especially in America, we have split experience into two: whereas life could be a steady stream of work intermingled with pleasure, we have disengaged the two, often preferring to lavish 'serious' attention only on the first.

2. COMPUTER SCIENCE IS COMPUTATIONAL TAYLORISM (BUT DOESN'T NEED TO BE)

A similar split and imbalance has occurred in computer science. Taylorism is, at heart, simply engineering applied to human behaviour; hence it is no surprise that computer scientists tend to approach work processes the same way as a Taylorist. We break complex processes down into simple steps, we figure out optimal procedures for each work step, and we eliminate wasteful steps and problems.

This process is most clearly seen in Artificial Intelligence, in which both classical planning and the newer behaviour-based approaches attempt to engineer experience by increasing the efficiency and optimality of algorithms and to maximize their functionality (Sengers 1998, Sengers forthcoming). But we see similar emphases in human-computer interaction (HCI). On the one hand, it has a strong emphasis on work-related tasks and increasing the efficiency of their execution. On the other hand, it often focuses on rationalized and optimised techniques to understand and engineer human experience – even when the goal is fun.

Engineering is the correct approach to take when there is a well-defined task to be solved. But designing systems that open a space for new kinds of experience is not an engineering task per se. Instead, one must consider the technical challenges to be overcome in the context of the kinds of cultural and social meaning that the system may take on and the ways in which users may choose to interact with it. This necessitates a shift from a pure, task-oriented engineering approach to an interdisciplinary approach that combines socially-oriented approaches such as the social sciences or literary and cultural studies with more traditional human-computer interaction and computer science. Such hybrid approaches are becoming popular both within HCI and in the media art community (see e.g. Ehn 1998; Wilson 2002).

3.   THINK BEYOND BOTH WORK AND FUN

The pendulum between work and play is beginning to swing in the other direction. The recent interest in 'fun' as manifested by this volume is important in opening up an understanding of some of the unstated work-related assumptions underlying HCI methods. Funology will necessitate fundamental rethinking of some HCI approaches and the development of new techniques that are less about efficiency and more about quality of experience.

Nevertheless, funology is not enough. Rather than continuing the bifurcation of experience into work vs. play (traditional HCI vs. funology), as a culture we need to consider systems that take a more integrative approach to experience. This may mean on the one hand systems like that of Hohl, Wissmann and Burger in this volume that combine work-related task achievement with pleasurable experience. More fundamentally, it also means that we need to explore the vast and utterly neglected territory of possible systems that are really *neither* work *nor* fun. Such systems may support reflection by users on their lives and activities; they may give users new ways to experience the world; they may make cultural comments in the form of interactive artworks. These systems are neither directly task-related, nor intended simply to entertain. They have a serious point, but they may bring their point across in a playful manner. Examples of such work include Bill Gaver and Heather Martin's conceptual information appliances (Gaver and Martin 2000), which explore the role of technology in our everyday lives; Tony Dunne and Fiona Raby's electronic furniture (Dunne and Raby 2001), which provide people with different ways to sense and respond to activity in the electromagnetic spectrum; and Simon Penny's Petit Mal (Penny 2000), an artwork exploring the nature of artificial agents through a gangly and not very bright robot whose complex and graceful physical activity is almost entirely triggered by human bodily interaction. What these systems have in common is not a desire to engineer experience, but to build thoughtful artefacts that create opportunities for thinking about and engaging in new kinds of experiences. We need to shift from engineering experiences – whether work or fun – to designing them, using principles that draw on both technology design methods and social and cultural analysis.

4.   SOME EXPERIENCES DESIGNING EXPERIENCES

In this section, I will describe some experiences in designing systems that are intended to support richer and more meaningful notions of human experience than those traditionally used in computer science by using a broader, interdisciplinary approach combining computer science with cultural analysis. My first work in this area was in designing Artificial Intelligence (AI) architectures for interactive computer characters. Traditionally, AI focuses on activity in the world as problem-solving rationality. The goal for autonomous agents is often to behave optimally rationally in approaching some goal. For interactive computer characters, this focus is problematic, since characters do not need to be particularly smart or rational, instead needing to project emotion and personality in a way that is understandable to users. In the Industrial Graveyard (Figure 1), I explored how to create agents, not as rational problem-solvers, but as experienced by human users (Sengers 1999). Users observe the antics of a discarded lamp in a junkyard, while controlling the behaviour of its unsympathetic overseer. The technology is based on narrative psychology, which argues that humans interpret activity by organizing it into narrative. I support human interpretation of character action by providing visible cues for narrative interpretation of agent behaviour, most notably through transitions between behaviours that connect them by expressing the reason for the behaviour change to the user.

Figure 1. *The hero of the Industrial Graveyard*

With the Industrial Graveyard, I started out being interested in how human experience was represented in agents; but in the course of building the system, I began to realize that what was central was the way in which the *user* experienced the system. The next system I worked on explored ways to generate engaging user experiences. With a team of 5 researchers led by Simon Penny, I explored the construction of physical experiences in virtual reality (Penny et al. 2001). In Traces, users' body movements generate 3-dimensional traces which share their physical space, and with which they can interact (Figure 2).

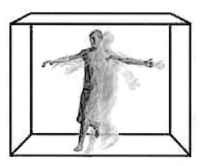

Figure 2. *Concept of Traces: user movement through space leaves behind 3-dimensional traces*

In traditional VR systems, the body is an afterthought, left behind when the headset is put on. The goal of Traces was to develop a kind of VR installation where it is possible instead to have strong bodily experiences. Traces is an installation for the CAVE VR display, a small room onto whose walls 3D images are projected. When users enter wearing 3D glasses, they have the illusion of being surrounded by virtual objects in real, physical space, while they can still look down and see their own bodies. In Traces, vision cameras detect the movement of users, allowing them to leave behind and interact with traces of physical movements that seem to surround them (*Figure 3*).

Figure 3. *A user (body model shown in black) moving through Traces leaves behind tracks of physical movement (grey). In the CAVE the voxel model is not shown; instead, the user's own body leaves behind colourful 3-dimensional traces in the space surrounding him or her. Users are surrounded by the trace they create*

Figure 4. *A user (body model shown in black) being chased by a set of Chinese dragons (grey). In the actual experience in the CAVE, the user does not see their voxel model, but only sees Chinese dragons sharing their physical space and responding directly to their physical movemen.*

Gradually, the traces become more autonomous, turning into "Chinese dragons" which flock together and sense and react to users' physical movements (Figure 4).

Traces was installed at Ars Electronica '99, where users leapt, ran, skipped, did cartwheels, and came out of the CAVE sweating. Users had strong reactions to the Chinese dragons; though the dragons were not particularly intelligent, they seemed strongly alive and present to human users because they shared the same physical space. With Traces, it became clear that physical interaction and shared physical space with (embodied) users is a way to create meaningful, powerful experiences.

The Influencing Machine (Sengers et al. 2002) explores the human experience of affective computing, or computational systems that recognize, reason about, or can express emotions. It was developed by the author, Rainer Liesendahl, Werner Magar, and Christoph Seibert at the MARS Exploratory Media Lab as part of the EU SAFIRA project. In the Influencing Machine installation, users enter a small room, on one wall of which childlike drawings are being created in real-time, accompanied by an abstract soundscape. In the middle of the room, they discover a wooden mailbox, into which they can put art or coloured postcards. By choosing postcards, they can change the "mood" of the drawings and sounds as they are being created. Users explore the postcards, asking themselves what the picture means to them, and exploring what it means to the machine. With the Influencing Machine, we came up with ways to engineer *enigmatic* experience: the interaction is deliberately open-ended and open to interpretation, yet through the interaction of postcards, graphics, and sound, we can create experiences which have concrete meaning for many users. The Influencing Machine was formally evaluated by Gerd Andersson, Pia Mårtensson, and Kristina Höök, who developed new techniques for non-task-oriented evaluation for this project, most notably by using groups of users and recording their conversations in order to better understand the nature of user experience of the system.

Figure 5. *Input and output of the Influencing Machine*

These three systems are all examples of critical technical practices (Agre 1997), or practices of technology development which incorporate a cultural, critical component. In all three cases, we built on an analysis of what was missing in the cultural assumptions about human experience that were unconsciously built into previous technology. The Industrial Graveyard twists the notions of optimality, correctness, and action-selection inherent in many algorithms for autonomous agents. Traces alters the assumption of bodilessness behind many VR applications. The Influencing Machine plays off of the assumption in many affective interfaces that "affect" is something to be extracted through surveillance or skin contact, and instead places the user's own choices at the centre of affective interaction. I believe building rich, meaningful experiences will require not just engineering competence but also cultural analysis, design, and art perspectives.

5.   HOW TO DESIGN EXPERIENCE

A pure engineering approach suggests that one can understand human experience by building formal models of it – the traditional approach taken by computer science. In

AI, for example, we build conceptual models of people, implement these in code, and run them, in the hopes of better understanding what human experience is like. In HCI, we similarly often build cognitive models of users, allowing software to reason about what users may be experiencing by comparing their behaviour with expectations of human behaviour built into the cognitive models. In many ways these attempts to make human experience computational mimic the efforts of the Taylorists, as we try to clean up, formalize, and organize what is an inherently messy and perhaps fundamentally incomprehensible phenomenon. In my own work as an AI researcher, I became frustrated by the fact that my clean, beautiful models of behaviour always seem to miss the point – they can somehow never generate the complexity and richness of natural behaviour of humans or animals.

The perspectives of the arts and humanities also suggest the futility of trying to formally represent experience. Many humanists and artists feel that complexity, messiness, ill-definedness, and enigmatics are fundamental to the nature of human experience, and that therefore all clean and formal models fundamentally distort that nature. Winograd and Flores's rejection of AI (Winograd and Flores, 1986), for example, is fundamentally based on this point. If this is the case, then how can we design systems that can create rich, meaningful, and complex experience for users? I believe we must do so by realizing that we cannot fully represent experience within the software, and instead try to set up more nuanced relationships between (internal, formal, clean) code and (external, messy, complicated) experiences. More concretely, I suggest the following (nonexhaustive) set of heuristics:

– *Instead of representing complexity, trigger it in the mind of the user*.
Instead of trying to contain the complexity of user experience in formal structures such as user models, one should focus on shaping the *actual* (not modelled) experience of the user, which will hopefully be much more complex than its internal, logical representation. One way to do this is to focus on the user's strength: an ability to engage in complex interpretation using a vast amount of cultural background knowledge. By focusing on how users react, rather than on the internal content of the software, a simple computational artefact can be used to communicate a rich and complex idea. In the Industrial Graveyard, I take advantage of the user's 'narrative intelligence' by providing 'hooks' that support narrative understanding of agent behaviour. The agent architecture is structured to support symbolic, narrative interpretation, rather than internal optimality, efficiency, and completeness. Systems built using this heuristic have behaviour that is internally simple, but appears complex to users thanks to the complexity of human interpretation.

– *Instead of representing complexity, bootstrap off it*.
Human behaviour is rich, complex, messy, and hard to organize into rules and formal models. This insight can be used to create rich, complex, messy, and subtle *computational* behaviour with little computational cost simply by driving it directly from human behaviour. For example, in Traces the motion of the Chinese dragons is based on simple rules that respond to human movement. Because human movement is complex and the dragons are responding to it in real time, the movement of the dragons is similarly complex. Unlike the previous heuristic, systems built using this

heuristic truly have complex behaviour – but only because they are driven by complex input.

– *Think of meaning, not information.* Computers care about information. Humans care less about raw data than they do about what information means to *them*. Focusing on meaning instead of information in the design of computational objects means that we adapt to user experience of information rather than to its internal representation. With the Influencing Machine, for example, we tried to move away from the standard affective computing model in which 'emotion' is fundamentally a unit of information to be extracted, manipulated, and communicated, to one in which user interpretation of emotionally valenced postcards, graphics, and sound is central, with the internal informational representation of emotion playing only a supporting role.

6. THE ENGINEERING OF EVERYDAY LIFE, OR WHERE'S THE FUN?

How do these heuristics extend to work outside of the museum and beyond AI? One domain in which non-engineering approaches are clearly needed is in everyday life in the home. In current discussions in HCI, the move of computation from desktops and factories into the home and everyday life is considered motivation to alter the efficiency- and task-oriented approaches on which HCI has largely concentrated in favour of fun- and pleasure-based approaches. Underlying this argument is an assumption that Taylorist models may be appropriate for work, but that they do not apply to the home. Yet the historical record makes clear that Taylorist models are central to current home life in the West, especially in America – to the detriment of our quality of life (Bell and Kaye, 2002).

Already at the turn of the century, the popularity of Taylorism and the model of factory production which was rapidly and fundamentally changing the American way of life led to attempts to adapt Taylorism to home life (Strasser 1982). Home economist Christine Frederick was perhaps its most ardent proponent; she proposed that housewives engage in motion studies to minimize the amount of movement they spent on household chores such as washing the dishes or doing the laundry. This attempt to adapt Taylorism to the home ran into resistance, for several reasons. First, many home tasks, such as minding children, are not amenable to being fully engineered and controlled. Second, there was no clear reason why housewives needed to be so efficient. Focusing purely on efficiency causes a great reduction in the experience of work, and many housewives saw no need to get more done at the cost of less pleasure and a more unnatural work process.

The situation today has changed. As Ralph Keyes notes,

> At one time the home was considered a refuge from work pressures. Now its inhabitants march to a businesslike beat. The pace at home has become little different from that at work. It calls for huge calendars on the kitchen wall, constant cross-checking of everyone's schedules, and sophisticated use of complex telephone systems so everyone can stay coordinated…. The tempo of the office and much of its paraphernalia – datebooks, Rolodexes, phone systems, computers, even faxes – have invaded the home. (p. 141)

In fact, especially for two-career families, efficiency and engineering an optimal task schedule are as important at home as at work. What role will HCI play in this? Will we continue the engineering approach, building domestic technology that will allow harried families to cram yet one more activity into a busy schedule, alternating with stress reduction through mindless fun? Or will we design experiences for users that counteract these cultural forces, developing an alternative vision of what home life could be like?

7.   DON'T JUST ENGINEER - LEARN TO LOVE COMPLEXITY AND SPEAK ITS LANGUAGE

Building computational artefacts that support rich and meaningful human experience requires a variety of perspectives to be combined. Engineering, including technology and algorithm design, is essential in order to be able to turn the vision of an interaction into a functioning system. Traditional and newly created human-computer interaction techniques are needed to support the fine-tuning of interaction and to evaluate the effect the system may have on users. But 'engineering' truly rich experiences requires more of system designers than just technical skills. System designers also need to understand and design for the ways in which user experience exceeds our abilities to formalize it. They can't just love their code; they must learn to love the complexity of user experience as well and be conversant in it. This suggests the incorporation of practices like cultural studies, anthropology, speculative design, surreal art, culture jamming, story-telling, cultural history, sociology, improvisation, and autobiographies, which have found ways to address and understand the complexity of human experience without needing to create complete and formal models of it. Most importantly, it means recognizing the role, not just of fun but of serious *play* as a form of opening the conceptual space for designing, building, and interacting with the new systems with which we will share our lives.

8.   ACKNOWLEDGEMENTS

The Industrial Graveyard was supported in part by an ONR Allen Newell Fellowship. My work on Traces was supported by a Fulbright fellowship. The Influencing Machine is part of the EU SAFIRA project. The systems described here were built at Carnegie Mellon University, the Center for Art and Media Technology (ZKM), the MARS Exploratory Media Lab at the German National Information Technology Research Center (GMD), and Cornell University.

9.   REFERENCES

Agre, P. E. (1977) *Computation and Human Experience*. Cambridge: Cambridge UP.
Bell, G. and Kaye, J. (2002). Designing Technology for Domestic Spaces: A Kitchen Manifesto. *Gastronomica*, 2(2).

Dunne, A. and Raby, F. (2001) *Design Noir: The Secret Life of Electronic Objects*. Basel, Switzerland: August / Birkhaeuser.

Ehn, P. (1998) Manifesto for a Digital Bauhaus. *Digital Creativity*, *9* No 4:207-216.

Gaver, B.l and Martin, H. (2000) Alternatives: Exploring information appliances through conceptual design proposals. *Proceedings of the CHI 2000 conference on Human factors in computing systems*. pp 209-216. ACM Press.

Keyes, R. (1991) *Timelock*. HarperCollins.

Penny, S. (2000) Agents as Artworks and Agent Design as Artistic Practice. In Kerstin Dautenhahn, ed., *Human Cognition and Social Agent Technology*. Amsterdam: John Benjamins.

Penny, S., Smith, J. Sengers, P., Bernhardt, A. and Schulte, J. (2001) Traces: Embodied Immersive Interaction with Semi-Autonomous Avatars. Convergence. Vol 7, No 2, Summer.

Sengers, P. (1998). *Anti-Boxology: Agent Design in Cultural Context*. PhD Thesis, Carnegie Mellon Department of Computer Science.

Sengers, P. (1999). Designing Comprehensible Agents. 1999 International Joint Conference on Artificial Intelligence (IJCAI-99). Stockholm, Sweden.

Sengers, P. (forthcoming) The Agents of McDonaldization. In Sabine Payr, ed., *Agents and Culture*.

Sengers, P., Liesendahl, R., Magar, W., Seibert, C., Müller, B., Joachims, T., Geng, W., Mårtensson, P. and Höök, K. (2002) The Enigmatics of Affect. 2002 Conference on Designing Interactive Systems. ACM Press.

Strasser, S. (1982) *Never Done; A History of American Housework*. NY: Pantheon Books.

Wilson, S. (2002) *Information Arts: Intersections of Art, Science and Technology*. Cambridge, MA: MIT Press.

Winograd, T. and Flores, F. (1986) *Understanding Computers and Cognition*. Norwood, NJ: Ablex.

MARC HASSENZAHL

CHAPTER 3

THE THING AND I: UNDERSTANDING THE RELATIONSHIP BETWEEN
USER AND PRODUCT

1. INTRODUCTION

We currently witness a growing interest of the Human-Computer Interaction (HCI) community in *user experience*. It has become a catchphrase, calling for a holistic perspective and an enrichment of traditional quality models with non-utilitarian concepts, such as fun (Monk & Frohlich, 1999; Draper, 1999), joy (Glass, 1997), pleasure (Jordan, 2000), hedonic value (Hassenzahl, 2002a) or ludic value (Gaver & Martin, 2000). In the same vein, literature on experiential marketing stresses that a product should not longer be seen as simply delivering a bundle of functional features and benefits - it provides experiences. Customers want products "that dazzle their senses, touch their hearts and stimulate their minds" (Schmitt, 1999, p. 22). Experiential marketing assumes that customers take functional features, benefits, and product quality as a given.

Even though the HCI community seems to embrace the notion that functionality and usability is just not enough, we are far from having a coherent understanding of what user experience actually is. The few existing models (e.g., Logan, 1984; Jordan, 2000) of user experience in HCI that incorporate aspects such as pleasure are rare and often overly simplistic. In the present chapter, I will propose a more complex model that defines key elements of user experience and their functional relations. Specifically, it aims at addressing aspects, such as (a) the subjective nature of experience *per se*; (b) perception of a product; (c) emotional responses to products in (d) varying situations. It is a more detailed and further developed version of a research model, I previously presented in Hassenzahl (2002a). I view it as a first step towards a better understanding of how people experience products and a valuable starting point for further in-depth theoretical discussions.

2. A MODEL OF USER EXPERIENCE

Figure 1 shows an overview of the key elements of the model of user experience from (a) a designer perspective and (b) a user perspective.

Mark A. Blythe, Andrew F. Monk, Kees Overbeeke and Peter C. Wright *(eds.)*,
Funology: From Usability to Enjoyment, 31—42

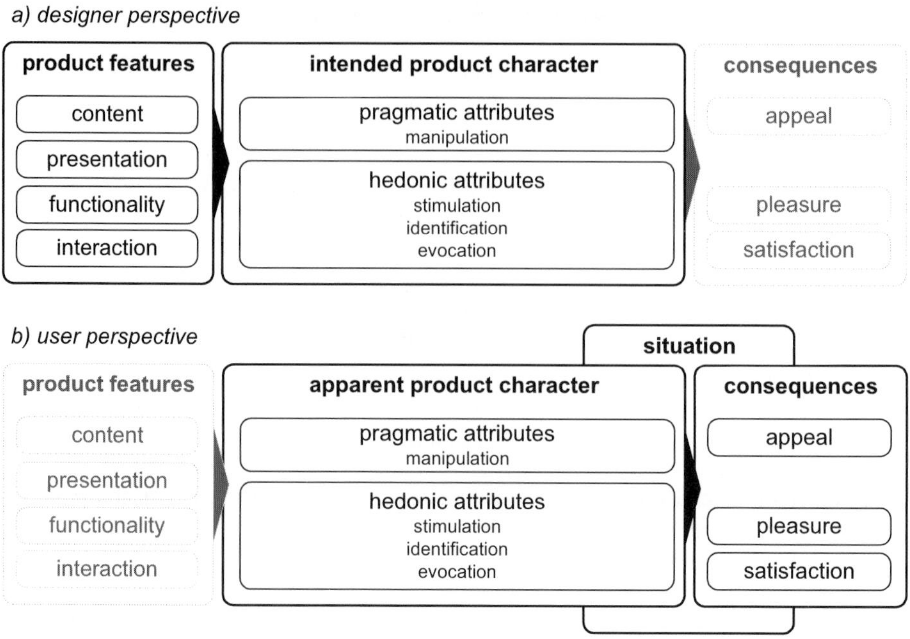

a) designer perspective

product features	intended product character	consequences
content	pragmatic attributes manipulation	appeal
presentation		
functionality	hedonic attributes stimulation identification evocation	pleasure
interaction		satisfaction

b) user perspective

		situation
product features	apparent product character	consequences
content	pragmatic attributes manipulation	appeal
presentation		
functionality	hedonic attributes stimulation identification evocation	pleasure
interaction		satisfaction

Figure 1. *Key elements of the model of user experience from (a) a designer perspective and (b) a user perspective (for details refer to text).*

A product has certain *features* (content, presentational style, functionality, interactional style) chosen and combined by a designer to convey a particular, *intended* product character (or gestalt; Janlert & Stolterman, 1997; Monö, 1997). A character is a high-level description. It summarizes a product's attributes, e.g., novel, interesting, useful, predictable. The character's function is to reduce cognitive complexity and to trigger particular strategies for handling the product. When individuals come in contact with a product, a process is triggered. First, people perceive the product's features. Based on this, each individual constructs a personal version of the product character - the *apparent* product character. This character consists of groups of *pragmatic* and *hedonic* attributes. Second, the apparent product character leads to *consequences*: a judgment about the product's appeal (e.g., "It is good/bad"), emotional consequences (e.g., pleasure, satisfaction) and behavioural consequences (e.g., increased time spend with the product). However, the consequences of a particular product character are not always the same. They are moderated by the specific usage situation. In the following, each key element is discussed in detail.

2.1 From the intended and apparent product character to consequences

A product designer "fabricates" a character by choosing and combining specific product features, i.e., content, presentational style, functionality, interactional style. However, the character is subjective and only *intended* by the designer. There is no guarantee that users will actually perceive and appreciate the product the way designers wanted it to be perceived and appreciated. For example, a product with a specific screen layout intended to be "clear" will not necessarily be perceived as "clear." A suitable design process must assure that an appropriate product character is selected and that this character is properly communicated to the user (see Hassenzahl, 2002b). For online banking, for example, an appropriate character may consist of attributes such as "trustworthy", "sober", and "clear". The features (e.g., tone of voice, screen layout, colours, news ticker) have then to be chosen and combined by the designer according to the character to be communicated.

When users are confronted with a product, a process is triggered: First, an apparent product character is constructed. It is a user's personal reconstruction of the designer's intended product character. Second, the fit of the apparent character and the current situation will lead to consequences, such as a judgment about the momentary appealingness of the product, and emotional or behavioural consequences.

➤ People *construct* the apparent product character based on the particular combination of product features and their personal standards and expectations. A personal standard most likely consists of other objects the product can be compared to. Variations of the character *between* individuals can be explained by differing standards. The apparent character can also change *within* a person over time. This change is due to increasing experiences with the product. For example, a product that was perceived as new and stimulating in the beginning may lose some novelty and ability to stimulate over time. Conversely, with increasing experiences products originally perceived as unusable may become more familiar and, thus, might be perceived as easier to handle. To date, not much is known about how perceptions of products will change over time. However, the specific way of change, i.e., direction and rate may be an integral part of a product's character extended over time.

Using a product with a particular product character in a particular situation has certain emotional and behavioural *consequences.* In some situations, for instance, to be novel is appreciated in a product; in others it can be neglected or even unwanted. Depending on the situation, character attributes become more or less relevant. The value of a product can be expressed by the user as judgments of appealingness or may manifest itself as emotions (see section 2.3). Compared to perceptions, consequences do vary more strongly because of their embedding into a particular usage situation. Consider, for example, an automated teller machine (ATM) designed to be highly understandable. To achieve this, the designers divided the process of receiving money into a number of small steps. If they got it right, you will perceive the ATM as highly understandable. The first time you try to get money from the ATM, you will certainly value this attribute. It will add to you satisfaction. Now imagine yourself being more experienced with the ATM or even under time pressure. The succession of small steps slows down interaction, and although you still perceive the ATM as understandable, this attribute is not relevant at the moment. It may even frustrate you. In this example, an individual's (your) appraisal of the ATM strongly varies (from satisfaction to frustration) because of the particular usage situation, whereas the perception of the ATM as understandable remains relatively stable.

The whole process of perceiving and constructing the character and experiencing consequences will *always* take place, no matter how insufficient the available information about the product seems to be. A study using the Repertory Grid Technique to gather product characters, for example, showed that people make far reaching inferences about quality and behaviour of online banking Web sites on the basis of simple screen shots or very short interaction sequences (Hassenzahl & Trautmann, 2001). However, the outcome of the process, i.e., the inferences made about the product character and the resulting consequences, may change with growing knowledge and experience of the product. This also implies that the process is repeated over and over again.

In the following section, I will take a closer look at two universal groups of attributes that define the product character and the underlying human needs they address.

2.2 Product character: Pragmatic and hedonic attribute

An apparent product character is a cognitive structure. It represents product attributes and relations that specify the co-variation of attributes. It allows inferences beyond the merely perceived. For example, a product with a simple user interface may also be thought of as easy to operate, although the user has no actual hands-on experience. But what groups of attributes can be distinguished? This is best answered by considering the major functions of products: They enable people to manipulate their environments, to stimulate personal development (growth) and to express identity. Moreover, a product can provoke memories and, thus, has a symbolic value.

2.2.1   Pragmatic attributes: manipulation

Manipulation of the environment requires relevant functionality (i.e., utility) and ways to access this functionality (i.e., usability). I call this group of product attributes *pragmatic*. Typical pragmatic attributes of software products are "clear", "supporting", "useful" and "controllable". A pragmatic product is primarily instrumental. It is used to fulfil externally given or internally generated behavioural goals. If, for example, somebody asks you to drive a nail into a wall to put up a picture, you use a tool to do so. From a pragmatic perspective, the only requirements for the tool are that it can in principle be used to drive in a nail and that you are able to figure out how to do so.

2.2.2   *Hedonic attributes: stimulation, identification, and evocation*

All other remaining product attributes I subsume as *hedonic*. I have chosen this term for two reasons: first, it is meant to highlight that hedonic attributes and the underlying functions of the product strongly differ from pragmatic attributes. Whereas pragmatic attributes emphasize the fulfilment of individuals' behavioural goals, hedonic attributes emphasize individuals' psychological well-being. Second, the American Heritage Dictionary of the English Language defines something that is hedonic as "of, relating to, or marked by pleasure". Thus, "hedonic" expresses my belief that the functions and attributes it subsumes are strong potentials for pleasure - - much stronger than pragmatic functions and attributes. Typical hedonic attributes of software products are "outstanding", "impressive", "exciting" and "interesting".

The hedonic function of products can be further subdivided into providing stimulation, communicating identity, and provoking valued memories.

- Stimulation

Individuals strive for personal development, i.e., proliferation of knowledge and development of skills. To do so, products have to be *stimulating*. They have to provide new impressions, opportunities, and insights. McGrenere (2000), for example, found in a study on "bloat" (i.e., "creeping featurism") in Microsoft's Word that on average only 27% of the available functionality was used. However, only 25% of the participants (13 of 53) wanted to have unused functionality entirely removed. I argue that these unused functions are viewed as future opportunities for personal development. They are not needed to fulfil current behavioural goals, but nevertheless wanted for future perfection of the way current goals are accomplished or for future generation of entirely new goals. Thus, functionality that is used and works well will be perceived as pragmatic, whereas functionality not *yet* used but interesting will be perceived as hedonic. The stimulation provided by novel, interesting or even exciting functionality, content, presentation or interaction style will also indirectly help goal fulfilment. It may raises attention, compensates for a lack of motivation to fulfil externally given goals, or facilitates new solutions to problems.

- Identification

Individuals express their self through physical objects – their possessions (Prentice, 1987). This self-expressive function is entirely social. Individuals want to be seen in specific ways by relevant others. To be socially recognized and to exert power over others is a basic domain of human motives (Schwartz & Bilsky, 1987). To fulfil this need, a product has to *communicate identity*. For example, personal homepages can be used to present the self to others. Borcherding and Schumacher (2002) found that students who believed that others hold unfavourable opinions about them, such as a lack of humour and few social contacts, presented more information about family and friends and humorous links on their homepages. In this case, the possession – a personal homepage – is deliberately shaped to communicate an advantageous identity. In general, people may prefer products that communicate advantageous identities to others.

- Evocation

Products can *provoke memories*. In this case the product represents past events, relationships or thoughts that are important to the individual (Prentice, 1987). For example, souvenirs are a whole product category that provides only symbolic value by keeping memories of a pleasant journey alive. Mackenzie (1997) presented the example of wine collectors, who may appreciate the wine in their cellar because of the aroma *and* the memories and effort attached to each single bottle. A more technology related example might be the trend to play vintage computer games. What do they provide? Definitely neither complex game play nor striking graphics. Their value comes from triggering memories of the good old days, when these games were exciting and kept people captive for hours.

To summarize, a product may be perceived as pragmatic because it provides effective and efficient means to manipulate the environment. A product may be perceived as hedonic because it provides stimulation, identification or provokes memories. Reconsider the example of driving in a nail. From a pragmatic perspective you prefer a tool that allows driving in the nail without much effort. You decide to buy a hammer. From a hedonic perspective you may buy a certain brand that communicates professionalism to others. Or you buy a whole set of tools instead of only a hammer. Although your current goal is to drive in a nail, you anticipate that do-it-yourself may become your new, most exciting hobby. Or you prefer to use an old hammer your mother once gave you as a present. Using it reminds you of the pleasant hours you spent with her as a child in her workshop. What you actually prefer to do depends on what is relevant to you. You then decide for the product which character suggests realization of your needs (i.e., the cheapest hammer that works, a professional hammer, a hammer and other tools, the hammer your mother once gave you).

2.2.3   *ACT and SELF product characters*

I view pragmatic and hedonic attributes as independent of each other. In combination they are the product character. If we take into account that peoples' perception of pragmatic and hedonic attributes can be either weak or strong, four types of product characters will emerge (see Figure 2). Notice, that products can be pragmatic or hedonic for different reasons. For example, a tool of a certain brand may be hedonic because this tool communicates professionalism to relevant others (i.e., communicates identity). Other tools may be hedonic because they are an innovation, which stimulates its user to do exciting new things.

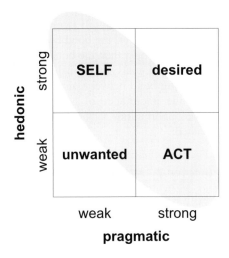

Figure 2. *Product characters emerging from specific combinations of pragmatic and hedonic attributes*

The combination of weak pragmatic and weak hedonic attributes is simply unwanted. It is a character implying a product that is neither able to satisfy pragmatic nor hedonic needs of potential users. The combination of strong pragmatic and strong hedonic attributes signifies the desired product. An uncompromising combination of both is the ultimate design goal. Most likely, both attribute groups will be not in balance. I call a primarily pragmatic product (i.e., "strong pragmatic / weak hedonic") an ACT product and a primarily hedonic product (i.e., "weak pragmatic / strong hedonic product") a SELF product.

The ACT product is inextricably linked to its users' behavioural goals. As already stated above, goals vary. They can be externally given by others or internally generated by the individual. Moreover, they can be of different importance to the user. Depending on the actual status of goals the appealingness of an ACT product varies (i.e., the importance of pragmatic attributes is decreased). Imagine: to reduce commuting time you bought a downright pragmatic car instead of going to your office by train. Unexpectedly, shortly after you purchase somebody offers you a new, cheap and attractive apartment only a five-minute walk from your office. You accept and suddenly your new car is not as appealing as before, because the main behavioural goal you have meant to fulfil with the car ceased to exist.

On contrary, the SELF product is inextricably linked to users' self, e.g., their ideals, memories, and relationships. If, for example, the car you have bought had been a luxurious sports car that not only stimulates your senses but also communicates success to others, the move would not have decreased the car's appeal. The appreciation of SELF products is much more stable than the appreciation of ACT products, because the probability that individuals change what they require from a product to satisfy their self is much lower than the probability that behavioural goals change. Moreover, the bond between a SELF product and its user should in general be much stronger than the bond between an ACT product and its user. Only when the behavioural goals accomplished with the ACT product are of high personal relevance a strong bond between an ACT product and a user can be expected. This emphasizes the importance of hedonic attributes. Only products, which provide at least some opportunities for being related to the self, are likely to be truly and stably appreciated.

2.3 Consequences: Satisfaction, pleasure and appealingness

Experiencing a product with a certain character will have emotional consequences, such as satisfaction or pleasure. They are momentary and take the usage situation into account. Note that these consequences (i.e., satisfaction, pleasure, appeal) are viewed as outcomes of experience with or through technology (see also Wright, McCarthy, & Meekison elsewhere in this book).

Human-Computer Interaction regards satisfaction with a product as a major design goal (e.g., ISO 9241-11). However, its definition as a "positive attitude towards the product" remains superficial. Moreover, attitudes differ from emotions in several aspects. Ortony and Clore (1988, pp 118, see Desmet & Hekkert, 2002 for a further application of Ortony et al.'s theory) define satisfaction as being pleased about the confirmation of the prospects of a desirable event. In other words, if people hold expectations about the outcome of using a particular product and these expectations are confirmed they will feel satisfied. In contrast to satisfaction, joy or pleasure requires no expectations. It is defined as being pleased about a desirable event *per se* (Ortony et al., 1988, pp. 86). The more unexpected the event is, the more intense will be the pleasure. In other words, if people use a particular product and experience desired deviations from expectations, they will be pleased.

In practice, one is likely to experience combinations of satisfaction and joy. To give an illustrative example, consider software for playing MP3 music files. You expected that it support you in managing the files on your computer hard disk by giving you an easy possibility to generate and save play lists. Indeed, the software provides this functionality and you feel satisfied whenever you use it. Moreover, you unexpectedly discover that it is possible to produce standard audio compact discs from the play list by only one click. You are pleased about the unexpected benefit you discovered. Satisfaction is linked to the success in using a product to achieve particular desirable behavioural goals. Pleasure is linked to using a product in a particular situation and encountering something desirable but unexpected.

If a product is able to trigger positive emotional reactions it is appealing. Appealingness is a group of product attributes such as good, sympathetic, pleasant, attractive, motivating, desirable, and inviting. Appealingness weights and integrates perceptions of product attributes by *taking particular situations (i.e., contexts) into account*. For example, individuals may consider an ACT product as appealing because the goals achievable by the product are of high relevance to them in a particular situation. However, other individuals (or even the same individual) can consider the same product as less appealing, maybe because people were rather interested in communicating a favourable identity to others than achieving behavioural goals. In short, appealingness integrates experiences with and feelings towards a product in a particular situation into an evaluative judgment.

In practice, I argue that particular product characters will render some emotional reactions more likely. ACT products emphasize fulfilment of behavioural goals. This can be interpreted as an expectation, which – given that goals had been reached – is more likely to lead to a positive expectation-based emotion, namely satisfaction. With an ACT product, pleasure may additionally be experienced if expectations about goal achievement (e.g., ease of achieving a goal) are excelled. SELF products are used to fulfil psychological needs rather than behavioural goals. Because of the weak connection to goals and expectations about fulfilling these goals, these products are more likely to lead to a positive well-being based emotion, namely pleasure. Satisfaction will only play a role, if hedonic functions are explicitly called for and expected, for example, if a person buys a product to impress a particular other person and is successful in doing so.

The susceptibility of emotional reactions and the judgment of appealingness to variation caused by situation is an argument for separating *potentials* for consequences (i.e., the product character) from the *actual* consequences -- the former is simply more stable and, thus, more reliable. Furthermore, in a product design process it is important to know why users judge a product as appealing, pleased by or satisfied by and thus one should rather focus on the product character and the usage situations than the consequences. However, this is not meant to imply that appealingness and the emotional reactions are unimportant. Both will certainly affect future use of the product.

2.4 Situation: Goal and action mode

I have repeatedly stressed the importance of different *situations* for understanding both judgments of appealingness and emotional reactions. A usage situation combines the perceived product character with a particular set of aspirations, such as specific behavioural goals or need for stimulation. Obviously, these situations can be quite diverse, which poses a serious problem for predicting emotional reactions or appealingness in particular usage situations. As a solution to this problem, I propose to focus on the mental state of the user by defining different *usage modes* (see Hassenzahl, Kekez, & Burmester, 2002). Specifically, I distinguish a goal and an action mode. Usage modes were inspired by Apter's reversal theory (Apter, 1989). In the present chapter I, however, use the term "action" instead of Apter's term "activity" to avoid a potential confusion with "activity theory" (see Figure 3 for an illustration).

Usage *always* consists of behavioural goals and actions to fulfil these goals. In *goal mode* goal fulfilment is in the fore. The current goal has a certain importance and determines all actions. The product is therefore just "a means to an end".

Individuals try to be effective and efficient. They describe themselves as "serious" and "planning". Low arousal is preferred and experienced as relaxation. If arousal increases (e.g., because of a usability problem that circumvents goal fulfilment), it is experienced as mounting anxiety (frustration). In *action mode* the action is in the fore. The current action determines goals "on the fly"; the goals are "volatile". Using the product can be an "end in itself". Effectiveness and efficiency do not play an important role. Individuals describe themselves as "playful" and "spontaneous". High arousal is preferred and experienced as excitement. If arousal decreases (because of a lack of stimulation) it is experienced as increasing boredom.

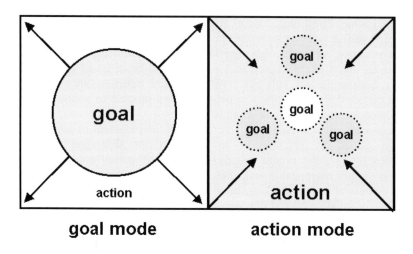

Figure 3. *Goal and action mode (inspired by Apter, 1989)*

The particular usage mode is triggered by the situation itself. If, for example, your boss wants you to do an important task that must be finished within two hours you most likely will be in goal mode. In contrast, if there is not much to do at the moment and you start exploring the new software you just got, you are more likely to be in action mode. In principle, I view usage modes as psychological states and every product can be experienced in either state. The perception of a product character as primarily pragmatic or hedonic will not be influenced by usage modes. However, appealingness and emotional reactions depend on the product's momentary fit to the usage mode. Thus, usage modes become the moderator between the product character and consequences. Usage modes can be chronic, i.e., a part of an individual's self-concept, too; to be in a particular usage mode becomes a stable personal trait.

To conclude, usage modes are certainly a more helpful distinction between ways of approaching a product than the classical "tool" and "toy" or "leisure" and "work"-dichotomy. The advantage lies in the emphasis on the fact that each product, irrespective of whether it is a computer game or a word processor, can be used in both modes.

3. SUMMARY AND CONCLUSION

User experience encompasses all aspects of interacting with a product. Its psychological complexity cannot be underestimated. First of all, user experience is subjective. Consequently, actual experiences with products may considerably differ from experiences intended by the designer. Experiences vary between individuals because of different personal standards. In addition, they vary between situations and they may change over time. Products have a character that suggests a capability to manipulate the environment, to stimulate, to communicate identity or to provoke memories. The first capability is pragmatic, i.e., inextricably tied to internally generated or externally given behavioural goals. The other three are hedonic, i.e., tied to individuals' self and their psychological well being. People value products on the basis of how it satisfies needs in particular situations. As a consequence, products have a certain appealingness and cause emotional reactions. Different emotional reactions may be distinguished: Satisfaction may be related to the fulfilment of expectations (i.e., behavioural goals), whereas pleasure may be related to the unexpected.

Approaches to user experience in HCI lack theory and empirical investigation. It seems important to better understand user experience itself, its determinants and situational/personal mediation *and* to validate this understanding. So far, several studies tested key elements of the model (e.g., Hassenzahl, Platz, Burmester, & Lehner, 2000; Hassenzahl, 2002a) and used the concept of "hedonic" attributes in product evaluation (e.g., Kunze, 2001; Sandweg, Hassenzahl, & Kuhn, 2000; Seifert, Baumgarten, Kuhnt, & Hassenzahl, 2001).

I view the benefit of the suggested preliminary model of user experience as two-fold: First, designers may better understand how people perceive and value objects. Second, it allows operationalisation and measurement of key elements. Both will inform design and lead to better, more satisfying and more pleasurable products.

4. ACKNOWLEDGEMENTS

I would like to thank Annette Amon, Kai-Christoph Hamborg, James Kalbach, Sara Ljungblad, Andrew Monk, Jürgen Sauer and Peter Wright for their helpful comments on earlier drafts of this chapter, and Katrin Borcherding for bringing the importance of the distinction between potentials for pleasure/satisfaction and their actual realization to my attention.

5. REFERENCES

Apter, M.J. (1989). Reversal theory: Motivation, emotion and personality. London, New York: Routledge.

Borcherding, K., & Schumacher, M. (2002). Symbolic self-completion on personal homepages. In *Proceedings of the 6th international conference on Work With Display Units (WWDU 2002)* (pp. 270-271). Berlin: ERGONOMIC Institut für Arbeits- und Sozialforschung.

Desmet, P.M.A., & Hekkert, P. (2002). The basis of product emotions. In W. Green & P. Jordan (Eds.), *Pleasure with products: beyond usability*. London: Taylor & Francis.

Draper, S.W. (1999). Analysing fun as a candidate software requirement. *Personal Technology*, 3(1), 1-6.

Gaver, W.W., & Martin, H. (2000). Alternatives. Exploring Information Appliances through Conceptual Design Proposals. In *Proceedings of the CHI 2000 Conference on Human Factors in Computing* (pp. 209-216). New York: ACM, Addison-Wesley.

Glass, B. (1997). Swept away in a sea of evolution: new challenges and opportunities for usability professionals. In R. Liskowsky, B. M. Velichkovsky, & W. Wünschmann (Eds.), *Software-Ergonomie '97. Usability Engineering: Integration von Mensch-Computer-Interaktion und Software-Entwicklung* (pp. 17-26). Stuttgart: B.G. Teubner.

Hassenzahl, M. (2002a). The effect of perceived hedonic quality on product appealingness. *International Journal of Human-Computer Interaction,* 13(4), 479-497.

Hassenzahl, M. (2002b). Character Grid: a Simple Repertory Grid Technique for Web Site Analysis and Evaluation. In J. Ratner (Ed.), *Human Factors and Web Development*. Lawrence Erlbaum.

Hassenzahl, M., Kekez, R., & Burmester, M. (2002). The importance of a software's pragmatic quality depends on usage modes. In *Proceedings of the 6th international conference on Work With Display Units (WWDU 2002)* (pp. 275-276). Berlin: ERGONOMIC Institut für Arbeits- und Sozialforschung.

Hassenzahl, M., Platz, A., Burmester, M., & Lehner, K. (2000). Hedonic and Ergonomic Quality Aspects Determine a Software's Appeal. In *Proceedings of the CHI 2000 Conference on Human Factors in Computing* (pp. 201-208). New York: ACM, Addison-Wesley.

Hassenzahl, M., & Trautmann, T. (2001). Analysis of web sites with the Repertory Grid Technique. In Proceedings of the CHI 2001 *Conference on Human Factors in Computing. Extended abstracts* (pp. 167-168). New York: ACM Press, Addison-Wesley.

ISO (1998). ISO 9241: Ergonomic requirements for office work with visual display terminals (VDTs) -- Part 11: Guidance on usability. Geneva: International Organization for Standardization.

Janlert L.-E., & Stolterman, E. (1997). The character of things. *Design Studies*, 18, 297-314.

Jordan, P. (2000). *Designing pleasurable products. An introduction to the new human factors*. London, New York: Taylor & Francis.

Kunze, E.-N. (2001). How to get rid of boredom in waiting-time-gaps of terminal-systems. In *Proceedings of the International Conference on Affective Human Factors Design*. London: Asean Academic Press.

Logan, R.J. (1994). Behavioral and emotional usability: Thomson Consumer Electronics. In M. Wiklund (Ed.), *Usability in Practice*. Cambridge, MA: Academic Press.

Mackenzie, C. (1997). Where are the motives? A problem with evidence in the work of Richard Thaler. *Journal of Economic Psychology*, 18, 123-135.

McGrenere, J. (2000). "Bloat": The objective and subjective dimensions. In *Proceedings of the CHI 2000 Conference on Human Factors in Computing. Extended abstracts* (pp. 337-338). New York: ACM Press, Addison-Wesley.

Monk, A.F., & Frohlich, D. (1999). Computers and Fun. *Personal Technology*, 3(1), 91

Monö, R.W. (1997). *Design for Product Understanding: The Aesthetics of Design from a Semiotic Approach*. Stockholm: Liber AB.

Ortony, A., Clore, G.L., & Collins, A. (1988). *The cognitive structure of emotions*. Cambridge, MA: Cambridge University Press.

Prentice, D.A. (1987). Psychological correspondence of possessions, attitudes, and values. *Journal of Personality and Social Psychology*, 53(6), 993-1003.

Sandweg, N., Hassenzahl, M., & Kuhn, K. (2000). Designing a telephone-based interface for a home automation system. *International Journal of Human-Computer Interaction*, 12(3&4), 401-414.

Schmitt, B.H. (1999). *Experiential marketing*. New York: Free Press.

Schwartz, S.H., & Bilsky, W. (1987). Toward a universal psychological structure of human values. *Journal of Personality and Social Psychology*, 53(3), 550-562.

Seifert, K., Baumgarten, T., Kuhnt, T., & Hassenzahl, M. (2001). Multimodale Mensch-Computer-Interaktion: tool oder gimmick? In K.-P. Timpe, R. Marzi, V. Karavezyris, H.-H. Erbe, & K.-P. Timpe (Eds.), *Bedienen und Verstehen. 4. Berliner Werkstatt Mensch-Maschine Systeme* (pp. 275-291). Düsseldorf: VDI-Verlag.

PETER WRIGHT, JOHN MCCARTHY AND LISA MEEKISON

CHAPTER 4

MAKING SENSE OF EXPERIENCE

1.   INTRODUCTION

Ehn and Löwgren (1997) use the term *quality-in-use* to refer to a range of aesthetic, ethic and functional qualities that need to be considered in design. Qualities such as enjoyment, fulfilment and fun are not properties of technology. They are better thought of as outcomes of certain kinds of experience with- or through- technology. So if we are to understand what might make a particular product or design more pleasing or enjoyable to use, it would seem sensible to begin by trying to analyse experience of use.

There has of course already been much interest in experience. For example, Turkle (1995) explored the social meaning of computers, the cultures of computing and the impact of the Internet on our sense of self. The concept of *user experience* has also come to dominate in consumer arenas such as branding and electronic commerce (see Pu and Faltings, 2000 and Lee, Kim, and Moon, 2000, for example). There is however an uneasy silence as to what actually constitutes experience. Questions such as how to set boundaries distinguishing a specific user experience from a general flow of experience, how to account for subjectivity, and whether it is possible to design experience, have remained conspicuously unanswered. In short, despite a growing acceptance of the need to focus on experience, the concept of user experience is not well developed conceptually. Without conceptual development, there is a danger that user experience and related concepts such as trust, loyalty, identity, and engagement will not be fully realized in studies of people and technology.

Elsewhere in this volume, Hassenzahl adopts a psychological approach to modelling experience in order to answer some of these questions. He attempts to identify the components of experience and to map the external physical properties of the world of artefacts onto their psychological effects, in the context of the user's purposes. His work is a step towards an explanatory model of experience in the traditional scientific sense. Our project here is slightly different. Our aim is to explore an approach which is holistic, constructionist and pragmatic in Dewey's sense of the term. Our theorising is thus of different quality but nevertheless aimed at being practically useful. Rather than isolate the elements of experience we seek to

Mark A. Blythe, Andrew F. Monk, Kees Overbeeke and Peter C. Wright *(eds.),*
Funology: From Usability to Enjoyment, 43—53

understand their interaction and how they mutually constitute each other. We also seek a stronger account of sense-making as the central process of experiencing.

2. CONCEPTUALISING EXPERIENCE

The turn to experience that we have outlined above reflects an attempt to engage with the 'felt life' of people participating in activities with- and through- technology. Worthy though this aspiration is, there is also a risk. 'Experience' is an elusive concept that resists specification and finalisation. In recent attempts to introduce 'experience' into consideration of relations between people and technology, it has been confused with subjective feelings, behaviour, activity, social practice, and knowledge. Thus the first major task in developing an experiential theory is to provide a basis for understanding experience that is not confused with any of these.

Dewey's philosophy of experience was geared towards a clarification that would end the tendency to reduce. For example, he pointed out that the most debilitating reduction to private, subjective experience is a feature of modern times.

> " To the Greeks, experience was the outcome of accumulation of practical acts, sufferings and perception gradually built up into …skill…There was nothing merely personal or subjective about it." (Dewey 1934, p.198)

He argued that experience is the irreducible totality of people acting, sensing, thinking, feeling, and meaning-making in a setting, including their perception and sensation of their own actions. He offered a useful definition along these lines. Experience, he wrote,

> " …. includes *what* men do and suffer, *what* they strive for, love, believe and endure, and also *how* men act and are acted upon, the ways in which they do and suffer, desire and enjoy, see, believe, imagine - in short, processes of experiencing. ….. It is "double barreled" in that it recognises in its primary integrity no division between act and material, subject and object, but contains them both in an unanalyzed totality" (Dewey, 1925, p.10/11).

According to Dewey experience is constituted by the relationship between self and object, where the self is always already engaged and comes to every situation with personal interests and ideologies. People and setting are also changed by experience, and the unity of any experience is itself a moving, fragile, fleeting event. He also made a distinction between experience and *an* experience, where we have *an* experience only when the material experienced runs its course to fulfilment and has its own individualising quality and self-sufficiency, an emotional unity that gives experience aesthetic quality.

In a move that is particularly useful for our purposes, Dewey also described the conditions of aesthetic form as an analytic tool to be used when we encounter problems with the unfolding of an experience - what went wrong, why we lost interest, why others got restless, etc. His conditions include: continuity, cumulation, conservation, tension, anticipation, and fulfilment. As the framework we describe in the next section draws heavily on Dewey's conditions, we will not dwell on them here.

Bakhtin (1986, 1993), a philosopher with a more literary bent than Dewey, provided a complementary account of the relationship between experience and meaning-making, through which we have read Dewey's conditions. Bakhtin's work is most useful in our consideration of the personal qualities of experience such as trust, identification, loyalty, and commitment. In terms of ongoing experiences of technology, Bakhtin's work shifts our focus from the immediate quality of an experience (absorbing, captivating, irritating) to the sense we make of an experience in terms of our experience of our selves, our culture, and our lives. Specifically, I might find a particular web site absorbing during my first few visits but if it is not integrated into 'my life' - if it does not fit with my sense of my self - it is likely to become less absorbing as time goes on.

For Bakhtin, the unity of an experience in action and an account of the meaning made of it is never available a priori but must always be accomplished. To understand how it is accomplished we must understand Bakhtin's central contribution in this area, the idea of dialogicality. Dialogicality refers to the presumption that in human activity there are always at least two consciousnesses involved. The activity of an individual sitting reading a book involves dialogues between the consciousnesses of the reader and writer and it is possible to argue, the consciousnesses of the characters in the book. We argue that web sites and other technology touchpoints can also be seen as abstractions from dialogues and that attention to the dialogical may yield fresh insights. The site of dialogical knowledge is never unitary. It is always relationally based. That is to say that knowledge of the self always emerges as an expression of self-other relations and similarly knowledge of an object always emerges as an expression of subject-object relations.

What dialogism means for this paper is that any discursive account of an experience, including a person's own account to themselves of an experience of buying through the internet, is incurably social, plural, and perspectival. In Bakhtin's terms, it is *interanimated* with the discourses of others. For example, my sense of myself as someone who supports small local bookshops is interanimated by discourses on the values of global capitalism, the importance of choice provided by small specialist booksellers, and the centrality of a personal relationship in choosing which books to buy. These discourses however might be accommodating of an Internet bookseller who appears to try to develop a buyer-seller relationship with me based on an understanding of my reading preferences, provides specialist choices, and seems to support small specialist booksellers. If my book buying activity moves from the small local bookshop to an internet seller who present themselves as engaging meaningfully with some of these discourses and also has other qualities of interest to me - e.g. speedy fulfilment of an order- then my sense of my self is subtly changed through dialogue with that bookseller.

This relational subjectivity is also reflected in the analyses of reflective practitioners. For example, writers and film-makers practice their craft under the influence of a practical understanding of experience and how they might influence or help create experience. Elsewhere in this volume, we appeal to Boorstin's (1995) analysis of Hollywood movie making as inspiration for an account of the enchantments of technology.

Our aim in drawing together the writings of philosophers such as Dewey and Bakhtin and reflective practitioners such as Boorstin is to try to understand experience well enough to understand how Internet shopping designers and brand managers deploy technical knowledge to help their user-consumers create a fulfilling interactive experience. To do this we created a framework, based on the above work, that pulls together a set of concepts that can be used as tools to analyse user experience with emerging technologies.

3.   THE FRAMEWORK

We will describe the framework in two parts, the first is concerned with describing experience from four points of view which we refer to as the four threads of experience. The second part is concerned with how we *make sense* in experience. Before describing these it is important to make some observations which we hope will avoid some possible misinterpretations of what is written here.

There is no simple mapping between the framework and the concepts of Dewey and Bakhtin. Dewey's concern for a holistic and interactionist approach is manifest in our characterisation of the four threads of experience, some of Boorstin's perspectivalism is reflected in this too. In terms of sense making, Dewey's concepts of anticipation, reflection and the pre-linguistic sense of meaning are echoed in our account. Bakhtin's concern for unity as an active accomplishment is reflected in our characterisation of appropriating, reflecting and recounting. But more subtly, what we have tried to do is understand Dewey through Bakhtin's dialogical lens. Thus self-other relations as continually constructed, permeates our account throughout.

Dewey's pragmatic account of experience emphasised that experience cannot be reduced to fundamental elements but only exists as relations. Experience is essentially holistic, situated and constructed. Thus it would be mistaken to approach experience in a way a classical physicist might approach the study of matter- to identify a substance, define it in terms of molecules, atoms and sub-atomic particles. We share Dewey's view on the holistic nature of experience, yet we see the need to be able talk about and describe experience in ways that can be understood. The analytical prose we use in this report to talk about the framework might suggest we are attempting such a reductive approach. This is not our intention. Rather we intend to connote a space within which things can be juxtaposed, related, separated, coalesced but never isolated.

3.1 The Four threads of experience

First of all we begin by identifying four threads of experience. We have found it helpful to think of these as four aspects as four inter-twined threads making up a braid.

3.1.1 The compositional thread

The compositional structure of an experience is that aspect which is concerned with part-whole structure of an experience. In an unfolding interaction involving self and other this could be thought of as narrative structure, action possibility, plausibility, consequences and explanations of actions. In an experience of an artwork, a poster or brand image it can be thought of as the compositional elements of the image their relations and implied agency. If you are asking questions like; "what is this about?", "what has happened?", "what will happen next?", "does this make sense?", "I wonder what would happen if?" then you are thinking about the compositional structure of experience.

3.1.2 The sensual thread

The 'look and feel' of a physical artefact or a web page are part of what we refer to as the sensual thread of experience. More generally, the sensual thread of experience is concerned with our sensory engagement with a situation. The sensations in an experience which we variously term thrill, fear, excitement are sensual, as are feelings such as walking into a room and finding it welcoming, a sense of belonging, a slight sense of unease or awkwardness in a conversation. Sometimes the sensual defies precise description but can affect our willingness become involved. The look and feel of a mobile phone may be as important a determinant of our decision to become (or not to become) a mobile phone user as the functional possibilities it offers.

3.1.3 The emotional thread

The emotional thread of experience includes anger, joy, disappointment, frustration, desperation and so on. These are stark examples, but other more subtle things that are included here are fulfilment, satisfaction, fun and so on. We can reflect on the emotional thread of our own experience or we can through empathy relate to the emotional thread of others' experiences. Relating to a character, in a movie is an obvious example, but we might also empathise with the designer or retailer of an e-shopping site even though they are not materially present.

We need to distinguish between the sensual and emotional threads since we can engender emotions associated with achievement through the exercise of control over sensations such as fear or anxiety. This is this case for example when a rock climber climbs a dangerous peak. For Csikszentimihalyi (1990), flow states result from precisely this kind of balancing. We can also engender emotional states such as bliss through the deliberate neutralisation of sensual states such as excitement and anxiety as is the case with meditation.

Emotions are not just passive responses to a situation. Our actions and our understandings may be motivated by emotional aspects just as surely as they may be motivated by our intellectual or rational understandings of action possibilities and consequences. We may act through compassion or morality just as surely as we may act through a rational assessment of actions and their likely consequences or some other utilitarian process.

3.1.4   The spatio-temporal thread

All experience has a spatio-temporal thread. Actions and events unfold in a particular time and place. When we are rushed we may feel frustrated and perceive space as confined, closeting. In addition, emotional engagement can make our sense of time change, hours can fly by in minutes. Pace may increase or decrease and our sense of space may open up or close down. Both space and time may become connected or disconnected as an experience unfolds. We might also distinguish between public and private space, we may recognise comfort zones and boundaries between self and other, or present and future. Such constructions affect experiential outcomes such as willingness to linger or to re-visit places or our willingness to engage in an exchange of information, services or goods.

3.2   Making sense in experience

People do not simply engage in experiences as ready-made, they actively construct them through a process of sense making. This process of sense making is reflexive and recursive. It is reflexive in the sense that we are always viewing experience through a person. Whether that is the first person or the third person or whether it is by recounting an experience to oneself or for others. This is not to be understood in some scientific way as an unfortunate consequence of our means of measurement. Rather it is central to what it means for something to be an experience. Without self and other, or subject and object interacting reflexively, there can be no experience. It is recursive in the sense that we are always engaged in sense making. Even when we reflect on experience as a completed object, we are having an experience.

Before describing sense making in detail however, we should note that the different sense making processes we describe are not linearly related in cause and effect terms. For example, in anticipation of some future planned action we may reflect on the consequences of that action, which may engender a certain sensual response. How we recount our experience to others may change how we reflect on it and so on.

3.2.1   Anticipating

When we think of the form of experience we need to extend our account beyond the beginning and the end of an episode. When experiencing on-line for the first time a well-known off-line brand we do not come unprejudiced to that on-line experience. We bring with us all sorts of expectations, possibilities and ways of making sense of an episode. In anticipation we may have a sensation of apprehension or possibly excitement. We may expect the experience to offer certain possibilities for action or outcome and may raise questions to be resolved. We will also anticipate the temporal and spatial character of the experience. We may come to the experience with a desire for fulfilling certain needs or we may be looking for inspiration. It is natural to think of anticipation as something that is prior to what ever it is an anticipation of, and this is true. But anticipation is not just prior. The sensual and emotional aspects of anticipation and our expectation of the compositional structure and spatio-temporal fabric of what follows, shapes later parts of the same experience, it is the relation between our continually revised anticipation and actuality that creates the space of experience.

3.2.2   Connecting

When a situation first impacts our senses before even giving meaning to it, the material components impact on us to generate some response, pre-linguistically. In the spatio-temporal aspect this may be an apprehension of speed or confusing movement or openness and stillness for example. An immediate impression of one frequently visited web-site is of redness and flesh tones which immediately gives an impression of sleaziness, yet on closer inspection it is a quite respectable e-commerce site. For the sensual aspect materially connecting may engender an immediate sense of tension or perhaps a thrill of novelty. For the emotional and causal aspects connecting may engender nothing more than a sense of relief or anticipation at something happening.

3.2.3   Interpreting

Giving meaning to an unfolding experience implies for the compositional and emotional threads, discerning the narrative structure, the agents and the action possibilities, what has happened, what is likely to happen and how this relates to our desires, hopes and fears and our previous experiences. We may sense the thrill of excitement or the anxiety of not knowing how to proceed or what will happen or where we are. At an emotional level, on the basis of our anticipation we may feel frustration or disappointment at thwarted expectations or we may regret being in this situation and have a desire to remove ourselves from it. On the basis of our interpretation falling short of our anticipation we may reflect on our expectations and alter them to be more in line with the new situation.

3.2.4   Reflecting

At the same time as interpreting we may also make judgements about the experience as it unfolds and place a value on it. In reflecting on causal aspects, can we make any sense of things? Are we satisfied with a sense of progress or movement towards completion? From an emotional aspect, do we feel we are getting any sense of fulfilment or achievement? How does the experience tally with our anticipation and how do we feel about being in this situation at this time? From a sensual perspective are we anxious, bored, or excited. In addition to reflecting *in* an experience, we also reflect *on* an experience after it has run its course to completion. This often takes the form of an inner dialogue with oneself or with others. It is a kind of inner recounting. It serves to help us relate the experience to others in an evaluative way in support of appropriation and recounting which in their turn help us reflect.

3.2.5 *Appropriating*

A key part of sense making is relating an experience to previous and future experiences. In appropriating an experience we make it our own. We relate it to our sense of self, our personal history and our hoped for future. We may change our sense of self as a consequence of the experience, or we may simply see this experience as 'just another one of those'. The degree to which an experience changes our sense of self may also be the extent to which we see it as something we identify with and want to experience again. In relating experience to our future and past we also may look afresh at the experience or the setting engendering the experience. Sensual aspects of an experience may become just another "white knuckle ride" or they may become unique moments such as the unforgettable sense of immersion in pure translucent colour when as a first-time scuba diver we descend into "the blue". The emotional aspects of flow and engagement during a session of the computer game "unreal tournament" may be quintessentially cathartic, providing a means of escape from the mundanities of everyday life. The compositional aspects of an experience may relate positively to our sense of self or not. Do we feel it is morally right or socially acceptable to go shopping at a virtual supermarket? How do we reconcile shopping at amazon.com with our commitment to 'the small bookshop' and to the concept of personal service? Is the experience of using a mobile phone one on which new possibilities for action in our everyday life become apparent or is it yet another concession to an undesirable technological future?

3.2.6 *Recounting*

Like reflecting and appropriating, recounting, takes us beyond the immediate experience to consider it in the context of other experiences. It is through a process of internal recounting that we reflect and appropriate experiences, but having appropriated an experience it is also natural to recount it to others. In this way we savour it again, find new possibilities and new meanings in it and this often leads us to want to repeat an experience- to go shopping again, to buy another book or to take another holiday. Experience often takes on different meanings or is giving different value when recounted in a different place at a different time- Marco Polo is reputed to have once said that adventures are hardships and sufferings had in the re-telling. Through recounting to others we draw out an evaluative response from others which changes our own valuation of it. We might for example relate our experience of mobile phones or e-shopping as a zealot but through dialogue with others become something of an apologist.

4. THE FRAMEWORK IN USE

We have used the framework as a starting point for data collection in a study of brand and online experience with the consultants Siegelgale UK. We presented the framework to the company as a written report and an audio-visual presentation. The presentations indicated how the framework could be used to assess the qualities of an on-line shopping site. The company, with our assistance then went on to design its own evaluation exercise using the framework. The context of use we chose involved a variety of experiences of a particular highly branded organisation, Virgin. In a small qualitative study, seven participants were asked to use Virgin services in a number of channels including 'bricks and mortar', web, and WAP. Each of these involved different activities like buying a CD, getting advice on savings for retirement and so on.

They introduced their participants to the ideas of the framework and provided them with a notebook -come- checklist which they called a diary. Each notebook page was divided into sections corresponding to the sense making processes (e.g. anticipating, connecting, interpreting, etc.) and was accompanied by a checklist of concepts and guidewords from the framework. Participants were then asked to go off and have their virgin experiences. In addition to their diary, they provided an oral account during a one-on-one debriefing afterwards. Both the contemporaneous notes and the debriefing were informed by a series of relatively open-ended questions. These were designed to facilitate the construction of a narrative of the experience that would engage with the concepts of the framework.

The study is reported elsewhere (McCarthy, Wright and Meekison 2002), but to give a flavour of the results, we present here an example of a user's experience of buying a CD at Virgin Megastores on-line. He wanted to find out the cost of a Nelly Furtado album and when it will be out and also the price of the Coldplay album.

Anticipating
Expecting it to do all the things as in the store and more…find out information about artists, albums, gig information…….download free or pay audio and visuals, magazines books…..order on line, reserve on line.

Connecting/interpreting/reflecting
Very busy site- lots of flashing and whizzing going on [this in relation to virgin.com portal page] scanning to find search or section. I selected the Megastore link, I've gone somewhere but not sure where as nothing is orienting me. In fact, what is the relationship between the tab and the Megastore link on the left hand side?… Is this an American site of a British site? Not much use to me- I'll find a review of coldplay and buy it from a music store instead. Pity though there are no star ratings for the album. Nothing on Nelly.

Recounting
Not that useful to me as it is very US oriented. Not as rewarding an experience as I had hoped for, it was more of an information site as opposed to an interactive site. Cannot download audio or video cannot buy online or reserve online. Disappointed and unlikely to recommend the site to anyone.

Siegelgale also recounted to us their own reflections about their experiences with the framework. One of the most important features for them was the importance of being able to question expectations and anticipations. They also concluded that aesthetics (by which they meant the sensual and emotional aspects of experience) is the key to being able to articulate user experience. Their view was that although they could understand the idea of sense-making and its components (connecting, interpreting, reflection and so on) these were difficult to work with and often enough it was sufficient to talk about three of the four threads of experience (sensual appearance, compositional structure, emotional unity). They also suggested that a concept of physicality or embodiment seemed to be lacking in the framework. While we might consider such issues within the spatial-temporal thread, our participants wanted something more direct to capture the similarities and differences between on-line and offline, between actually physically handling objects and reading about their descriptions.

Although some of the difficulties experienced by Siegelgale suggest to us that the framework approach requires some fine-tuning and some clarification of concepts if it is to be used as a tool for analysing experience, nevertheless these results are promising. They suggest that the underlying concepts are manageable and usable by practitioners as a way of thinking about user experience.

5. CONCLUSIONS

It is common these days to hear the term experience in connection with theme parks, Hollywood blockbusters, pre-packaged adventure holidays and so on. Experience is used to sell. We are guaranteed an 'experience of a life time' all we need to do is show up with the right amount of money. But Dewey and Bakhtin show us that experience is as much a product of what the user brings to the situation as it is about the artefacts that participate in the experience. What this position implies is that we cannot design an experience. But with a sensitive and skilled way of understanding our users, we can design *for* experience.

Design for experience requires the designer to have ways of seeing experience, to talk about it, to analyse the relations between its parts and to understand how technology does or could participate to make that experience satisfying. The framework we have presented here is not a method for analysing experience, rather it is a set of conceptual tools or a language for thinking and talking about experience. It is intended to help make visible what we consider to be the essential characteristics of experience. Characteristics that differentiate from behaviour, practice, knowledge and other more familiar psychological categories. The case study, informal though it was, suggests that the framework can provide practitioners with an understanding of the concept of experience that would help them design for experience.

6. REFERENCES

Bakhtin, M. (1986). *Speech Genres and Other Late Essays.* Austin, TX: University of Texas Press
Bakhtin, M. (1993). *Toward a Philosophy of the Act.* Austin, TX: University of Texas Press
Boorstin, J. (1995). *Making Movies Work: Thinking like a Filmmaker.* Beverley Hills CA:Salaman James Press.
Csikszentimihalyi (1990). *Flow: The psychology of optimal experience.* NY: Harper and Row.
Dewey, J. (1925). *Experience and Nature.* LaSalle, Illinois: Open Court.
Dewey, J. (1934). *Art as Experience.* New York: Perigree.
Ehn, P., and Löwgren, J. (1997) Design for quality-in-use: Human-computer interaction meets information systems development. In Helander, M., Landauer, T.K. and Prabhu, P. (Eds.), *Handbook of human-computer interaction (2nd edition).* pp. 299-313.Amsterdam, NL: Elsevier Science.

Lee, J., Kim, J. and Moon J.Y. (2000). What makes internet users visit cyber stores again? Key design factors for customer loyalty. Proceedings of CHI'2000, The Hague, Amsterdam, p. 305-312. New York: ACM Press.

McCarthy, J., Wright, P., Meekison, L (2002) Characteristics of user experience of brand and e-shopping. Paper presented at the International Symposium of Cultural Research and Activity Theory, ISCRAT 2002. Amsterdam: Netherlands.

Pu, P. and Faltings, B. (2000). Enriching buyers' experiences: the SmartClient approach. Proceedings of CHI'2000, The Hague, Amsterdam, p. 289-296. New York: ACM Press.

Turkle, S. (1995). *Life on the Screen: Identity in the Age of the Internet.* London: Phoenix.

PETTER BAE BRANDTZÆG, ASBJØRN FØLSTAD AND
JAN HEIM

CHAPTER 5

ENJOYMENT: LESSONS FROM KARASEK

1. INTRODUCTION

What makes some experiences enjoyable, and other experiences not? How can we understand enjoyment in human factors design; what components should we consider when we are designing for enjoyment? This chapter explores a theoretical model for understanding the components and nature of enjoyment, and how HCI (Human Computer Interaction) professionals can use the model to predict and evaluate enjoyment. The model is a modified version of Robert Karasek's well-known *demand-control-support model* used in work and organisational psychology (Karsek & Theorell, 1990).

Enjoyment is a subjective experience that may be understood in relation to theories of motivation. Two distinct types of motivation for engaging in an activity may be distinguished. Extrinsic motivation depends on the reinforcement value of the outcome of the activity, and parallels the idea of 'technology as tool'; in a traditional usability perspective, whether or not the technology functions as a means to complete well-defined tasks, particularly work related tasks. Intrinsically motivated action is perceived as rewarding in it self, and is a parallel to the idea of 'technology as a toy'. In their study of motivation and computers in the workplace, Davis et al. (1992) conclude that both intrinsic and extrinsic motivation explain workers' intentions when using computers.

It is central to the understanding of user behaviour that a complex pattern of behaviour may consist of both extrinsically motivated tasks and intrinsically motivated activity. As an example, search behaviour on the WWW will often not follow a strict goal oriented pattern. Rather the user may soon be lured away from her search task by an interesting piece of information that diverts her attention in a joyous short-lived oasis of distraction before she returns to her original search chore; probably only to be lured away a second time. Even the most boring tasks may include refuges of intrinsically motivated activity, in the same way, joyous activities may involve extrinsically motivated tasks. These two kinds of behaviour may be close in time and space; but they still involve dissimilar sets of human factors issues and different theoretical assumptions.

Mark A. Blythe, Andrew F. Monk, Kees Overbeeke and Peter C. Wright *(eds.),*
Funology: From Usability to Enjoyment, 55—65

1.1 Karaseks demand-control-support model

Karasek's paradigm describes a simple theoretical framework of good and healthy work. The model postulates that job satisfaction and well-being result not from a single aspect of the work environment, but from the joint effects of the experienced demands of the work situation, the decision latitude available to the worker, and finally the degree of social support from co-workers and management. Job satisfaction and well-being occur when job demands, job decision latitude and social support, are high (Karasek & Theorell, 1990).

The goal structure of a good working life in Karasek's terms is similar to the goal structure of enjoyable activities. A good working life is not seen as the engagement in a series of well-defined tasks, achieving well-defined goals. Rather it consists of an interwoven complexity of activities in dynamic environments with several actors and conflicting interests. Jacob Nielsen (1996) has proposed that in business or work it is becoming common to cater to subjective whims and satisfaction. It is also interesting that work has been referred to as "hard fun" (Jensen, 1999). Traditional usability assessment does not address this aspect of work life at all, but is mainly focused on optimising task performance for the lonely worker in a static work environment. However, it should be noted that Shneiderman (1987) refers to "subjective satisfaction" as one of several usability goals.

We contend that the demand-control-support model will be useful in the investigation and understanding of the enjoyable experience, because the model includes components that seem to be universal in the understanding of activities associated with well-being. Csikszentmihalyi (1992) states: "It would be a mistake to assume that only art and leisure provide optimal experience" (p. 52). It should then be reasonable to expect that an adjusted version of the Karasekian model may help to understand and predict fun and enjoyment in human factors design. Literature on the theory of fun and enjoyment in support of the proposed model will be reviewed below.

2. DEMANDS AND ENJOYMENT: CHALLENGE AND VARIATION

Challenges and variation of procedures and tasks are regarded as important aspects of the demands of a work situation. Variation reflects the degree of an active experience, which is essential to the design of good jobs (Karasek, 1979; Karasek &Theorell, 1990). The concept of demands is understood as the degree of variation and challenge experienced by users of technology, and is also an important aspect of enjoyment. Products and services for enjoyment do not necessarily provide a given task to be performed, but rather a notion of "a good experience". The central element in the optimal experience is that the activity is a goal in itself (Csikszentmihalyi, 1992).

The concept of challenging demands is not unknown in the human factors literature. According to Skelly (1995) variation is a well-known means of exploiting the element of curiosity or surprise. It has similarly been argued that a certain degree of unpredictability is important for the experience of fun (Davenport et al., 1998).

Thackara (2000) points out that future human factors design should take into consideration the fact that people enjoy being stimulated.

2.1 Challenges

"A lot of pieces that you deal with are very straightforward ... and you don't find anything exciting about them ... but there are other pieces that have some sort of challenge ... those are the pieces that stay in your mind, that are the most interesting."
Csikszentmihalyi (1992, p. 51).

Many people use their leisure and spare times to solve hard puzzles or seek out difficult challenges. As an example, computer games are often experienced as fun when they have a certain level of difficulty. This can be explained by the notion that a dynamic environment is associated with challenges that invites activity and involvement. Those users meet challenges that are stimulating and encourage creativity. The users get the opportunity to test their own skills (Holmquist, 1997).

Csikszentmihalyi (1975) refers to other examples of challenging demands: surgeons performing difficult operations or rock climbers struggling to scale an unclimbed mountain peak. Situations like these may be intensely demanding, but at the same time they may elevate the individual to a level of optimal experience or a "flow" experience: An experience that takes the individual to a state of absorbing engagement. In literature, "demands" in terms of challenges and variations are connected to the opportunity and motivation to learn (Karasek & Theorell, 1990). The opportunity to acquire mastery may promote a feeling of self-confidence and an intrinsic motivation to use a particular technology.

Figure 1. *BigBrother in Norway - one of the most watched and successful TV programmes ever shown on Norwegian Television.*

Correspondingly, Springel (1999) argues that the computer is becoming a device for stimulation. Springel suggests that the growing interest in games, web-entertainment, online chat etc. foreshadows a new attitude towards media. In turn this may shape a different form of media, which directly engages and challenges users and allows them to take active roles in co-creating the new media experience. A variant of this is the concept of reality TV, such as "Big Brother" (see Figure 1). As a viewer you can vote for the participants you like or dislike. You can also choose to follow the program in different media channels such as the Internet and mobile phones and you have the opportunity to e-mail and chat with the participants in the show. The same tendency is reflected in other media channels such as MUDs (Multi User Domains). This trend is moving users away from being passive consumers to becoming active collaborators.

2.2 Variation – and the surpassing of users' expectations

In the face of routine and repetitiveness, people easily get bored. Variation may be seen as hinged on assuming a universal human interest in novelty and fascination for surprises, spontaneity, freshness and a certain degree of unpredictability. The importance of variation is congruent with the meaning of demands stated in the Karasek-model.

From a human factors perspective, the concept of variation involves the prediction that products or services with a static design, and at the same time no novelties or change, will lose users' interest. Today we see an increasing rate in the turnover of news, trends, systems, applications and products to meet the demands for variation and novelty. Karasek and Theorell claim that "new challenges must constantly be confronted - and offering them will be a significant challenge for work designers" (Karasek & Theorell, 1990, p. 173). The same challenges will probably be significant for the human factors designer.

Unpredictability, or the element of surprise, is an important facet of variation. There are of course different levels of unpredictability. Regarding human factors design, it is unpredictability just on the edge of security, involving no more than minor risks or possible penalties, which will be of central relevance to fun (Davenport, Holmquist & Thomas, 1998). Psychoanalytic theory also emphasises the importance of risk to jokes and fun (Freud, 1960). Hassenzhal et al. (2000) state that products should have elements added in order to make them interesting, novel, or surprising. Designing for fun may involve the inclusion of something unexpected, an element of surprise and unrelated or opposing events. Surprise and unpredictability are also well-known approaches in marketing research to gauge consumer experience. Consumer experience is often understood in terms of the discrepancies between *ex ante* expectations of a product and the products *ex post* performance. The best predictors of a good experience are when the product actually exceeds the users' expectations (Oliver, 1981).

Unpredictability and challenges may partially be in conflict with principles of traditional usability (Hassenzahl et al., 2000). Making something as simple as possible may make it boring. In the Karasek model the importance of the joint effects of demands and decision latitude is addressed. Karasek (1979) stresses the importance of matching challenges with individual skills and control. Csikszentmihalyi (1975) states that "flow" requires a subtle balance of not being too simple and not being too challenging. Demands without the experience of control will result in a stressful and frustrating experience, rather than the experiences of joy. Decision latitude or control without any demands will probably imply a passive and probably boring interaction. An enjoyable experience is dependent on the balance between demands and control.

3. DECISION LATITUDE AND ENJOYMENT: SKILL DISCRETION AND DECISON AUTHORITY

User control is regarded as an important aspect of an enjoyable experience and is addressed through the concept of decision latitude. In consonance with the Karasek model, the concept is defined as including: the ability to use and develop skills, and the availability of decision-making authority or freedom of action. Decision latitude can also be seen in the light of engagement, a concept discussed by Brenda Laurel (1991). Engagement refers to the user's feeling of being in control of the interaction. Laurel writes about computer fiction, games, etc. and addresses the subject "I" who interacts in a virtual world. There should be nothing to mediate the communication between the user and the system. "I do, what I myself want and feel involved in what I am doing." (p. 116). Laurel suggests that the frequency of interaction, the range of possible alternatives available for selection at a given time and the effectiveness of the inputs influence engagement. The interface should enable the user to see the effects of her or his actions, to give a sense of agency or personal power.

3.1 Skill discretion: the opportunity to use and develop skills

Getting to use one's own skills in the fullest range possible helps to make activities enjoyable. Everyone knows the truly intrinsic joy attached to engagement in activities that invite the utilisation of acquired skills. The ability to use and develop skills may be seen as related to the term "self-efficacy". Within social cognitive theory self-efficacy is the belief "in one's capabilities to organise and execute the courses of action required to produce given attainments" (Bandura, 1997, p. 3). Self-efficacy involves monitoring and evaluating one's own actions, and influences the individual's decision about what activities to engage in, whether to proceed with the activity when faced with obstacles, and the mastery of that particular activity. Self-efficacy is not a measure of skill, but is closely related to the likelihood of the individual to reach the ability to using a given technology at a level of contentment. Factors such as unwanted complexity, unrealistic tolls on the knowledge of potential users, and other comfort issues faced by the users, may be construed as self-efficacy deficits. Low self-efficacy is likely to mean that the use of technology is not perceived as rewarding, following which it is less likely that the technology will be used in the future (Eastin & LaRose, 2000). Conversely, high self-efficacy will be correlated with the tendency of increased technology use, and also the development of skill and mastery.

The development of skills may be seen as a path winding from the first faint attempts of the novice, to the full-blown repertoire of skills of the expert. Dreyfus, Dreyfus and Athanasiou (1986) describe progress from novice to expert as going through qualitatively different stages; from early efforts of learning rules and repetitive training, to the non-reflective mastery of the expert. As skills develop, the engaged-in activities will gradually become intrinsically satisfying.

3.2 The decision-making authority of the user

According to Karasek, elevating the level of the decision-making authority of the worker improves wellbeing at work. Similarly, providing the user with extended powers of decision-making may enhance the fun experienced in a user-technology interaction. The level of decision-making authority of the user is a consequence of constraints inherent in the relation between the user and the technology. Unlike constraints on decision-making in a workplace, rules, strict routines, organisational hierarchy and repetitiveness, the constraints of the user-technology relation are a consequence of the user not seeing or understanding the possibilities represented by the technology. Choi et al. (1999) address this point in their analysis of computer-game design factors. They suggest that fun computer games are characterised by the gamers freedom and leadership in the progression of the game's story. In order to make possible the leadership of the gamer, computer-games must give hints in a manner the gamers can perceive and understand. This, of course, without giving away the complete solution to the game.

Another example of user control is the opportunity of "fun design" through *personalization* of the technology. Nokia have served their users with products they can personalize with tremendous success. In the case of, for example, the Nokia 3350, users can personalize their phones by using a ringing tone as an SMS alert or compose their own SMS alerts for originality. A picture editor allows users to create and personalize picture messages for all occasions. The phone's rhythmic backlight alert accompanying a ringing tone also makes it fun to receive a call. Users can also opt for a fully personalized look by downloading profile names, logos and ringing tones. Other personalization options include an exclusive range of changeable Xpress-on covers in new and exciting colours.

These opportunities to personalize the technology give the user decision-making authority over the technology. It enables the user to influence and to create their own experience in a dialogue with the technology. The role of personalization may also be seen in relation to another phenomena, social cohesion or social identity; that you give the user a feeling of being part of a group, which will be discussed further in section 4.2.

4. SOCIAL SUPPORT AS ENJOYMENT: CO-ACTIVITY AND SOCIAL COHESION

Many leisure activities may be characterised as socialising. Thackara (2000) states that providing the user with a sort of community is important in designing for a good user experience. Also an awareness of the conditions that support enjoyable social interaction is important in the design of systems (Monk, 2000). The parallel in Karasek is social support. Karasek and Theorell (1990) define social support as "the overall levels of helpful social interaction available on the job from both co-workers and supervisors" (p.69). Two element of this may be useful in explaining enjoyment: co-activity and social cohesion.

4.1 Co-activity

The concept of co-activity implies collective action; a user's social behaviour, not just human-computer interaction as a single user of the system. User studies have pinpointed the fun of doing things together (Mäkelä & Battarbee, 1999; Mäkelä, et al, 2000; Battarbee, et al, 2000), and technology that promotes an opportunity for social interaction probably supports an enjoyable user experience.

Figure 2. *Game boy Advanced: with multi-player opportunities*

Communication and interaction are identified as the most popular activities on the Internet (December, 1996). Likewise, the spread and use of mobile telephones can be seen as an example of a social need. Studies indicate that young people and adults use mobile telephones differently, where young people engage in expressive rather than informative use (Ling, 1999). A Swedish field study that mapped the use of mobile telephones among youngsters, found that both the mobile phone and the information on it is often shared among users and made public in various ways. Young people use mobile phones for doing things together in collaborative, social action, rather than task-related communication (Weilenmann & Larsson, 2000). The sharing of experiences, feelings and information is considered to be rewarding, pleasant and enjoyable. However, there may also be an element of competition or contest, which by nature is seen in relation to fun. Studies show that young people are likely to use the computer for playing games together, rather than playing in isolation (Wartella et al., 2000). These findings may be explained by the *social facilitation effect;* it is easier, and more rewarding and motivating to do things in the presence of others, because mere presence of others is arousing (Zajonc, 1965). Children play more enthusiastically if a playmate is near by, even if only engaged in parallel play

4.2 Social cohesion

Social cohesion is related to a social expression of being part of or attracted to a community. Social psychologists define cohesion as the attraction towards the group and motivation to participate in the activities of a group (Cartwright & Zander, 1960,). Being part of groups with high levels of social cohesiveness is positively related to individual wellbeing (Sonnentag, 1996). The term *affiliation* is related to social cohesion. Affiliation occurs because social contact is rewarding. The rewarding aspect of affiliation includes emotional happiness and cognitive stimulation, opportunity for self-confirmation through the attention of others, opportunity for relevant self-knowledge through social comparison, and the opportunity of emotional support and sympathy (Hogg & Abrams, 1993). Individually experienced rewards associated with social cohesion may be important to understand fun in human factors design. Mäkelä et al. (2000) found that children use digital images for joking, storytelling and sharing art. One of the purposes of sending images seemed to be to maintain attraction between group members. The social nature of technology use is also reflected in the boom of communities of young media users who create their own web pages (Wartella et al., 2000). Such personal online publishing offers a fun way for young people to connect with their peers and others interested in the same topic. Jordan (1997) considers 'pleasure with products' to be characterised by social relations and communication enabled by the product. These products bring people together and provide topics of discussion or conversation.

Interactive technology is not, and should not be, socially isolating. On the contrary, it should be used for important social activity. High levels of social support are, according to Karasek and Theorell (1990), important in providing favourable effects in the interaction between demands and decision latitude. Human factors design should focus on the development of design, which provides more social opportunities, to facilitate enjoyable experiences.

5. CONCLUSION

Karasek's demands-control-support model, which predicts wellbeing and motivation in the context of work, is useful for understanding enjoyment in human factors design. When designing for enjoyment, professionals should consider demands, but at the same time allow a high degree of decision latitude and socially rewarding activity. The factors of demands and decision latitude have been treated separately, but it is important to address the crucial interaction effects between these. It has been explained that an enjoyable user-technology interaction depends on the interaction effects of challenge and use and the development of skills, as well as variation and the enabling of the decision-making authority of the user. How these joint effects enable an enjoyable experience will of course depend on the context. In addition, the effects of co-activity and design in support of social cohesion have been discussed. On this basis, three implications for the design of enjoyable technology may be formulated:

- *User control and participation, with appropriate challenges:* to enjoy technology the user should be enabled to carry out challenging activities. These activities should attract the user's attention and test his or her skills. Besides being challenging the design should allow the user to feel in control of the interaction. The user also needs to see the effects of her actions in order to give a sense of agency or personal power. To give the users an experience of active participation is central to an enjoyable experience.
- *Variation and multiple opportunities*: the user should be provided with a high level of variation by offering multiple possibilities and services. There should be an opportunity to personalise the product. This should be under direct user control, where the user explicitly selects between certain options. A key point is to give the user more than they actually expect.
- *Social opportunities in terms of co-activity and social cohesion*: the technology should give the user a feeling of being part of a group. The technology should also enable the users to do things together in social activities. A socially rewarding environment is necessary and essential for all humans, also when it comes to enjoyment.

Future research should focus on the development of reliable and valid measures of the factors and aspects that have been introduced. In addition the question of integrating knowledge and the evaluation of fun in the design process will be a major challenge in the future.

6. ACKNOWLEDGEMENT

We would like to thank our colleague Anne Lund.

7. REFERENCES

Bandura A. (1997). *Self-efficacy: The exercise of control*. New York: W.H. Freeman.
Battarbee, K, Mattelmäki, T., & Mäkelä, A., (2000). Design for user experience, method lessons form a design student workshop. *Proceedings of the 1th Nordic CHI*. Stockholm.
Cartwright, D., & Zander, A. (1960). *Group dynamics. Research and Theory.*(2nd ed.). Evanstone: Row, Peterson and Company.
Choi, D., Kim, H., & Kim, J. (1999). Toward the Construction of Fun Computer Games: Differences in the Views of Developers and Players. *Personal Technologies, 3*, 92-104.
Csikszentmihalyi, M. (1975). *Beyond boredom and anxiety*. San Francisco: Jossey-Bass Publisher.
Csikszentmihalyi, M. (1992). *Flow. The psychology of happiness*. London: Rider.
Davenport, G., Holmquist, L. E., & Thomas, M. (1998). Fun: A Condition of Creative Research. *IEEE MultiMedia, 5,3*, 10-15.
Davis, F. D., Bagozzi, R. P., & Warshaw, P. R. (1992). Extrinsic and intrinsic motivation to use computers in the workplace. *Journal of Applied Social Psychology, 22*, 1111-1132.
December, J. (1996). Units of analysis for Internet communication. *Journal of Communication, 46,1*, 14-38.
Draper, S.W. (1999). Analysing Fun as a Candidate Software Requirement. *Personal Technologies, 3*, 117-122.

Dreyfus, H.L., Dreyfus S.E., & Athanasiou. (1986) Mind over machine : the power of human intuition and expertise in the era of the computer. Oxford: Basil Blackwell.

Eastin, M. S., & LaRose, R. (2000). Internet Self-Efficacy and the Psychology of the Digital Divide. *JCMC, 6,1.* Retrieved April 16, 2001 from the World Wide Web: *http://www.ascusc.org/jcmc/vol6/issue1/eastin.html*

Freud, S. (1960). Jokes and their relations to the unconscious. London: Routledge & Kegan Paul.

Hassenzhal, M., Platz, A., Burmester, M. and Lehner, K. (2000). Hedonic and Ergonomic Quality Aspects Determine a Software's Appeal.(pp. 201-208) *Proceedings of the CHI 2000 conference on Human factors in computing systems.* April 1 - 6, 2000, The Hague Netherlands.

Hogg, M., & Abrams, D. (1993). Towards a single-process uncertainty-reduction model of social motivation in groups. In Hogg, M., & Abrams, D. (Eds.), *Group Motivation. Social Psychological Perspectives.* New York: Harvester Wheatsheaf.

Holmquist, L.E. (1997). The right kind of challenge. . In (Eds.) Braa, K., & Monteiro, E., *Proceedings of the 20th Informations systems Research seminar in Scandinavia. IRIS 20.* Department of Informatics, University of Oslo.

Igbaria, M.; Schiffman, S. J., & Wieckowski, T. J. (1994). The respective roles of perceived usefulness and perceived fun in the acceptance of microcomputer technology. *Behaviour & Information Technology, 13,6,* 349-361.

Jensen, R. (1999). *Dream Society. The Coming Shift from Information to Imagination.* London: McGraw-Hill Book Company.

Jordan, P. W. (1997). The four pleasures – taking human factors beyond usability. *Proceedings of the 13th Triennial Congress of the International Ergonomics Association, 2,* 364-365. Helsinki: Finnish Institute for Occupational Health.

Karasek, R. (1979). Job demands, job decision latitude, and mental strain: Implications for job redesign. *Administrative Science Quarterly, 24,* 258-307.

Karasek, R., & Theorell, T. (1990). *Healthy work: stress, productivity, and the reconstruction of working life.* New York: Basic books.

Laurel, B. (1991). *Computer as Theatre.* Reading, MA: Addison-Wesley.

Ling, R (1999). We release them little by little. Maturation and gender identity as seen in the use of mobile telephony, *Telenor R&D Report 5/99.*

Mäkelä, A., & Battarbee (1999). It's Fun to do Things Together: Two Cases of Explorative User Studies. *Personal Technologies,* 3-137-140.

Mäkelä, A., Giller, V. Tscheligi, V., & Sefelin, R. (2000). Joking, storytelling, artsharing, expressing affection: a field trial of how children and their social network communicate with digital images in leisure time. (pp. 548-555). *Proceedings of the CHI 2000 conference on Human factors in computing systems.* April 1 - 6, 2000, The Hague Netherlands.

Monk, A.F. (2000) User-centred design: the home use challenge. In Sloane,A., & van Rijn, F. (Eds.), *Home informatics and telematics: information technology and society* (pp. 181-190). Boston: Kluwer Academic Publishers.

Nielsen, J. (1996). *Seductive user interface.* Retrieved April 12, 2001 from the World Wide Web: http://www.useit.com/papers/seductiveui.html

Oliver, R. L. (1981). "Measurement and Evaluation of Satisfaction in Retail Settings." Journal of Retailing 57 (Fall). 25-48.Peppers, D. and Rogers, M. (1993). *The One to One Future: Building Relationships One Customer at a Time.* New York. Currency/Doubleday.

Shneiderman, B. (1987*).Designing the User Interface: Strategies for Effective Human-Computer Interaction*, Addison-Wesley Publ. Co., Reading, MA

Skelly, T. (1995). Seductive Interfaces – Engaging, Not Enraging the user. *Microsoft Interactive Media Conference.* Retrieved April 10, 2001 from the World Wide Web: *http://www.designhappy.com/sedint/TheMaze.htm*

Springel, S. (1999). The New Media Paradigm: Users as Creators of Content. *Personal Technologies, 3,* 153-159.

Sonnentag, S. (1996). Work Group Factors and Individual Well-being. In West, M. A. (Ed.), *Handbook of Work Group Psychology* (pp. 345-367). Chichester: John Wiley & Sons.

Thackara, J. (2000). The design challenge of pervasive computing. *CHI, 2000 .* Retrieved April 1, 2001 from the World Wide Web: *http://www.doorsofperception.com/projects/chi/*

Wartella, E., O'Keefe, B., & Scantlin, R. (2000), Children and Interactive Media. A compendium of current research and directions for the future. *A report to the Markle Foundation. Markle*

Foundation. Retrieved February 2, 2001 from the World Wide Web:
  http://www.markle.org/news/digital_kids.pdf
Weilenmann, A., & Larsson, C. (2000). Collaborative Use of Mobile Telephones: A Field Study of
  Swedish Teenagers. *Proceedings of the 1th Nordic CHI*. Stockholm.
Zajonc, R. B. (1965). Social facilitation. *Science, 149*, 269-274.

DARREN J. REED

CHAPTER 6

FUN ON THE PHON: THE SITUATED EXPERIENCE OF RECREATIONAL TELEPHONE CONFERENCES

1. INTRODUCTION

How do we know when we are having fun? A psychological approach can tell you what it feels like or how it is perceived; a sociological approach, on the other hand, can show how, as active participants in structures of social relevance, members of society *have fun together.*

We take the view that 'having fun' is a *situated and interactional experience.* By which we mean that particular identifiable social arrangements encourage, allow for, or engender a collective sense of enjoyable engagement. That they are identifiable means they are available for empirical observation. We have therefore a specific notion of fun in mind that might contrast with others (Blythe and Hassenzahl this volume).

Goffman's notion of 'situated experience' is enlisted as a theoretical and conceptual basis, and Conversation Analysis (henceforth CA) as a methodology in our investigation of technologically mediated interaction. CA is a form of detailed 'naturalistic observation' that seeks to understand structures of meaning generated sequentially through interaction between individuals – typically in 'talk-in-action'. The combination of CA and Goffman – what we might call directed or applied CA – is seen in Hopper's (1992) analysis of play on the phone. Our contribution builds on this example in the situation of recreational telephone conferences, and aims to provide a viable approach for product development. Our efforts are preliminary, and offer only exemplars of analytic findings, but start to build a case for an empirical sociological account of technologically mediated experience.

2. FUN AS SITUATED EXPERIENCE

Erving Goffman is credited with bringing the individual into sociology and developing, according to Williams (1998), 'a distinctly sociological account of the

Mark A. Blythe, Andrew F. Monk, Kees Overbeeke and Peter C. Wright *(eds.),*
Funology: From Usability to Enjoyment, 67—79

person'. He does this by moving attention away from the individual's 'inner' life and toward 'externally observable forms of conduct' (ibid). He builds his notions of fun on the related area of play.

In sociology play has historically been contrasted with work (Slater, 1998) or conceived as meeting a range of social functions: from the socialisation of children to the large-scale development of culture (Bruner, 1976; Huizinga, 1949). By contrast, for Schwartzman (1978) play is a 'context of activity rather than a structure' (Sutton-Smith 1988:xi). Play is the product of action, creates its own context and is freed from specified space and time.

Sociology's 'linguistic turn' in the 1960's (Lemert and Branaman, 1997) brought an emphasis on the individual and an acceptance of communication based notions of play. Stephenson (1967) sees media consumption as a form of play in which potential 'communication pleasure' involves complete and effortless engrossment. Bateson (1972) conceives of 'metacommunicative' cues that 'frame' behaviour beyond what is actually said or done; an example being the cue 'this is play' seen in the play fighting of animals. In what might be seen as a combination of these ideas, Goffman (1961) conceives of fun in terms of mutual engrossment in a social 'encounter' or 'focused gathering'. He says, 'When an individual becomes engaged in an activity … it is possible for him to become caught up by it, carried away by it, engrossed in it - to be, as we say, spontaneously involved in it' (Goffman, 1961:38). Fun is the sense of euphoria possible when there is 'spontaneous co-involvement', when all are engrossed in the commonly understood encounter.

Goffman therefore looks to identify the social propensities of experience: not as cognitive processes, but as sociological arrangements, as *situated experience*. He does this by developing Bateson's idea of frames to cover all social meaning. Frames become 'principles of organization which govern events – at least social ones – and our subjective involvement in them' (Goffman, 1974:10-11). Goffman defines frame analysis as an examination of 'the organization of experience' (ibid:11). Individual experiences in socially organized frameworks of meaning are more than mental emotions:

> 'frameworks are not merely a matter of mind but correspond …to the way in which an aspect of the activity itself is organized…Organizational premises are involved, and these are something cognition somehow arrives at, not something cognition creates or generates. Given their understanding of what it is that is going on, individuals fit their actions to this understanding and ordinarily find that the ongoing world supports this fitting. These organizational premises – sustained both in the mind and in activity – I call the frame of the activity.

> …activity interpreted by the application of particular rules and inducing fitting actions from the interpreter, activity, in short, that organizes matter for the interpreter, itself is located in a physical, biological, and social world' (Goffman, 1974:247).

To Goffman frames of meaningful experience are cognitive ('a matter of mind'), social (organized activity) *and* material (physical, spatial, temporal). What's more they are contextual and temporal: worked out in ongoing social activity.

2.1 Schemata of frame analysis

All social experience is made meaningful by frames, the most fundamental being 'primary frameworks'. There are two kinds of primary framework: *natural* and *social*. The first set of frameworks define situations in terms of physical contingencies that are not controlled by humans, such as the weather (1974:22); the second make sense of situations in terms of human intervention, activities, motives and the like. A barbecue, in which a number of friends talk chat and eat, can be understood in terms of a social frame. Success or failure of the event might similarly be decided through a social frame of interpretation: people might not get on with each other. On the other hand a sudden downpour that sends guests scurrying inside without eating could be explained in terms of a natural frame, beyond the control of human actors.

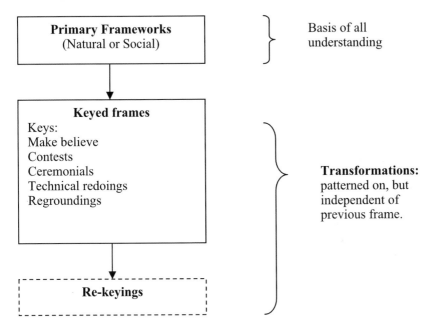

Figure 1. *A schemata of frame analysis*

These primary frameworks however can be transformed into a new meaning. For example the host of the barbecue might be held responsible for organising the event on the particular day if he or she was a professional weather person. The failure of the event might then be a matter of poor planning. Goffman says the meaningful experience can be 're-keyed'. A key is,

'the set of conventions by which a given activity, one already meaningful in terms of some primary framework, is transformed into something patterned on this activity but seen by the participants to be something quite else. The process of transcription [or transformation] can be called keying' (Goffman, 1974:43-44).

Goffman identifies five basic keyed frames: make believe, contests, ceremonials, technical redoings, regroundings (1974:48). The first of these the *make-believe key* playfully transforms a serious frame into a non-serious one and is normally for the benefit of an audience. However daydreaming is an example of when the person employing the key and the person understanding the meaning are the same. Radio, television and theatre are examples of make believe keys because they involve 'dramatic scripting' according to Goffman. According to Manning (1992) 'Make-believe [keys are] only sustained by a considerable collective engrossment in the transformed frame, and as a result, spontaneous make-believe keys are likely to be short-lived' (ibid:214).

An important point to be made about keys is they can also be transformed into new meaning - they can be *re*-keyed. Each re-keying is a transformation, a new frame patterned on the one preceding it. A situation may have many layers of meaning, or 'laminations',

> '… the outermost lamination of a frame of a [theatrical] play tells us that what is happening is make-believe, even though an inner lamination tells us, perhaps, that Romeo and Juliet are very much in love' (Manning, 1992:126).

The potential confusion possible with multiple layers of meaning is avoided through clear frame 'anchors'; one example being 'brackets', which denote when a frame starts and ends. Like mathematical formula, brackets can be 'internal' or 'external': external brackets are not formally part of the activity to be framed, e.g. the raising of the theatrical curtain; internal brackets mark off 'strips' of the ongoing frame as having a separate meaning.

2.2 Frames as interactional achievements

An element that is underdeveloped in Goffman's frame analysis, is the *interactional achievement* of frames, specifically through the negotiation of bracketed meaning. When talking about playfulness, for example, Glenn and Knapp (1987) see 'a series of framing signals *mutually negotiated* by the participants' (emphasis added, p. 52). Frames of meaning are produced in real time interactive behaviour.

One way to extend Goffman's conceptual apparatus is to apply Conversation Analysis (CA), which is interested in the sense people make in sequences of action, as a temporal and emergent features of people's interaction.

2.2.1 Thick external bracket

Jason Rutter analyses comedy compéres' introduction talk in the 'Framing of Response' of the audience, which engenders 'alertness' and 'involvement' (2000:471). In this way the comedy routine is framed as a particular comedic strip of experience,

> 'The introduction sequence is invariably a feature of stand-up openings and holds a position as forerunner to the entrance of comedians and their first joke. It provides a

foundation for the performance and prepares the audience by establishing stand-up conventions, expectations and situation for the comedy to take place' (2000:482).

He makes a point about the keyed nature of jokes, in relation to the broader bracketed comedy routine when he comments,

'Given this organization, jokes performed by stand-up comedians cannot be seen as isolated texts. They cannot be seen as being hermetically separated from the ongoing performance, as they are located within, and part of, the developing interaction of stand-up' (Rutter, 2000:481).

While compéres' introductions have a conventional nature, Rutter notes an introduction sequence by Johnny Vegas – himself a comedian – that completely undermines these conventions. In a Goffman sense, the introduction-keyed frame is itself re-keyed.

Compéres' introductions are sequences of interaction (between compéres and audience) that we might think of as 'thick' brackets. Goffman details such a thick bracket in a description of a radio broadcaster introducing a live concert (1974:263). The framing work is achieved over a period of time, and may itself include internal brackets. The jokes are themselves transformed frames within the comedic episode based upon the compére's external bracketing.

2.2.2   Internal brackets as an interactional achievement

In an explicit combination of Conversation Analysis (CA) Goffman and Bateson, Hopper (1992) uses the ideas of meta-communication and frames to understand the *interactive* nature of play on the phone. He underlines interactional achievement when he says 'Parties must … work out the course of play-in-progress' (Hopper, 1992:176). He notes that after ten years of looking for the 'elusive beginning bracket carrying the message 'this is play' he has instead come to the conclusion that it is misleading to think in terms of a single 'keying message signal' (p. 175). Instead, he says, telephone play takes the following form,

```
CAROL:      have you ate t'day?
(0.5)
CAROL:      Eaten?=
Rick:       =eh heh heh=
CAROL:      =day hay huh huh eated. .hhhh=
Rick:       =No I-I-I- already eated heh heh heh
```

Transcript 1. *Telephone play, Hopper, 1992:175-6*

Rather than a specific cue, the extract is shot through with 'play-relevant keying' in the form of a *speech error* in the first line, *laughter* after the error is corrected and *repetition* in the last two lines. Hopper concludes 'The play frame is created and sustained through each of these interactive details. There is no single front bracket for play in this episode, but rather play's interactive management occurs across this entire fragment' (Hopper 1992:176).

In short, 'Meta-communicative framing comes about not through individual message units that accomplish bracketing, but by interactive displays across speakers' turns. Each such indication of play's possible relevance may be confirmed, denied, ignored, or transformed by what happens next' (Hopper 1992:177).

The example of CA and frame analysis allows for an appreciation of a number of specific interactional details such as episodic bracketing which may involve 'thick brackets' of interaction, and the play relevant keying of activity in a series of interactional turns. In each instance successful framing is a transformation of the underlying frame.

3.   ANALYSING FUN ON THE PHONE

Goffman's concepts of fun and frame analysis and their application to real instances of activity through Conversation Analytic method inform our analysis of fun on the phone. This analysis is part of the ethnographic stage of work carried out at York University in an initiative investigating the 'good recreational experience' in technologically mediated interactions funded by PACCIT[1].

The Friendship Links scheme[2] provides telephone conferences for isolated older people in London. Groups of four to eight people come together for an informal half hour chat each week and a trained coordinator or 'facilitator' encourages a friendly and lively atmosphere. With the consent of participants a number of calls were recorded, transcribed[3] and analysed. This analysis involved combing the concepts in frame analysis and directed Conversation Analysis. Rather than a one-way methodological process (i.e. concept informing observation), there developed a 'mutual elaboration' of concept and analysis (Reed, 2002). Wherein at times the concept of frames motivated looking at the data in a particular (directed) way and at other times CA provided the lead for conceptual development. Indeed 'analysis' and 'conceptual basis' developed together in a continual circular manner, i.e.,

Frames & fun

CA analysis

Figure 2. *Mutual elaboration of conception and analysis*

For purposes of narrative integrity the following section contains exemplar 'findings' from this process that necessarily simplifies this relationship.

3.1 From formal to fluid interaction

General observation of the telephone conferences revealed an interesting feature: facilitated calls started out stilted and formal but at some point became a relaxed interaction between the whole group. The move from one to the other was highly relevant to us; the question being how it occurred. What became apparent was that we could understand this move in terms of particular interaction that framed the behaviour in different ways. We began to talk about this in terms of the move from 'formality' to 'fluidity'.

3.1.1   The primary frame of the telephone

One way in which CA helped the conceptual development was in understanding the primary frame of the telephone conference. There has been a great deal of work on telephone conversations in CA that recognises the limitations of the audio channel and the consequences for behaviour. Emanuel Schegloff for example (1986) shows that there is a ritualised sequence of interaction – what he calls the 'canonical telephone opening' - at the beginning of a two person telephone call to deal with questions about who is speaking to whom, about what, and who gets to speak first:

Example telephone opening	Sequence elements
((Telephone ring)) R: Hello C: Hello Ida? R: Yeah C: Hi, =This is Carla R: Hi Carla. C: How are you. R: Okay:. C: Good.= R: =How about you. C: Fine. Don wants to know….	Summons/Answer Identification/Recognition Greetings Initial inquiries or 'how-are-you's' Caller's move to first topic

Figure .3. *Canonical opening of telephone call – adapted from Schegloff, 1986*

The need to deal with such issues as 'access', 'recognition' and 'turn ordering' are exaggerated with telephone conferences when there are more people involved in the call. In face-to-face conversation the more people in an interaction the more difficult a conversation is. Atkinson (1982) explains that ordered conversation is based upon 'solutions being found to what can be characterized as the problem of achieving and sustaining the shared attentiveness of co-present parties to a single sequence of actions' (Atkinson, 1982:97). The greater the number of people in a group the more difficult shared attentiveness is to generate, and the greater likelihood of formal methods of coordination (ibid.). So for example successful classroom interaction often depends upon rules about who gets to speak when. Wayne Beach suggests that facilitated group discussions lie toward the formal end of a continuum of formal and informal talk, what he calls a 'casual-institutional continuum' (Beach, 1990:201) - All of which goes towards explaining why business meetings and telephone conferences have formal agendas.

Recreational telephone conferences have a natural frame of meaning based upon the physical (visual) limitations of the technology. From this *natural* frame, there needs to develop a *social* frame of socialising. This is achieved through particular social rituals.

3.1.2   Framing the call –Introductions as thick external brackets

Given the primary frame of the telephone conference a number of issues have to be addressed immediately upon the arrival of each new participant. Rituals have developed played out between Operator, Facilitator and new participant to do this.

In the calls we examined, an Operator gains access to the ongoing call and introduces each new participant by directly addressing the Facilitator. This 'direct introduction' leads to a 'directed welcome' segment between new participant and Facilitator, which follows many of the ritualistic elements of a two person call (greetings, how-are-you's, move to first topic). Here is an example,

```
1     O:     [Excuse me lisa ]=
2     L:=y ↑Yes ↓Op[erator
3     O:        [It's the operator I've got ida joining you ↑now=
4     L: =ok R ROse had to go because she's not very well this
5     L: [morning
6     D: [oh poor thing
7     L: alright?=
8     D:=mmm=
9     L:=He↑llo Ida
10    I: Hello dear
11    L: hwa=
12    I: =i've got a dreadful coawd
13    L: ↑O↑h dear
14    I: Yeah I started off with hay>Fever Last< (.) week an I
15    I: finished up with larynGitis
```

Transcript 2.*Friendship links*

In the above example the Facilitator Lisa gives the merest hint of a how-are-you 'hwa' (line 11) and Ida immediately replies with news about her health (denoted by the latching convention '='). In the next example it is the Facilitator who formulates the current topic at the end of the 'access/directed introduction/directed welcome' sequence with 'we were just saying it's a lovely morning…' (line 12),

```
1   O:   [ek (.) scyoos me again lisa Dorothy joining you?
2   L:   thank you very much
3   R:   >I dint have to put an extra blanket on<
4   L:   aahh [hhh
5   D:        [hhh
6   L:   morning dorothy?
7   D:   good morning lisa how are you
8   L:   I'm fine an an you alright?
9   D:   a:n so an so
10  L:   oh [oh]
11  D:      [ah] hh hh hh hh
12  L:   w we were just saying it's a lovely morning and its not so
13  L:   hot
14  D:   yeah dats right dis the humid weder doesn't agree with me hh
15  D:   hh hh hh
```

Transcript 3. *Friendship links*

In both cases – and indeed on every occasion of new participant introduction in this tape – the access/directed introduction/directed welcome sequence lead to a period of two person (Facilitator/new participant) conversation. At times these periods were extensive, leaving the remaining participants to just listen. The access/directed introduction/directed welcome sequence also engenders the ongoing conversation as mediated by the Facilitator.

3.1.3   Two forms of internal brackets – formal and fluid

Within the call we identified two forms of framing activity, both aimed toward multiparty interaction. The first is a coordination effort on the part of the Facilitator; the second form of 'frame breaking' initiated by participants.

Part of the Facilitator role – engendered, as we noted, by the opening sequences of new participants - is the coordination of ongoing talk. A rather nice example of this coordination is a form of 'next turn allocation' we have called 'participation in the round'. The following table shoes some examples, the 'in-the-round' character being most apparent in the first example:

```
L: so what did you do over the weekend, if we start off with you
L: renie.(.) did you do anything excitin(0.2)

((16 lines of interaction between Renie and Facilitator in which the
topic moves to the tennis, followed by …))

L:[ .hh what about] (.) dorothy do you watch the did you watch the
tennis

((23 lines of interaction between Dorothy and Facilitator))
```

```
L: (0.2) dorthy when you were at school obviously it was a different
process to the one we had=

((42 line of interaction between Dorothy and Facilitator))
```

```
L: .h y you were saying um d d dorothy do do do you read a lot.

((9 lines of interaction between Dorothy and Facilitator, followed
by....))

L: WHAT ABOUT YOU RENIE you read novels?

((29 lines of interaction between Renie and Facilitator))
```

Figure 4. *Participation in the round*

Evidently the Facilitator's wish is to encourage talk from all; by allocating turns to each person their participation is ensured[4]. With each next-turn-allocation by the Facilitator comes an extended spate of two-person interaction. So while geared toward equality of activity, it does not in the first instance encourage multi-person interaction. This form of framing through internal brackets leaves the interaction with a formal structure.

In some way these strips of formalised two-person interaction give way to more relaxed interaction. One way to understand how this occurs is to say that the current formal frame must be 'broken'. An example of frame breaking is through the 'flooding out' of laughter (see Goffman, 1974: 350-9 for an account of 'flooding out').

Laughter is an accountable matter if placed wrongly; even one turn distance brings questions such as 'what's funny?' (Sacks, 1995 VI:746) and there is an imperative to 'get the laughter in' immediately upon its relevance. However it is one activity that is available to people that, while 'tied' to the previous utterance, does not have to respect the general conversation rule of 'one person at a time' (Sacks, 1995: V1:745).

```
1    L: w there you go (.) there's was I going to talk about the tennis
2    L: an I've been
3    L: squashed .hh [hh
4    D:           [hh hh hh hh hh hh hh hh [hh hh hh hh hh] hh
5    I:           [hh hh hh hh hh hh hh hh [hh hh hh hh hh] hh ahh
6    R:                         [well never mind dea:r]
7    I: wait a minute I gotta geta hanki
8    L: ok
9    R: (.) No well I think if it hadn't been for the raining I think
10   R: he would have won
```

Transcript 4. *Friendship links*

In the above extract, multi-person overlapping laughter (denoted by laughter tokens 'hh' in square brackets) appears to free up the interaction. This is one of the few occasions early in the interaction, for example, in which a participant jumps in to the conversation – or 'self selects' - (Renie at line 9) when others have been speaking in a period of two party interaction.

In the above example the Facilitator Lisa takes an in breath at line 3 ('.hh') that signals the onset of laughter. This is a minimal form of 'invitation to laughter'. A clearer example can be seen in the following example,

```
1    R: my grandchildren wont get m(hh)arried [hh hh hh
2    D:                             [ah hi h h h >h h h<
3    L: [they wont get ↑married]
4    R: yeah my grandson keeps saying (.)you gotta wait gran
5    R: she'll ave you'll ave we're ave great grandson (.) .hh you
6    R: gotta ang on till then [so i said ↑ow long do you think i'm=
7    D:                        [Yeah
8    R: =gonna w(hh)ait [so he said i've got you on for the first=
9    D:                 [exactly
10   R: =babys(hh)iter
11   D: [huh huh huh huh huh huh huh
12   L: [hh hh hh hh hh
13   R: i woont care i'm ninete:
14   L: [hh hh hh hh h
15   D: [oh: nn a:n
16   L: oh well you got a way to go ye:t
```

Transcript 5. *Friendship links*

Renie signals the humorous nature of her comment about her grandchildren not getting married with an inserted laughter token at line 1 with 'm(hh)arried', in what might be called a 'laughter voice' ('hh' denotes out breath). Renie goes on to explain the relevance of the comment in lines 4-10 and again signals with an inserted laughter tokens in 'w(hh)ait' and ''baby(hh)iter'. The 'punchline' comes at line 13 'i woont care i'm ninete:'. Instances such as these provide for the interactional achievement of playful keying according to Hopper,

'The first laugh raises the question 'is this play' and the second laugh ratifies play as a live possibility. The play frame is keyed not by just the first laugh, but by the shared laugher' (Hopper, 1992:180).

Interactionally achieved play frames are fragile and can easily be undermined with a serious comment (Drew, 1987). In the above extract Renie's comment about her age is turned into a comment about longevity by Lisa the Facilitator. Alternatively initial invitation laughter tokens may not be 'picked up' in the first place. More than this, Hopper says that the play frame must 'periodically be resustained' (Hopper, 1992:180) with further laughter.

At times in the interaction the tension between the need for coordination and fluidity is marked by the first countering the second. In the following example, the 'serious' talk that signals the end of the play frame is the self same turn allocation of the Facilitator. Another participant has been introduced into the group but is not feeling very well, she leaves immediately. To which Renie comments,

```
1    R: sounds if she's got dehidratid
2    L: (0.2) year dear that's (.) a shame ↑is'nt tit
3    R: yeah
4    D: (  )
5    L: right well there's just the three of us then girls
6    R: ah [he he he he ]he he he
7    D:    [he he he he]
8    R: ge:rwls loveley
9    L: so what did you do over the weekend, if we start
10   L: off with you rose.(.)
```

Transcript 6. Friendship links

The description 'girls' is keyed as funny by Renie's 'invitation to laughter' at line 6 ('ah') and ratified by Dorothy at line 7. Lisa's 'so what did you do…' re-keys the interaction as a formal matter of coordination.

We see throughout our conference, then, small segments of flooding out of the two party interaction at moments of shared laughter. At those moments it is possible for the formalized two-party interaction to be undermined and there occurs a momentary 'free-for-all'. Segments of shared laughter and play-framing in combination with other elements can precipitate longer segments of fluidity in which the generic two party structure is turned to a multi-party interaction with much overlapping speech. These instances of spontaneous co-involvement are based upon these earlier moments of framing.

Summing up, These telephone conferences have a primary frame of seriousness due to the need for coordinated activity with the constraints of the telephone: opening sequences of telephone conferences along with coordination efforts, characterize them as formalized two-party frames of interaction. The ideal state for a recreational telephone conference is spontaneous co-involvement, which is worked toward through frame breaking activities such as shared and invited laughter.

4.   CONCLUSION

Fun in telephone conferences in this analysis is defined in relation to what it is not: having fun is a matter of transforming the (necessarily) formal structured basis of activity into moments of triviality and playfulness. And as such it complements early sociological appreciation of play as not work. However by understanding fun as the consequence of particular interpretive transformations in ongoing interaction, our sociology of fun becomes a dynamic conceptualisation: fun is always interactionally achieved by active social actors.

Our investigation of telephone conferences through applied or directed CA allows an appreciation of the interactionally situated experience of fun. A question might be how these insights benefit the future design effort. One way is that they can be recruited to inform experimental interventions. For example we might ask how changes in the opening routines affect interaction patterns and see if fluidity can be reached more quickly.

On a more general note, we might ask how we can make telephone conferences more 'fun'. Initial answers appear counter-intuitive: fun is tied to engendering structure, and allowing for its re-framing; to have fun, we have to have seriousness first.

5. FOOTNOTES

[1] People at the Centre of Communication and Information Technology
[2] We would like to thank and acknowledge Community Network, the organisers of this scheme for their invaluable help.
[3] An integral part of the Conversation Analytic method is the detailed transcription of talk. Rather than a 'record' of the talk, transcripts and their generation are viewed as an essential part of the analysis process. However at all stages the original recording is regarded as the primary data and is re-turned to when reading the transcript.
[4] Facilitator professionals characterise such turn allocation as a form of 'ice-breaker' that gets the participants talking.

6. REFERENCES

Atkinson, J.M. (1982). Understanding Formality: Notes on the Categorisation and Production of 'Formal' Interaction. *British Journal of Sociology* 33, 86-117.
Bateson, G. (1972). *Steps To An Ecology of Mind*, New York: Ballantine Books.
Beach, W.A. (1990). Language As and In Technology: Facilitating Topic Organization in Videotex Focus Group Meeting. In: Medhurst, M.J., Gonzalez, A. and Peterson, T.R., (Eds.) *Communication and the Culture of Technology*, pp. 197-219. Pullman: Washington State University Press
Bruner, J.S. (1976). Nature and uses of immaturity. In: Bruner, J.S., Jolly, A. and Sylva, K., (Eds.) *Play. Its role in development and evolution*, pp. 28-64. New York: Penguin Books.
Drew, P. (1987) Po-faced receipts of teases. *Linguistics* 25, 219-53.
Glenn, P.J. and Knapp, M.L. (1987). The interactive framing of play in adult conversation. *Communication Quarterly* 35, 48-66.
Goffman, E. (1974). *Frame Analysis. An Essay on the Organization of Experience*, Boston: North Eastern University Press.
Goffman, E. (1961). Fun in Games. In: Goffman, E., (Ed.) *Encounters: two studies in the sociology of interaction*, pp. 15-81. Indianapolis: Bob Merril
Hopper, R. (1992). *Telephone Conversation*, Bloomington; Indianapolis: Indiana University Press.
Huizinga, J. (1949). *Homo Ludens*, Boston: Beacon Press.
Lemert, C. and Branaman, A. (1997). *The Goffman Reader*, Oxford, UK: Blackwell Publishers Ltd.
Manning, P. (1992). *Erving Goffman and Modern Sociology*, Cambridge: Polity Press.
Reed, D.J. (2002). Observing and Quoting Newsgroup Messages: Method and Phenomenon in the Hermeneutic Spiral. Unpublished Doctoral Thesis.
Rutter, J. (2000). The stand-up introduction sequence: Comparing comedy compéres. *Journal of Pragmatics* 32, 463-483.
Sacks, H. (1974). The Analysis of the Course of A Joke's Telling In Conversation. In: Bauman, R. and Sherzer, J., (Eds.) *Explorations in the ethnography of speaking*, pp. 337-353. Cambridge: Cambridge University Press.
Sacks, H. (1995). *Lectures on Conversation. Volume 1&2*, Oxford UK; Cambridge USA: Blackwell.
Schwartzman, H. (1978). *Transformations: The Anthropology of Children's Play*, New York: Plenum.
Slater, D. (1998). Work/Leisure. In: Jenks, C., (Ed.) *Core Sociological Dichotomies*, pp. 391-404. London: Sage Publications Ltd.
Stephenson, W. (1967). *The Play Theory of Mass Communication*, New Brunswick, NJ: Transaction Publishers.
Sutton-Smith, B. (1988). Introduction to the transaction edition. In: Stephenson, W., (Ed.) *The Play Theory of Mass Communication*, New Brunswick, NJ: Transaction Publishers.

Williams, R. (1998). Erving Goffman. In: Stones, R., (Ed.) *Key Sociological Thinkers*, pp. 151-162. London: Macmillan Press Ltd.

JOHN C. MCCARTHY AND PETER C. WRIGHT

CHAPTER 7

THE ENCHANTMENTS OF TECHNOLOGY

1. INTRODUCTION

Ask people about their enchantments and they will talk about being absorbed in a film or painting, glimpsing another world in a story, or being totally blown away by the engine of a motorbike. An artist might talk about the intense, sensuous experience of a single line in a painting. Having made the line, the artist is taken outside of herself for a moment, into the clarity of the line. A mechanic might talk about the pleasure of working with a particular motorbike. Mesmerised by the beauty of the engine, absorbed in each and every challenge, aware of the pleasure in a skill. Others may simply be enchanted by the stones on a beach, the smile on a baby's face, the view from the top of a hill.

There is no telling what holds the power to enchant any one of us. Whereas the motorbike engine would leave me cold, I can become absorbed in a painting or a person's smile. The things that have the power to enchant me, that grab my attention and shape my desires, seem written on me by the history of my experience in my culture. I trace my attachment to Apple computers to my enchantment with the Apple II, a computer that didn't seem like the ponderous computers we used at work. It was lively, engaging, different, the rave of another youth subculture. I loved and became hooked on the surface of it and the pleasure of transacting in what seemed to be a common language with something intelligent. DOS never did that for me. I found the requirement to communicate using the machine's language disenchanting.

Although our enchantments are our own, it is possible to clarify some aspects of the enchantments of technology. It is also worthwhile to do that. The dominance of function in the design of computer systems frequently produces disenchantment tales: stories of workers resisting new technology and students bored or cynical about it; stories of very powerful computational devices separated from the sensuousness of interaction and the meaningfulness of action. As a counterpoint to these tales of disenchantment, we explore the potential for people to be enchanted with technology by: clarifying what we mean by the experience we call enchantment; exploring sources of enchantment in film as an example of the experience of enchantment with a contemporary cultural form; and teasing out

Mark A. Blythe, Andrew F. Monk, Kees Overbeeke and Peter C. Wright *(eds.)*,
Funology: From Usability to Enjoyment, 81—90

implications of enchantment for feelings and imaginative activity in relationships between people and technology.

2.   WHAT DO WE MEAN BY ENCHANTMENT?

Rather than examine the relationship between people and technology through the study of form or function, we focus on experience. According to Dewey (1934), experience is constituted by the relationship between self and object, the concerned, feeling person acting and the materials and tools they use. It includes what people do and what is done to them, what they strive for and desire, and how they feel, fear, believe, hope, enjoy, and imagine. Experience registers life as lived and felt. In a companion chapter in this volume, Wright, McCarthy, and Meekison, we present a framework for analysing experience. In the current chapter we focus on the power of technology to enchant.

Our particular concern with the power of technology to enchant is motivated by the capacity of enchantment to evoke both the transformative openness and unfinalisability of experience and the capacious potential of imagination to power holistic engagement by bringing past or future meanings into present action, making the mundane creative. Rendering people's experience with technology as transformative, imaginative, and creatively meaningful is the proper corrective against pervasive disenchantment tales. Technology may indeed be used to oppress, suck meaning from activity, alienate people from communities, mechanise, monitor, and rationalise but it also enchants, pleases, energises and clarifies.

Enchantment is akin to Dewey's 'holistic engagement' between the sensing person and their environment, which Dewey sees as necessary for peoples' growth and development. At the heart of this holistic engagement is an integrated sensual experience, where the senses unite to reveal the qualitative immediacy of the situation. Dewey uses the example of a mechanic who, when wholly engaged in his job, sees, hears, smells, and touches the engine. He senses it, and through his engagement with it, senses what is wrong. He is completely attentive, engrossed, intensely concentrated, and immersed or lost in an activity. In contrast, Dewey argues that when the senses are compartmentalised, "we undergo sensations as mechanical stimuli or as irritated stimulations, without having a sense of the reality that is in them and behind them" (Dewey, 1934, p.21). As stimuli, sensations are robbed of their power to enchant.

Holistic engagement captures some of what it means to be caught up but not what it means to be carried away. According to Bennett (2001), when we are enchanted we are "both caught up and carried away" (p.5). When enchanted, although we are momentarily spellbound, our senses seem heightened. We notice lines, colours, and sounds that we have not previously noticed. And even as our senses are sharpened and intensify, as we see with heightened clarity, we are transfixed. Mesmerised by the sharpness with which we see the beauty of a scene, we are carried outside of ourselves. Caught up in wonder at the object and carried away by our senses.

According to Gell (1992) we are carried away by the power behind the enchanting object. For him, the enchantment of technology is in its becoming rather than its being. By this he means that the power of technology to enchant resides in our sense of wonder at the skill of the maker of the technology. For him, the Trobrianders' use of the prow-board of the Kula canoe is a case in point. The board is a visually intricate display or surface designed to dazzle anybody looking at it and put them off their stroke for a moment. Gell attributes the power of the canoe-board not to the visual appearance per se but to the fact that mild disturbances caused by the captivating visual effects of the board are interpreted by the viewer as evidence of magical power emanating from the board. They can't imagine how it came into being so it must be magic. The magical power is in the idea one has of the board coming into being.

Gell's analysis of the enchantment of technology describes a serious emotion, something like the awe one feels in a religious setting or in response to a mystery. Those seeing the prow-boards are in awe of the powers of those who had the power to make them. This disorients and frightens them. Without a sense of charm, delight, and pleasure, this description of enchantment is incomplete. Enchantment also describes a sense of pleasure borne of the experience of novelty. There is pleasure in the enchantment of seeing something new in a stone on the beach or a line in a painting. Perhaps it is the pleasure of experiencing becoming, the openness of everything. For us, enchantment is not only in the skill of the maker but also in the becoming that is all round us, the openness or unfinalisability of the world.

Imagine a world in which every-thing is open and unfinalised. In this world, we take no-thing for granted, for every-thing is always becoming, always on the way to being. We can't just assume that things are the way we see them. The stone on the beach, the computer on which I am writing, my body, our definition of personhood, the physical world, and time – all always becoming. Bakhtin, a philosopher and literary scholar, described a world in which all is always becoming, and reflected on how we can know and understand in such a world (see Bakhtin, 1981 and 1984, for example). For Bakhtin, the site of knowledge is never unitary, rather knowing is better seen in terms of dialogue. Dialogically, everything is perceived from a unique position in space and time. In a world in which knowing is decentred, whatever is observed is shaped by the position from which it is observed. Bakhtin goes so far as to refer to perception and observation as authorship, a constructive act of meaning making by an author, an "I" with no referent other than a person who is always changing and different. The 'thingness' of everything is worked at and is a provisional finalisation in a relational process between observer and observed. There is every possibility that, at a different time and from a different perspective, every-thing might be different. For Bakhtin, the world is an open place full of potentiality, freedom, newness, and surprise. In this world, the potential for enchantment rooted in the experience of novelty is everywhere.

The important point for us about Bakhtin's work is that he was describing what we seem to miss in the ordinary, everyday, world because we have already finalised it in our minds. We have closed our minds off to the potentiality of the physical, biological and social world, having already decided what everything is instead of looking closely. Because of this we fail to notice the essential creativity of our relationship with every-thing that is ordinary. In a world that is always becoming, we are compelled to create the thing-ness and event-ness of the world. And it is so ordinary that we miss it. For example, most of us already know what a body or a person is. We also know that the physical world is fairly solid. Instead of settling for this given knowledge, Bakhtin celebrates the human body in the act of becoming, never finished, continually built, swallowing and being swallowed by the world, and Prigogine and Stengers (1984) describe the physical world "as seething and bubbling with change, disorder, and process" (p. xv).

In the prosaic world in which we live, all encounters contain the possibility of something unexpected. Enchantment begins when engagement with the unexpected creates a 'moment of pure presence' (Fisher, 1998). According to Fisher, the object with the power to enchant "does not remind us of anything we know and we find ourselves delaying in its presence for a time in which the mind does not move on by association to something else". In a moment of enchantment, one of the millions of stones on a beach stands out as unique. We notice something about its shape, colour, or smoothness, the clarifying sensuous experience of which holds us in that time and place for a moment, totally engaged with and fascinated by the stone. According to Bennett (2001), the surprise of the encounter contains two feelings at the same time: the pleasurable feeling of being charmed by something that is new and singular, and not yet processed and categorised; and the disorientating feeling of being taken out of one's habitual sense-making dispositions. Bennett suggests that the effect of enchantment is a mood of fullness and liveliness, a sense of heightened perception and concentration, and a feeling of excitement about life.

In the account of enchantment that we have presented so far, sites of enchantment are everywhere to be found as long as we are prepared to encounter the novelty in things and events. The experience of enchantment is constituted by the relationship between a person who is fascinated by the singularity of objects and events and those objects and events. In terms of relations between people and technology, we might want to think of enchantment as a state of interactive fascination between the person enchanted and the source of enchantment. Our task in the next section then is to say something about how this interactive fascination can be evoked in interactive technologies.

3.   ENCHANTMENTS OF TECHNOLOGY

Some contemporary technologies are readily associated with the experience of enchantment. The settings, characters, and activities of computer games create worlds in which children become caught up and to which they are carried away. Handheld computer games, such as Gameboys, seem to absorb children and teenagers for hours on end. Teenagers are not just satisfied with their mobile phones. They are bewitched to the extent that the primitive input and output devices matter very little to them. In the magical world of text messaging, where new communication media and the cachet of the mobile are dazzling, enchantment overwhelms function. Adults also have moments of enchantment with mobiles such as when a father's experience of time, space, and presence are transformed by speaking to his young daughter who is on the London Eye when he is at his desk in York.

How do we design for the potentiality that makes something as ordinary as a phone enchanting? Elsewhere in this volume, Sengers argues that we do this by focusing on the user's ability to engage in complex interpretation using cultural background knowledge. In another chapter in this volume, Dix's deconstruction of people's experience of traditional Christmas crackers, which enables him to re-mediate the experience, can be seen in a similar light. Both seem to suggest that, if we understand the richness and complexity of users' responses, simple artefacts can be designed to facilitate rich experiences. In a similar spirit, we examine the richness and complexity of people's responses to film, not to re-mediate the film experience (many games manufacturers have already tried that) but to make visible aspects of experience with contemporary technologies at play that would otherwise remain unseen.

Boorstin (1990), a writer and producer of Hollwood films, describes the rich and complex response of filmgoers' to film that enables filmmakers to enchant with even the simplest filmic experience. He suggests that the key is to understand that we experience or watch movies in three ways. Each way has a distinct pleasure and magic associated with it. Boorstin refers to his three ways of seeing as the voyeuristic eye, the vicarious eye, and the visceral eye.

The *voyeuristic eye* is a way of experiencing film in terms of the simple joy of seeing the new and the wonderful. It refers to a way of looking that gets up close to things and really looking at them but becoming bored as soon as the experience of seeing the newness of the thing has run its course. As the mind's eye it can be quite sceptical, and it requires a high level of plausibility and credibility. When it experiences events that seem implausible, it is inclined to disengage. What appears on screen must contain surprise and plausibility to seduce and enchant the voyeuristic eye. There is no magic without a new look at things, but a new look that makes sense in the world being experienced even if it is a fictional or fantasy world.

In the early days of cinema the voyeuristic eye was seduced by the magic of the projected moving image. As the projected image became passé, more was required: talk to go with the action, more and more precise synchronisation of talk and action, high precision editing, adherence to a more sophisticated grammar of cinematic action that took account of how the audience would fill in the gaps, colour, action and images that could not be accomplished other than with film. As we viewers become more experienced with a medium, it takes more to enchant the voyeuristic eye. However designers should bear in mind that less can be more enchanting as long as it gives us something new and wonderful. For example, Boorstin describes films by Charles Eames as miniature masterpieces because they made us see anew simple objects like spinning tops. These short films did this without story, characters, or even a point. They stood or fell in terms of voyeuristic pleasure on the back of the visual logic threading through the images.

The *vicarious eye* is attentive to the emotional substrate of action rather than to its internal logic and plausibility. It may be an even more powerful factor in our experience than internal logic because we can make allowances for what seems illogical if we are made aware of an emotional truth underlying it. While the magic of film can be threatened voyeuristically if a viewer feels 'that could not happen', it is threatened vicariously if a viewer feels 'he wouldn't do that'. No matter how implausible the action, if we are won over by the character, we may be convinced that 'yes, *he* would do that'. But it can never be a character separate from the world created in the film. For the vicarious eye, the basic unit is not the beat of the story but the moment of the character. In great moments, story time stands still and the pleasure of the new and wonderful is irrelevant. But a film cannot be enchanting if it is made up of great moments alone. The editor has to create a rhythm and movement between the voyeuristic and vicarious to keep us engaged – intellectually, emotionally, and valuationally.

The *visceral eye* is attuned to first-hand experience of thrill, joy, fear and abandonment. Here the character is a conduit for the viewer's feelings rather than the other way around. Unlike the vicarious eye, the visceral eye is not interested in characters in the empathic sense, it is interested in having tokens for our sense of thrill or fear. As we feel the thrill and fear of people on a roller coaster ride we are not empathising with them, rather we are having our visceral experience through their activity. However it is a thrill or fear cosseted by the knowledge that it is not actually you that is being attacked by an alien or free-falling from 10, 000 feet. As character is not empathic in the visceral experience, it is closer to montage than story, narrative, or connectedness. It consists of moments of gut reaction and as viewers we are carried along by those moments as if on a roller-coaster.

Of course the magical experience can have visceral, vicarious, and voyeuristic elements. In film, visceral alone can't be enough. We build up resistance to every thrill the director creates for us so that, as Boorstin puts it, when evaluating the visceral aspect of the magic of film: twice as much comes off half as effective. The visceral impact of films like Psycho and Alien depend as much on the characters we identify with as the thrills of action. The visceral shock of the shower scene in Psycho depends on Hitchcock's manipulation of the story to that point such that a tale of love and embezzlement becomes a tale of murder. He builds up to the visceral moment by playing with our voyeuristic and vicarious pleasures.

Boorstin's (1990) analysis of the magic of movies suggests that, in a media-savvy world, a combination of wonder at the new, sensuous experience, and emotional response to characters is required to create an enchanting experience. In the context of our analysis of enchantment, we read this analysis as replacing a relatively undifferentiated, cognitive approach to seeing, such as Gell's, with an active, differentiated, aesthetic approach. In contrast with Gell's monological perspective on enchantment, Boorstin's analysis develops from an understanding of the play of appearance as dialogical, with multiple perspectives on novelty, emotional tone, and sensuousness in constant interaction with each other against a shifting magic standard.

This analysis of how people experience film may inform the design of technologies in a number of ways. Following Dix, we could treat this analysis as a deconstruction of experience with one of the most significant mediums of the twentieth century, with a view to informing design of experience with new media such as computer games, virtual reality, and the cyberspace of MUDs and MOOs. The re-mediation of film experience in new media (see Bolter and Grusin, 2001, for example). Alternatively, the analysis might be used to complement the application of concepts from experience of narrative in design with a set of concepts from experience with film. Or, following Sengers, we could use it to understand the abilities of people to interact with new technologies and media and to reveal the cultural resources we use to make these interactions personally meaningful. Film plays with our cultural knowledge of genre, storytelling conventions, visual logic, and the language of film. It creates a mediated inter-subjective experience by addressing itself to the ways in which we experience, see, and make sense and by assuming that we understand its modes of expression. Over time, new media will also have to nurture similar relationships and might benefit from an analysis of existing popular media such as film. Each of these uses of the analysis would take another chapter to develop. Our aim in presenting an analysis of enchantment with film here has been to take a first step by enhancing our sensibility to experience, especially enchanting experience with mediating technologies. One of the main ways in which we have done this is by illustrating the potential complexity of the user's response to and experience of these technologies, making visible the enchantment of novelty, emotional identification, and visceral thrill, which might otherwise remain unseen.

4.   ENCHANTMENT IN THE SPACE OF PUBLIC APPEARANCE

It is easy to dismiss enchantment as trivial as having to do with play or entertainment and not the important things in life. Or even to treat enchantment as a modern day opiate of the masses: enchantment as a stylistic marketing device to cover up deficiencies of function and woo the unsuspecting consumer. Our final move in this chapter is a brief defence of enchantment in the context of people's interactions with technology. Our defence argues against the disenchantment tale of enchanting technology inevitably mesmerising – in the sense of controlling - the person using it. Elsewhere in this volume, Blythe and Hassenzahl have usefully critiqued the political analysis that associates mass media enchantment with passivity and cultural duping, suggesting a psychological corrective to enquire into people's enjoyment of TV and other media of entertainment. We want to raise similar concerns with readings of enchantment that downplay the activity of subtle participation.

Internet stores are interested in customer loyalty and commitment and try to enchant each customer by making transactions personal. They engage with the identity of the shopper inferred from a history of transactions. With respect to product design and branding, it is not just the functionality but also the style of a mobile phone that matters to the owner. We can dismiss this as a matter of 'style over substance' or we can inquire into the substance of people's experience of enchantment with the style of a product. What vitality does a sense of style bring to people's relationships with their mobile phones? Attending to style in this way does not stop us being critical but it does stop us being dismissive.

Apple have made style central to the relationships people have with their computers. The colour and transparency of the IMac and the titanium casing, slim body, and lightness of the G4 are examples of computers marketed as something more than what we traditionally think of as computers. Indeed this has been Apple's stock in trade since the Apple II. For Apple, computers are not just computational devices they are objects to be with. We are encouraged to see them as sensuous objects that, in our presence, become sensing, sensual, sense-making subjects. Referring back to Boorstin's analysis, we can see in the Apple Mac style sensitivity to our desire for novelty with emotional integrity. The design becomes a meditation on the computer and computation itself, as Eames' films meditate on the spinning top and in the process on the medium of film. A computer dialogically interanimated with voices of adventure and mesmerising technology from the space age (titanium and very light, almost defying gravity) and of contemporary consumer product aesthetic. But do we passively consume this message or complete the experience ourselves? Do we, like the enemies of the Trobrianders, dazzled by the canoe prow board, take leave of our senses and give into the power behind the technology? Or do we retain our sense while enjoying the vivifying pleasure of something new and wonderful?

DeCerteau (1984) argued that people who are dismissed as passive consumers often resist definition of themselves by others through the use they make of what is given. They can be enchanted by the technology they buy and still make their mark by giving the technology a personal meaning, for example, creating sub-cultural text messaging languages or using electronic bookshops as handy bibliographic databases. The response of organisations such as the Billboard Liberation Front in editing Apple's (and many other company's) billboard advertisements suggests resistance to the message and raises questions about who owns the power to enchant. The Billboard Liberation Front and other culture jammers (Klein, 2000), who parody advertisements and billboards to radically alter their message, draw the advertisements, the brand, and the products into a moral-political discourse. Moreover they do it by trying to make better use of enchantment than the advertisers. The parodied advertisements evoke pleasure at the experience of novelty by creating images that are charming as well as damning. We are caught up and carried away by the metamorphing of the image and the movement between cultural worlds entailed in that morphing: is it an advertisement or not, is it the original or has it been changed?

Our approach to questions of the mindfulness or mindlessness of enchantment with technology turns on our understanding of the power of technological mediation of experience to press into the gap between feelings and expression or imaginative activity. This understanding offers up a range of possibilities that can take shape only as hypotheses at this stage. Table 1 provides a simple space in which to question about issues of interpassivity and interactivity, which we briefly address below in response to Zizek's critique of the enchantment of cyberspace as inevitably promoting passivity.

Zizek's (1999) critical analysis of interpassivity in cyberspace points to the potential for unhelpful passivity in relations with technology. He draws attention to people allowing themselves to be caught up in activity in order to avoid feelings. Zizek would argue that our enchantment with electronic pets and cyber friends is a form of *one-sided interpassivity* that enables us to engage in the activities of caring without having the responsibility and feelings of mutually relating. We have the experience of caring without the complexity of a relationship with another person, who may care in return or may be indifferent to being cared for.

Table 1. *An analysis of the possibilities of interactivity and interpassivity with technology playing in the gap between feelings and expression*

	Interactivity		
	Dialogue. Culture jamming. Christmas crackers (Dix this volume). The Influencing Machine (Sengers, this volume)	Acting through an agent. Electronic pet? Cyber friend?	
Mutual			One-sided
	Lovers being quiet together. Texting to just be in each other's presence.	Greek chorus doing the feeling for us. Throwing oneself into rituals of activity in order not to experience a feeling. Electronic pet? Cyber friend?	
	Interpassivity		

However, if the electronic pet is not fed, it dies. It can be argued that this context of caring with limited responsibility provides the kinds of experiences that enable children to learn about relationships. In contrast, Zizek sees it as promoting interpassivity, with the cyber and the virtual as agents of mediation sustaining the subject's desire while acting as agents of prohibition of its full expression and gratification. He sees *one-sided interactivity* as acting through another agent, so that my job is done while I remain passive. As we have seen in brief reflections on culture jamming and DeCerteau's treatment of the strategic action of consumers, these apparently one sided relationships may in fact involve a subtle, expressive response. One such response occurs when the technology mediating experience facilitates *mutual interactivity* as is the case in episodes of culture jamming, creative use of the technology given, and dialogue. The child who uses her mobile phone to call her father who is 200 miles away acts from feelings to imaginative use of technology. Another possibility, *mutual interpassivity*, points to the expressiveness of being quiet together. The clearest model is lovers being quiet together.

A jazz riff, a film, or a piece of technology might play me. I may be caught up and carried away by any of these things. However this does not render me passive or a victim to their powers of enchantment. Far from it, it may be that in recognising the creativity of my relationship with them, I begin to understand my emotions and the communication between me and others that makes me what I am and what they are – always becoming. Technology that enchants: a computer that allows me to question what it is to be a computer; textual communication, the limitation of which, requires me to be creative and expressive; objects or installations that are sensitive to the moment and to my sense of wonder and emotional integrity. Technology that enables me to change.

5. REFERENCES

Bakhtin, M.M. (1981). The Dialogic Imagination: Four Essays by M.M. Bakhtin, edited by M. Holquist. Austin, TX: University of Texas Press.

Bakhtin, M.M. (1984). Problems of Dostoevsky's Poetics, edited by C.Emerson. Minneapolis: University of Minnesota Press.

Bennett, J. (2001). The Enchantment of Modern Life: Attachments, Crossings, and Ethics. Princeton: Princeton University Press.

Bolter, J.D. and Grusin, R. (2001). Remediation: Understanding New Media. Cambridge, Mass.: MIT Press.

Boorstin (1990). Making Movies Work: Thinking Like a Filmmaker. Beverley Hills: Silman-James Press.

DeCerteau, M. (1984). The Practice of Everyday Life. Berkeley, California: University of California Press.

Dewey, J. (1934). Art as Experience. New York: Perigree.

Fisher, P. (1998). Wonder, the Rainbow, and the Aesthetics of Rare Experiences. Boston Mass.: Harvard University Press.

Gell, A. (1992). The technology of enchantment and the enchantment of technology. In J. Coote and A. Shelton (eds.), Anthropology, Art, and Aesthetics. Oxford: Clarendon Press, pp. 40-63.

Klein, M. (2000). No Logo. London: Flamingo.

Prigogine, I. and Stengers, I. (1984). Order Out of Chaos. London: Flamingo.

Zizek, S. (1999). The fantasy in cyberspace. In E.Wright and E. Wright (eds), The Zizek Reader. Oxford: Blackwell.

MARK BLYTHE AND MARC HASSENZAHL

CHAPTER 8

THE SEMANTICS OF FUN: DIFFERENTIATING ENJOYABLE
EXPERIENCES

1. INTRODUCTION

Over the last 20 years repeated attempts have been made in HCI to put enjoyment into focus. However, it is only recently that the importance of enjoyment, even in serious applications, has been widely recognised by the HCI community.

Typical of a relatively new area of investigation is the lack of an agreed set of terms: enjoyment, pleasure, fun and attraction are often used interchangeably. But do they really refer to the same experiences? Of course, in common speech pleasure, enjoyment and fun are almost synonymous and this is not an attempt to fix the language. None of these terms are reducible to single definitions but for the purposes of this chapter we will propose a difference between pleasure and fun in an attempt to delineate distinct forms of enjoyment.

The chapter begins with a consideration of the psychological account of peak experiences and how this might relate to less intense activities. After exploring the semantic and cultural connotations of the word fun the chapter goes on to consider the historical and political construction of leisure in the West. The final sections outlines distinctions between "fun" and "pleasure". It is argued that pleasure is closely related to degrees of absorption while fun can be usefully thought of in terms of distraction. The distinction has important implications for design. It is argued that repetitive and routine work can be made fun through design while non-routine and creative work must absorb rather than distract if they are to be enjoyable.

2. PLEASURE FROM A PSYCHOLOGICAL PERSPECTIVE: FLOW

Mihaly Csikszentmihalyi's (1975) study of "flow" is one of the few psychological accounts of pleasure. After studying diverse groups, such as rock climbers, chess players and dancers, who were engaged in self motivating activities, Csikszentmihalyi discovered a common characteristic of their experiences. "Flow" was a term used by the participants themselves to describe a peak experience of total absorption in an activity. Csikszentmihalyi identified the conditions for flow as: a close match between skill and challenge, clear goals and constant feedback on performance. It was characterized by a decrease in self-consciousness and time

Mark A. Blythe, Andrew F. Monk, Kees Overbeeke and Peter C. Wright *(eds.),*
Funology: From Usability to Enjoyment, 91—100
© 2003 *Kluwer Academic Publishers. Printed in the Netherlands.*

distortion in that an hour might seem like a minute (Csikszentmihalyi, 1975). Flow experiences may be experienced in non-leisure and serious contexts.

The term "micro-flow" was coined in order to catalogue small periods of activities which are not necessary, yet are engaged in routinely, for example, chatting, doodling and stretching. These activities are intrinsically satisfying, although they do not induce the deep and intense experience of flow. Csikszentmihalyi (1975) suggested that these apparently unnecessary activities are in fact vital to our well-being. Doodling, for example, may aid concentration in a dull meeting. However "micro-flow" is a less well defined concept than flow and does not adequately account for less intense experiences.

Flow addresses a "deep" kind of enjoyment which may be only rarely achieved (and actually called for). To experience flow, we have to go beyond our own limits. This, however desirable from a humanistic view, is not the type of enjoyment most people choose. Most of the time, more superficial, shallow, short-term and volatile "pleasures" are in the fore. Or as Seligman and Csikszentmihalyi (2000) put it:

> "Why do we choose to watch television over reading a challenging book, even when we know that our usual hedonic state during television is mild dysphoria while the book will produce flow?" (Seligman and Csikszentmihalyi 2000)

The answer to this question may be, in part, political. The next section considers the history of the word fun and offers an account of the leisure industry and mass media in relation to their development in the West.

3.   THE POLITICS OF FUN

An examination of the changing uses of the word "fun" as illustrated in the Oxford English Dictionary demonstrates that fun, meaning - diversion, amusement, jocularity - appears relatively late in the language. (The following citations are all taken from the OED http://dictionary.oed.com/). In the earliest records, its meaning is - to fool, to cheat or hoax: "She had fun'd him of his Coin" (1685). Although this usage continued it was superseded in the eighteenth century "Tho he talked much of virtue, his head always run upon something or other he found better fun" (1727). In the mid eighteenth century Samuel Johnson described it as a "low cant word", its disreputable aspect continued into the nineteenth century "His wit and humour delightful, when it does not degenerate into 'fun'" (1845). The use of the word in the phrase "to make fun of –" also appears in the eighteenth century: "I can't help making fun of myself" (1737). Similarly, fun as in exciting goings on appears relatively late: "The engineers officers who are engaged in carrying out some of the Sirdar's plans get much more than their fair share of 'the fun'" (1897).

It was, then, at the turn of the eighteenth century that the language required and developed the word fun in something like its current form. It is not fanciful to relate this semantic development to the industrial revolution. When British society was industrialised and class relations came to be organised around production and labour rather than feudal ties, a "low cant word" appeared which signified the absence of seriousness, work, labour. When production is mechanised, when labour processes are rationalised, when time is ossified to demarcate work and leisure, the word fun appears as its correlative. As EP Thompson (1963) pointed out, the working class was there at the moment of its own making. The word fun then has a political dimension. It still retains its "low" associations. Fun remains a form of resistance in the workplace, the fun of "the laff", the piss-take (Willis, 2000). Fun can be seen both as a resistance to the rigid demarcation between work and leisure and also as a means of reproducing that dichotomy.

The rigid division between work and leisure and the rise of the cultural industries are relatively recent phenomena. Writing on the cultural industries of the nineteen fifties, Adorno and Horkheimer (1986) pointed to the similarities between the ways in which leisure and work time were structured and monitored. For these authors, the cultural industries exacerbated the artificial division between enjoyment and the rest of life: "Amusement under late capitalism is the prolongation of work." (Ibid: 137). Although amusement is sought as an escape from mechanized work, mechanization determines the production of "amusement goods" with the result that leisure experiences are "inevitably after-images of the work process itself" (Ibid). For Adorno and Horkheimer, the cultural industries then encouraged passivity, operating as a hegemonic device and a means of mass deception.

These members of the Frankfurt school and other Marxist writers pointed out that leisure was structured to meet the demands of capitalist production and working days of alienated labour (Roijec, 1985). The Situationists of the nineteen sixties argued that the entertainment industry and mass media had formed a "society of the spectacle" which enchants, distracts and numbs us, transforming us into the passive spectators of our own lives (Debord, 1995). Fun is something we buy, something we consume, something that ultimately reproduces the situations of alienated labour that we are seeking to escape. This somewhat bleak view of fun can be related to the work of the cartoonist Bill Griffiths (see Figure 1).

Figure 1. *Zippy The Pinhead*

Bill Griffith's character *Zippy* wanders through consumer landscapes asking hopefully "Are we having fun yet?" There is something tragic about the look of these cartoons and about the question itself. The question suggests at once a promise and a betrayal. Like Seligman and Csikszentmihalyi's dysphoric TV viewers Zippy is probably not having fun even when he is told that he is.

Marxist analyses of the cultural industries and leisure are, of course, deeply unfashionable and have been criticized for their pessimism and elitism. Empirical studies on the actual uses of cultural products have show than consumption is not passive: private and individual meanings are invested in leisure activities despite hegemonic intent (Willis, 1990). We do not watch TV solely because we have become the numbed spectators of our own lives, passively and joylessly consuming spectacles as "cultural dupes". Dysphoria is not the only result of watching TV. The experience may not be the intense peak that Csikszentmihalyi's chess players would call flow or Adorno might approve of but it is nevertheless in some sense rewarding. We believe that Csikszentmihalyi's humanistic and Adorno's pessimistic views can neglect the psychological reality of individuals - their need to be *absorbed* sometimes and to be *distracted* at others.

4. CONTEXT DEPENDENCY

It is important to consider enjoyment as a context dependent and relational phenomena. Enjoyment is never guaranteed. Think of activities associated with enjoyment: sex, dancing, riding, swimming, taking drugs, playing a game, talking, joking, flirting, writing, listening to music, looking at a painting, reading, watching a play, movie, or other entertainment. Each of these activities is enjoyable or not depending on the situation that the activity is embedded in. Each situation is a unique constellation of a person's current goals, previous knowledge and experiences, the behaviour domain, and applicable social norms. A ride on a roller coaster can be enjoyable, but maybe not after an enormous dinner. Activities or objects normally appreciated by a person do not necessarily or deterministically lead to enjoyment. What may be enjoyable in one context (watching a soap opera with friends) might be utterly dull in another (watching a soap opera alone). A game we enjoyed playing yesterday might completely bore us today. Activities associated with enjoyment offer potentials for enjoyment rather than enjoyment itself (see Hassenzahl elsewhere in this book).

Enjoyment is, in the widest sense, context specific. Indeed the American philosopher John Dewey argued that all emotions are grounded in particular contexts of experience:

> "There is no such thing as the emotion of fear, hate, love ... The unique character of experienced events and situations impregnates the emotion that is evoked" (Dewey, cited in Jackson, 1998, p. 11).

In this sense enjoyment doesn't exist in and of itself. It's a relationship between ongoing activities and states of mind.

Is it then impossible to define or categorise different forms of enjoyment? Can there be a body of knowledge about enjoyment, a "pleasure-based human factors," (Jordan, 2000), a "funology" (Monk et al., 2002)? In Matt Groening's *Futurama* cartoon show there are theme parks on the moon designed by "fungineers". The idea is hilarious. How could fun be engineered? Taking enjoyment seriously is a paradox, which on the face of it, seems pretentious or simply silly. There are as many kinds of enjoyment as there are people in the world. In the novel *My Idea of Fun* Will Self assumes the character of a man who finds murdering tramps enjoyable (Self, 1994). It may or may not be the case that psychopaths experience violence as enjoyment and we are in no more a position of authority in this matter than the grandiloquent author. But the existence of theme parks, and indeed all popular culture, suggests that there is a degree of common ground in our ideas of enjoyment, culturally specific though they may be.

5.   THE EXPERIENCE OF FUN AND PLEASURE

There are connotational and experiential differences between fun and pleasure. Fun has quite specific and differential everyday meanings. Pleasure as a term is more problematic. It is, like enjoyment, a superordinate term. In the following sections we discuss pleasure as a specific type of enjoyment rather than as a superordinate category. This distinct use of the word can be related to Aristotle's view of pleasure as sense stimulation through action. Commentators have argued that Aristotle saw pleasure as "the perfect actualisation of a sentient being's natural capacities, operating on their proper objects" (Honderich, 1995: 688). This notion of pleasure as self-actualisation is echoed in Csikszentmihalyi's work and his emphasis on the importance of appropriate levels of challenge as a condition for flow. In the remaining sections then pleasure is thought of as distinct from fun in terms of intensity and its relation to action. More specifically we argue, that fun and pleasure can be thought of as experiences that generally differ in terms of distraction and absorption (see Table 1 for an overview of specific differences). This is not to suggest a polar dichotomy and it must be stressed that these experiences are fluid.

Table 1. *Experiential and cultural connotations of fun and pleasure*

Fun / Distraction		Pleasure / Absorption
Triviality	-	Relevance
Repetition	-	Progression
Spectacle	-	Aesthetics
Transgression	-	Commitment

During the fleeting and amorphous experience of fun, we are distracted from the self. Our self-definition, our concerns, our problems are no longer the focus. We distract ourselves from the constant clamour of the internal dialogue. This is not meant to imply that fun is unimportant or by any means "bad". Its ability to distract with short-lividness and superficiality satisfies an important underlying psychological need.

In contrast, pleasure is a deeper form of enjoyment. The main difference between pleasure and fun is its focus on an activity and a deep feeling of absorption.

Pleasure, in this sense, is not short-lived. It may not even be spontaneous. It happens when people are devoted to an object or activity. It happens when people try to make sense of themselves – explore and nourish their identities. The objects or activities an individual is absorbed by make a connection to his or her self. They become important, relevant.

It has been argued that the dichotomy between work and pleasure originates in the protestant work ethic (Willis, 2000). Clearly it is a false dichotomy: work can be a pleasure, it can be absorbing. But is it fun? The workplace can be the site of fun but it is generally in the context of a break from work. Fun cannot be serious and if it is then it ceases, in this sense, to be fun.

It is likely then that repetitive and routine work based tasks and technologies might be made fun through design but non-routine and creative work must absorb rather than distract if they are to be enjoyable. The infamous winking paperclip in word is clearly intended to be fun but most people find it annoying. It distracts rather than aiding concentration or absorption. A cute graphics approach may be appropriate to making repetitive or mundane tasks more enjoyable and Hohl et al describe a good example of this in their chapter for this book. But such an approach can be hazardous if the experience that is being designed for should be pleasurable rather than fun.

In the following sections we discuss differences between fun and pleasure in more detail.

5.1 Triviality and Relevance

The word fun in English carries cultural connotations of frivolity and triviality. Fun is an antonym of serious. In this sense science and art are not fun. Where there is an association with these endeavours and fun, it is with education. Occasionally pedagogues attempt to "make" science and art fun. The implication of this is, of course, that they are not already intrinsically fun themselves. Thus early educational software incorporated games to make the learning less serious, less unpleasant. But there is something uncomfortable about the yoking together of fun and serious applications. The fun elements in educational software can appear as bribes when they are not totally integrated (Laurel, 1993, p. 74). They are confidence tricks; they are the spoonful of sugar that helps the bad medicine go down.

It may be that where learning and high art are enjoyable it is when they are totally absorbing in and for themselves. Opera, ballet, classical music, poetry, do not carry cultural connotations of fun but of pleasure. "High" art is not a distraction, indeed if our powers of concentration are not up to it they may actively bore us and cause anxiety. Art demands absorption and we are not necessarily prepared to commit that much of our attention to it. Fun may be banal and in some respects morally suspect. It can be malicious – I was just having a bit of fun. Game shows, quiz shows, reality shows are increasingly absurd and surreal and those that decry a "dumbed down" mass media are accused of elitism. In this sense, fun can function as a moral imperative – western hedonistic culture frequently tells itself to - lighten up, live a little, get a life, have some fun.

Jordan distinguishes between needs pleasures, which move a person from discontentment to contentment, drinking a glass of water for example, and appreciation pleasures, where something is pleasurable no matter what the current level of contentment, drinking wine, for instance (Jordan, 2000: 14)

> "The important thing to note, then, is that pleasure can be thought of both as the elimination of, or absence of, pain and also as the provision of positive, joyful feelings" (Ibid: 15).

Fun is not necessarily the absence of pain or even the provision of a joy it is the absence of seriousness. An activity or object that is fun is trivial in the sense that it does not make a strong connection to the self. It is not necessarily personally relevant and meaningful. Distraction from the self requires this. A roller-coaster ride is fun, it dazzles the senses, but it is not revealing. After a roller-coaster ride you might realise that you have a weak stomach, but you are unlikely to uncover a hidden aspect of your personality. (However, if you take the roller-coaster ride in order to overcome strong personal fears then you will rather experience pleasure. This is also an example of the relational nature of experience.) Activities or objects that are absorbing, are personally meaningful. They become a part of one's self-definition. They are long-lived, i.e., people tend to stick to these objects and activities.

But how does relevance come about? One source of relevance has already been mentioned: opportunities for personal growth. Activities (and sometimes objects) can be self-revealing. For example, playing a part in a play may be a pleasure, because of the insights one gains while trying to relate to the figure in the play. Questions like 'How do I feel about the figure? Would I act the same or differently? How does it feel to give up my own personality for a while?' have the power to change ways of thinking about oneself. This is very different to the fun we get out of watching a second rate Sci-Fi movie such as *Barbarella*. Here distraction from the self is at the fore. It is important to note, that relevance does not depend on the activity or object *per se*. What seems to be a silly movie to us can be very relevant to others. A second source for relevance is memory. Every object or activity can have personally relevant meanings attached to it that go beyond the obvious. This can be a source of pleasure. Imagine a couple listening to *their* song – the song that reminds them of their first rendezvous. Besides the actual enjoyment of merely listening to the song, pleasant memories are triggered. These memories will add to the pleasure. This again, differs very much from listening to a radio playing in the background while doing the daily household chores. The former requires focus and absorption; the latter is a welcome distraction from an otherwise boring task. A third source of relevance is anticipation. Here fantasies about activities or objects that are about to happen are a source for pleasure. Both memory and anticipation require a high commitment to and focus on the activities and objects involved.

5.2 Repetition and Progression

Popular culture is based on repetition. Although there is repetition in "classical" music the repetition is focussed towards progression: the gradual change and development of themes and movements; pop music as a form, is based on repetition that does not necessarily progress: the alternation between verse and chorus and the relentless emphasis of a regular beat (Adorno 1991). The mainstays of popular entertainment are largely formulaic. Soap operas, sitcoms and game shows are all based on the repetition of particular themes. When sitcoms break the formulae – Niles finally getting together with his unrequited love in *Frasier* for instance, the show is rarely as popular. All popular sporting events endlessly repeat the same scenarios. Within all of these forms there must be infinite possible combinations which produce new events: the new pop song, the new episode of *Friends*, the next game of *Who Wants To Be A Millionaire*, the next world cup and so on. High culture may also depend on certain kinds of repetition, genre for instance, but it is not concerned with creating formulae. There could be no *Hamlet II*. High art is concerned with complete experiences. Popular culture is concerned with cycles of sameness, endless variation within self-replication. Games, whether physical or virtual, also depend on variable repetition. Consider the number of physical games that involve bouncing a ball, or the act of bouncing a ball itself. There is a comfort and a joy in the act. In computer games there is not only the physical repetition of hitting buttons on a keyboard or a joy pad but also the repetition of virtual action on the screen: running, jumping, hitting, shooting, dying.

Pleasure can be thought of in terms of progression rather than repetition Progression stimulates, it makes us think, it surprises. Surprise marks the central difference between satisfaction and pleasure. Satisfaction is the emotional consequence of *confirmed* expectations, whereas pleasure is the consequence of *deviations* from expectations. For example, a meeting with an important client that went better than expected or an unexpected pay rise. Here, the source of pleasure is not the actual outcome of the meeting or the size of pay rise – it is its unexpectedness. The notion that surprise may lead to pleasure, has an important implication, which can be circumscribed by the metaphor of a "hedonic treadmill" (Brickman & Campbell, 1971, cited in Kahneman, 1999). A novel object may be pleasurable but reactions to novel objects are not stable. The individual will adapt and the likelihood of pleasure derived from the novelty of a certain object will decrease. As Aristotle noted, pleasure decreases because the mind becomes less active, less stimulated as it becomes familiar with the novel object or experience. Instead of having fun by repeating familiar patterns, the pleasure-seeker will constantly explore new regions and domains in her pursuit of pleasure. Csikszentmihalyi's flow also depends on progression in this sense. It requires a close match between ability and challenge. Progression seems to be a necessary precondition for challenge; a challenge can only be set up, when there are things to do and it is clear what hasn't been done yet, pleasure involves the setting of plans and actions to meet these goals. Without the possibility of generating new and challenging goals pleasure, in this sense, is unthinkable.

5.3 Spectacle and Aesthetics

During fun the senses must be engaged, there must be spectacle. The bright and luminous colours of children's toys, the gaudy kitsch sets of the popular game show, the explosions of light and sound in popular film are instances of the spectacle of fun. Attention is "grabbed", we demand increasingly violent distraction; the leisure society is also the society of the spectacle. Spectacle and wild colour signal and signify fun. Subdued pastels do not. If there is an aesthetic of fun then it is gaudy, and fleeting, it bursts at the eye like a firework.

Aesthetic pleasures are more abstract and orderly (Duncker, 1941, cited in Rozin, 1999). The Gestalt of objects and activities, their regularity, symmetry, shapeliness, solidness reassures us. There is a danger of confusing aesthetics with *tastes*. It is now, more or less accepted in the field of Aesthetics that judgements of taste are not universal or timeless but historically, culturally and socially specific (Devereaux, 2001). However, within given cultures some aesthetic values can endure for a very long time as examples of "classic" architecture, sculpture and painting indicate. Thus, aesthetic values are something people share.

To return to the distinction between pleasure and fun, the fun of the spectacle is a result of the *intensity* of perceptual stimulation, whereas aesthetic value is concerned with the *quality* of perception

5.4 Transgression and Commitment

What, is the "fun" of the practical joke, the wind up, the "piss take" the unexpected appropriation of a situation? The fun of the "laff" in the workplace involves a transgression, albeit temporary and playful, of accepted forms of work behaviour. Goffman (1972, p. 59) describes this as the "flooding out" of one social frame to another. Perhaps then, transgression can be thought of as an element of fun, if only in a temporary deviation from seriousness. The mechanics of the joke are reduced by some writers on comedy, to category mistakes or the coming together of independent frames of reference creating a conflict or tension which is relieved in laughter; the essential basis of comic devices then, is conflict. Bergson considered satire to be "a social sanction against inflexible behaviour" (cited in Skynner & Cleese, 1993) The transgressions of "fun" like those of satire are "bites that are not bites" (Bateson, 1972). They are safe transgressions within particular contextual boundaries.

Again, in relation to fun and the distinction we are trying to outline, transgression can be fun but commitment may be pleasurable. Being absorbed in an activity requires - first of all - a general acceptance of the activity, a commitment to the basic assumptions and rules underlying this activity. Imagine two people playing a game. For the first the game is appealing. She figured out strategies to win in the context of the game. She accepts the game. The activity of playing, understanding and using the rules absorbs her. She will experience pleasure. The other person finds the game boring, but wants to oblige the first person. In order to distract herself from the boredom she finds a way to cheat, to bend the rules. By doing this, she ridicules the game but she may now have fun playing it. Both players enjoy themselves but their experiences will significantly differ in quality.

6. CONCLUSION

To summarise, this chapter has argued that although words like fun and pleasure are closely related and may each function as a superordinate category for the other, there are experiential and cultural differences between them. Fun has been considered in terms of distraction and pleasure in terms of absorption. This is not to suggest that pleasure is a more worthy pursuit than fun, it is rather an attempt to delineate different but equally important aspects of enjoyment. It is possible to appreciate Shakespeare and still acknowledge that *The Simpsons* is the greatest achievement of western civilisation. Both offer rich and fulfilling experiences but they are very different kinds of pleasures. As Peter Wright and John McCarthy argue elsewhere in this book, it is not possible to design an experience, only to design *for* an experience; but in order to do this it is necessary to have an understanding of that experience as it relates to and differs from others.

7. REFERENCES

Adorno, T., & Horkheimer, M. (1986). *Dialectic of Englightenment*. London: Verso.

Bateson, G. (Ed.). (1972). *Steps To An Ecology of Mind*. New York: Ballantine Books.

Csikszentmihalyi, M. (1975). *Beyond Boredom and Anxiety: The Experience of Work and Play in Games*. San Fancisco: Jossey Bass Publishers.

Debord, G. (1995). *The society of the spectacle*. New York: Zone Books.

Devereaux, M. (2001). *The Philosophical Status Of Aesthetics*. Available: http://aesthetics-online.org/ideas/devereaux.html.

Goffman, E. (1972). *Encounters : two studies in the sociology of interaction*. Harmondsworth: Penguin.

Jackson, P. (1998). *John Dewey and the Lessons of Art*: Yale University Press.

Jordan, P. (2000). *Designing Pleasurable Products: An Introduction to the New Human Factors*: Taylor and Francis.

Kahneman, D. (1999). Objective happiness. In D. Kahneman, E. Diener, & N. Schwarz (Eds.), *Well-being: The foundations of hedonic quality* (pp. 3-25). New York: Sage.

Laurel, B. (1993). *Computer as Theatre*. Reading, MA: Addison-Wesley.

Monk, A. F., Hassenzahl, M., Blythe, M., & Reed, D. (2002). *Funology: designing enjoyment*. Paper presented at the CHI. p.p. 924-5

Oxford English Dictionary. Available at: http://dictionary.oed.com/entrance.dtl

Roijec, C. (1985). *Capitalism and Leisure Theory*. London: Tavistock.

Rozin, P. (1999). Preadaption and the puzzles and properties of pleasure. In D. Kahneman, E. Diener, & N. Schwarz (Eds.), *Well-being: The foundations of hedonic psychology* (pp. 109-133). New York: Russell Sage Foundation.

Self, W. (1994). *My idea of Fun*. London: Penguin books.

Seligman, M. E. P., & Csikszentmihalyi, M. (2000). Positive Psychology: An Introduction. *American Psychologist, 55*, 5-14.

Skynner, R., & Cleese, J. (1993). *Life And How To Survive It*. London: Methuen.

Thompson, E. P. (1963). *The Making Of The English Working Class*. London: Gollancz.

Willis, P. (1990). *Common Culture*: Open University Press.

Willis, P. (2000). *The Ethnographic Imagination*. Cambridge: Polity Press.

SECTION TWO: METHODS AND TECHNIQUES

JAKOB NIELSEN

USER EMPOWERMENT AND THE FUN FACTOR

QUESTIONS AND ANSWERS WITH JAKOB NIELSEN

Q: The usability movement has been criticised for being dull and promoting boring designs. Why do you think this is?

A: The chief reason is that some people equate design conventions with creative restrictions. However, this equation doesn't add up. While it is true that usability is typically enhanced by consistency and adherence to design guidelines, this does not necessitate identical design. Rather, such conventions aim to create a vocabulary of building blocks that designers can combine in many vastly different, and often enjoyable, ways. Consider natural language. Each word has an established meaning, and we typically combine words using a defined grammar. Literature that follows these conventions is easier to read and has a bigger audience than avant-garde, experimental literature. Still, such "conventional" novels are definitely not the same: Although they use fully standardized language, they can reach any desired extreme on a variety of emotional scales.

Q: Do you think that concerns with fun, enjoyment and aesthetics are incompatible with traditional models of usability?

A: No, because the greatest joy of using computers comes through user empowerment and engagement. It's very enjoyable to visit a website that works, where everything just clicks for you. In contrast, a user interface that doesn't do things the way you want feels sluggish, unpleasant, and possibly even hostile, despite the designer's no doubt sincere attempt to invoke positive emotions. A user's personal experience trumps anything the designer is trying to communicate. In talking about a design's "look and feel," feel wins every time.

Q: Can you give us an example of a fun website?

A: Amazon.com uses associative links to create a fun and rewarding experience for users. Each book page offers associative links to five books frequently bought by other people who purchased the book you're interested in. Following these links can lead to a powerful feeling of discovery. As a result, you can easily spend much more time shopping on Amazon than is dictated by the simple efficiency metric of buying the book you came for as quickly as possible. Such engagement requires usability. If users can't master the interface, they'll feel oppressed rather than empowered, and are unlikely to explore or use anything beyond the absolute minimum. On the Web,

Mark A. Blythe, Andrew F. Monk, Kees Overbeeke and Peter C. Wright *(eds.)*,
Funology: From Usability to Enjoyment, 103—105.
© 2003 *Kluwer Academic Publishers. Printed in the Netherlands.*

this "minimum" often turns out to be one or two page views, and then users are gone -- never to return.

Q: Critics might say that there is more to an enjoyable activity than the ability to complete it.

A: Certainly, but at the same time, computers are currently difficult to use and much of the Web feels like a vast wasteland. Given this, people can and do derive considerable pleasure in finding a well-crafted user experience that empowers and engages them.

Q: Can traditional usability methods be adapted to address enjoyment, fun and so on?

A: Traditional user testing is great at debugging user interface designs to find the elements that make the system difficult to use. Testing methods are less well developed however, when it comes to determining the enjoyable aspects of a design. In the past, this was not much of a problem because user interfaces were so difficult to use that all we could hope for was that they'd improve to the level where using them was not actively unpleasant. Websites in particular were designed in such great contrast to users' needs that simply exterminating bloated and useless designs has been the usability movement's great achievement over the last ten years. Now, as we change from the negative endeavour of removing bad design to the positive pursuit of good design, we must modify the methodology to encompass more awareness of fulfilling, engaging, and fun design elements.

Q: How is enjoyment currently assessed?

A: Most studies currently rely on classic and not completely satisfactory ways of assessing user enjoyment: One method is subjective satisfaction questionnaire administered at the end of a study that provides a simple, overall system assessment. Another is observations of the user's body language for indications of satisfaction or displeasure (smiles or frowns), as well as for laughs, grunts, or explicit statements such as "cool" or "boring."

Q: Are these observations the kind of thing that anyone can do?

A: A skilled observer can gain much insight from the second approach, but it is a weak and possibly misleading source of data for less-skilled usability professionals, who constitute the vast majority of the world's test facilitators. As for the first approach, subjective satisfaction questionnaires suffer the standard problem of being administered out of context: They typically rely on users' recollection of enjoyment, rather than the actual experience of use in the moment. You can alleviate (though not eliminate) this by administering several small questionnaires throughout the test session rather than saving all the questions for one larger questionnaire at the end.

Q: Are user statements enough?

A: No. As always, you cannot rely on simple, literal interpretations of users' statements. For example, in testing company websites, users almost always say that they don't want fun or entertaining content: *Just give me the answers as straight and as fast as possible.* And, in observing actual user behaviour, we certainly do see negative reactions to frivolous content -- such as big photos of glamorous models or meaningless animations that bounce around the screen. But, at the same time, we also see users smile or exhibit other positive body language when they come across cleverly written content or moderately funny descriptions -- assuming they fall within the scope of users' expectations of professional writing in the website's genre. Thus, users seem to appreciate and enjoy a somewhat higher style to their content than they claim to prefer.

Q: What are the new challenges for HCI?

A: We need much better methods for testing enjoyable aspects of user interfaces. Such methods should be both robust and easy to apply, since people with relatively little expertise do the vast majority of user testing in the world. That said, ease of use must remain our first priority. Technology is just too difficult for us to abandon this goal. But hopefully it will soon be time to emphasise joy of use as well.

INTRODUCTION TO SECTION 2

As the Q&A with Jacob Nielsen makes clear, the idea of designing for enjoyment rather than simply designing to reduce frustration is a relatively new one for HCI. Usability evaluation methods have tended to concentrate on identifying usability black spots rather than beauty spots. But now it is no longer adequate just to avoid bad experiences, we have to find methods for designing good ones. As we noted in the introduction to this book, the move from principles, theory and concepts to practical methods and techniques has traditionally been quite a tricky one, involving as it does so many different interests, concerns, constraints and viewpoints. There would seem to be two possible fronts on which to advance. The first is to extend our existing armoury of user-centred design methods. The second is to do what HCI often does and borrow some ideas from disciplines new to HCI such as graphic design, art and literary theory. It's not surprising then, that the papers in this section provide examples of both of these ways forward.

The first three chapters in this section approach the problem by extending traditional user-centred design approaches.

In his chapter entitled **Measuring Emotion,** *Pieter Desmet*, describes the development of a psychological instrument for measuring emotional responses to products. The chapter is a good example of a classic psychometric approach to measurement. Key factors relating to emotion are first identified and refined down to a small set of measurable attributes. One of the interesting questions that Desmet asks is whether a product that is enjoyable in one culture will also be enjoyable in another. Consequently, he develops a *culture-free* test by using animated faces as stimuli. Using this tool, Desmet is able to show how different products engender different emotional responses in subjects.

In their chapter entitled **That's Entertainment!,** *John and Clare-Marie Karat* are concerned to find out whether the web has to be interactive to be entertaining. They show us how a traditional mix of focus groups, interviews, prototype evaluation and questionnaires can be used to design and assess the entertainment value of cultural web sites. They conclude that while the web is an interactive medium it is not exclusively so. Users can be satisfied by watchable experiences on the web too and a major factor in entertainment is *who* we are entertained by not how much control we have.

In their chapter entitled **Designing for Fun,** *Randy Pagulayan et al.* support Nielsen's argument that you need to get usability right before your product can be fun. Their work is concerned with the rapid evaluation cycles required to test games for Microsoft's *Xbox*. Like Karat and Karat's paper, their approach adapts traditional usability techniques to allow them to test various aspects of their games. They argue that by extending current usability design methods, games designers can get a handle on fun and improve the entertainment experience. Through a series of real product design examples, they show how standard usability tests highlighted problems which when solved, improved users' experiences.

Mark A. Blythe, Andrew F. Monk, Kees Overbeeke and Peter C. Wright *(eds.),*
Funology: From Usability to Enjoyment*, 107—109.*

In contrast to the first three chapters that extend traditional user-centred design methods, the next two chapters borrow from the disciplines of art and literary theory.

In their chapter entitled **Playing Games in the Emotional Space,** *Kristina Andersen et al* take on a rather daunting design challenge namely, how to ease the sense of privation felt by people who are emotionally close but physically distant from one another. In trying to solve this problem they set out on a fascinating journey, exploring what it means to be emotionally close. Inspired by the Surrealist art movement they develop a set of games that move people into the *emotional space* they wish to explore. They argue that fantasy games are, like art and poetry, valuable instruments for triggering sincere emotional responses in artificial situations. Once they have moved their participants into the emotional space they use what they call a *survey* to elicit responses from users about what it feels like and how technology might help, but it is certainly a survey with a difference! In contrast to Desmet, their approach is to focus on the *felt life* of individuals and what these feelings mean to them. By getting participants to consciously reflect on their feelings, Andersen et al. uncover what they call a universe of specific symbols and meanings that intimates share and which create a shared, but private, alternative emotional space.

In his chapter entitled **Deconstructing Experience,** *Alan Dix* provides us with a method for analysing experience. Taking as his starting point the literary concept of *deconstruction* and *reconstruction*, Dix shows us how a piece of poetry can be analysed in terms of resonances, dissonances and paradoxes at a number of different levels. He argues that this is precisely what strikes us about poetry. He then shows us how principles of reconstruction can be used to produce similar but novel poetic lines. Then he makes the interesting move of arguing that science can be regarded as a kind of deconstruction while design can be seen as a kind of reconstruction. He shows us how these same literary principles can be used to analyse graphic design problems and to deconstruct everyday experiences and reconstruct them in new media. What Dix is offering us then, is a simple but powerful technique for analysing and designing for experience. His point in all of this is not only that literary theory may have a lot to tell us about design but also that in an age when digital media change at such a rate, there is a real need to understand how experience can be re-mediated.

And finally, the last two chapters of this section take an approach somewhere in between the two extremes. In some ways they use traditional HCI concepts and methods but they apply them to artistic and imaginative activities, and they bring together engineers, designers and artists in interesting ways. These two chapters also fall naturally together because they are both concerned with designing for children.

In their chapter entitled **Designing Engaging Experiences with Children and Artists,** *Richard Hull and Jo Reid,* show us some inspired design concepts for ubiquitous applications. They bring together low-cost technologies to provide interactive multimedia experiences in a number of settings and show how it is possible to deliver engaging experiences with artful combinations of simple functionality. They argue that engaging experiences share in varying combinations, a number of features including *self-expression, social interaction, bonding, sharing, drama* and *sensation.* In order to iteratively design the tools and explore user experience they adapt participatory design techniques. In particular they bring engineers, artists and children together to work as full design partners. One outcome of their experiences as designers is a provisional model of consumer experience that they use to situate their products and to identify future design concepts.

In their Chapter entitled **Building Narrative Experiences for Children through Real Time Media Manipulation: POGO world**, *Antonio Rizzo et al* describe their approach to building POGO world. Where Hull and Reid gave us a lightning tour of their experiences of participatory design with artists and children over a range of products, Rizzo et al focus on describing in detail how they went about modelling and providing tool support for one pedagogic activity. They argue that narrative construction of experience is a central pedagogical technique in European schools. Through an analysis of children at a number of schools they developed a model of this activity based on Vygotsky's conception of the *cycle of creative imagination*. Using this framework, Rizzo et al describe how they developed and evaluated a set of novel interactive tools the aim of which is to augment the more familiar media of pencil and paper. In so doing the tools re-mediate the experience of narrative construction. One of the interesting points made by Rizzo et al, is that before the introduction of POGO world teachers saw traditional desktop technology as a potential risk to successful narrative activity. In contrast, POGO world by transforming those same activities into something more, positively enhanced the teachers' and children's experiences and perceptions of technology. Surely it is this kind of transformation which is at the heart of what designing for enjoyment should be about.

PIETER DESMET

CHAPTER 9

MEASURING EMOTION: DEVELOPMENT AND APPLICATION OF AN
INSTRUMENT TO MEASURE EMOTIONAL RESPONSES TO PRODUCTS

1.   INTRODUCTION

Emotions enrich virtually all our waking moments with either a pleasant or unpleasant quality. Cacioppo and his colleagues wrote,

> "emotions guide, enrich and ennoble life; they provide meaning to everyday existence; they render the valuation placed on life and property" (Cacioppo et al. 2001 p. 173).

These words illustrate that our relationship with the physical world is an emotional one. Clearly, the 'fun of use,' i.e. the fun one experiences from owning or using a product, also belongs to the affective rather than rational domain. The difficulty in studying affective concepts as 'enjoyment of use' and 'fun of use' is that they seem to be as intangible as they are appealing. Even more, rather than being an emotion as such, 'having fun' is probably the outcome of a wide range of possible emotional responses. Imagine, for example, the fun one has when watching a movie. This person will experience all kinds of emotions, such as fear, amusement, anger, relief, disappointment, and hope. Instead of one isolated emotion, it is the *combination* of these emotions that contributes to the experience of fun. It is not implausible that the same applies to other instances of fun, whether it is sharing a joke, using a product, or interacting with a computer.

So far, little is known about how people respond emotionally to products and what aspects of design or interaction trigger emotional responses. In order to support the study of these responses, a measurement instrument was developed that is capable to measure combinations of simultaneously experienced emotions: the Product Emotion Measurement Instrument (PrEmo). This chapter discusses the development of PrEmo in the context of existing instruments. In addition, an illustrative cross-culture study is reported, in which emotions evoked by car models have been measured in Japan and in The Netherlands.

2.   APPROACHES TO MEASURE EMOTION

Before one can measure emotions, one must be able to characterise emotions and distinguish them from other states. Unfortunately, although the concept of emotion

Mark A. Blythe, Andrew F. Monk, Kees Overbeeke and Peter C. Wright *(eds.),*
Funology: From Usability to Enjoyment, 111—123.

appears to be generally understood, it is surprisingly difficult to come up with a solid definition. In the last 100 years, psychologists have offered a variety of definitions, each focussing on different manifestations or components of the emotion. As there seems to be no empirical solution to the debate on which component is sufficient or necessary to define emotions, at present the most favoured solution is to say that emotions are best treated as multifaceted phenomena consisting of the following components: behavioural reactions (e.g. retreating), expressive reactions (e.g. smiling), physiological reactions (e.g. heart pounding), and subjective feelings (e.g. feeling amused). Each instrument that is claimed to measure emotions in fact measures one of these components. As a consequence, both the number of reported instruments and the diversity in approaches to measure emotions is abundant. In this chapter, the basic distinction is made between non-verbal (objective) instruments and verbal (subjective) instruments.

2.1 Non-verbal instruments to measure emotions

This category comprises instruments that measure either the expressive or the physiological component of emotion. An expressive reaction (e.g. smiling or frowning) is the facial, vocal, and postural expression that accompanies the emotion. Each emotion is associated with a particular pattern of expression (Ekman, 1994): for example, anger comes with a fixed stare, contracted eyebrows, compressed lips, vigorous and brisk movements and, usually, a raised voice, almost shouting (Ekman & Friesen, 1975). Instruments that measure this component of emotion fall into two major categories: those measuring facial and those measuring vocal expressions. Facial expression instruments are based on theories that link expression features to distinct emotions. Examples of such theories are the Facial Action Coding System (FACS; Ekman & Friesen, 1978), and the Maximally Discriminative Facial Moving Coding System (MAX; Izard, 1979). Generally, visible expressions captured on stills or short video sequences are analysed. An example is the Facial Expression Analysis Tool (FEAT; Kaiser & Wehrle, 2001), which automatically codes videotaped facial actions in terms of FACS. Like the facial expression instruments, vocal instruments are based on theories that link patterns of vocal cues to emotions (e.g. Johnstone & Scherer, 2001). These instruments measure the effects of emotion in multiple vocal cues such as average pitch, pitch changes, intensity colour, speaking rate, voice quality, and articulation.

   A physiological reaction (e.g. increases in heart rate) is the change in activity in the autonomic nervous system (ANS) that accompanies emotions. Emotions show a variety of physiological manifestations that can be measured with a diverse array of techniques. Examples are instruments that measure blood pressure responses, skin responses, pupillary responses, brain waves, and heart responses. Researchers in the field of affective computing are most active in developing ANS instruments, such as IBM's emotion mouse (Ark, Dryer, & Lu, 1999) and a variety of wearable sensors designed by the Affective Computing Group at MIT (e.g. Picard, 2000). With these instruments, computers can gather multiple physiological signals while a person is experiencing an emotion, and learn which pattern is most indicative of which emotion.

The major advantage of non-verbal instruments is that, as they are language-independent, they can be used in different cultures. A second advantage is that they are unobtrusive because they do not disturb participants during the measurement. In addition, these instruments are often claimed to be less subjective than self-report instruments because they do not rely on the participants' own assessment of the emotional experience. For the current application however, this class of instruments has several limitations. First, these instruments can only reliably assess a limited set of 'basic' emotions (such as anger, fear, and surprise). Reported studies find a recognition accuracy of around 60-80% for six to eight basic emotions (see Cacioppo et al. 2001). Moreover, these instruments cannot assess combinations of simultaneously experienced emotions. Given these limitations, it was decided not to use this approach for measuring emotions evoked by products.

2.2 *Verbal instruments to measure emotions*

The limitations of non-verbal instruments as discussed above are overcome by verbal self-report instruments, which typically assess the subjective feeling component of emotions. A subjective feeling (e.g. feeling happy or feeling inspired) is the conscious awareness of the emotional state one is in, i.e. the subjective emotional experience. Subjective feelings can only be measured through self-report. The most often used self-report instruments require respondents to report their emotions with the use of a set of rating scales or verbal protocols.

The two major advantages of the verbal instruments is that rating scales can be assembled to represent any set of emotions, and can be used to measure combinations of emotions. The main disadvantage is that they are difficult to apply between cultures. In emotion research, translating emotion words is known to be difficult because for many emotion words a one-to-one, 'straight' translation is not available. Between-culture comparisons are therefore notoriously problematic. To overcome this problem, a handful of non-verbal self-report instruments have recently been developed that use pictograms instead of words to represent emotional responses. An example is the Self-Assessment Manikin (SAM; Lang, 1985). With SAM, respondents point out the puppets that in their opinion best portray their emotion. Although applicable in between-culture studies, these non-verbal scales also have an important limitation, which is that they do not measure distinct emotions but only generalised emotional states (in terms of underlying dimensions such as pleasantness and arousal). Consequently, a new instrument for measuring the emotions evoked by products was developed. This instrument combines the advantages of existing non-verbal and verbal self-report instruments: it measures distinct emotions and combinations of emotions but does not require the participants to verbalise their emotions.

3.   THE PRODUCT EMOTION MEASUREMENT INSTRUMENT

Does my question annoy him? Is she amused by my story? In the face-to-face encounters of everyday life we constantly monitor and interpret the emotions of others (see Ettcoff & Magee, 1992). This interpretation skill was the starting point for the development of PrEmo. PrEmo is a non-verbal self-report instrument that measures 14 emotions that are often elicited by product design. Of these 14 emotions, seven are pleasant (i.e. desire, pleasant surprise, inspiration, amusement, admiration, satisfaction, fascination), and seven are unpleasant (i.e. indignation, contempt, disgust, unpleasant surprise, dissatisfaction, disappointment, and boredom). Instead of relying on the use of words, respondents can report their emotions with the use of expressive cartoon animations. In the instrument, each of the 14 measured emotions is portrayed by an animation by means of dynamic facial, bodily, and vocal expressions. Figure 1 shows the measurement interface.

Figure 2. *Product Emotion Measurement instrument interface*

The procedure of a PrEmo experiment is self-running. The computer screen displays instructions that guide respondents through the procedure, which includes an explanation of the experiment and an exercise. The program's heart is the measurement interface, which was designed to be simple and intuitive in use. The top section of this interface depicts stills of the 14 animations. Each still is accompanied by a (hidden) three-point scale. These scales represent the following ratings: "I do feel the emotion," "to some extent I feel the emotion," and "I do not feel the emotion expressed by this animation." The rating scales are 'hidden behind' the animation frames. A scale appears on the side of the animation frame only after the animation is activated by clicking on the particular still. The lower section of the interface displays a picture of the stimulus and an operation button. During an experiment, the respondents are first shown a (picture of a) product and subsequently instructed to use the animations to report their emotion(s) evoked by the product. While they view an animation, they must ask themselves the following question: "does this animation express what I feel?" Subsequently, they use the three-point scale to answer this question. Visual feedback of the scorings is provided by the background colour of the animation frame.

Note that earlier PrEmo versions have been discussed in previous publications (e.g. Desmet, Overbeeke, & Tax 2001; Desmet, Hekkert, & Jacobs 2000; Desmet & Hekkert 1998). See www.DesigningEmotion.nl for a dynamic animation example and information regarding PrEmo usage.

3.1 Emotions measured by PrEmo

The 14 measured emotions were selected to represent a manageable cross-section of all emotions that can be elicited by consumer products. For this selection, a multistage method was used. First, a set of emotions was assembled that is sufficiently extensive to represent a general overview of the full repertoire of human emotions. This set of 347 emotions was compiled by merging and translating reported lists of emotions. In the first study, participants (N = 20) rated these emotions on the dimensions 'pleasantness' and 'arousal,' which represent the dimensions of the 'Circumplex of Affect' developed by Russell (1980). Both dimensions were rated on a three-point scale: pleasant-neutral-unpleasant, and calm-moderate-excited respectively. In addition, participants marked emotion words with which they were not familiar. On the basis of these ratings, the set emotions was divided in eight categories (see Table 1). Note that one combination, i.e. moderate-neutral is not included. It is left out because it is not considered to be an emotional category in the Circumplex model. Emotions that were ambiguous or marked as unfamiliar were omitted from the set.

In order to further reduce the set, the second study was designed to select those emotions that are most often elicited by products. In this study, participants (N = 22) used a rating procedure to indicate which emotions they often, and which they do not often experience in response to product design. They were instructed to do this for each of the eight emotion sets. On the basis of the sum scores, 69 emotions were selected that are evoked regularly by product design (the sum scores of these emotions were significantly higher than the average score).

Table 1. *Emotion categories*

Category	Amount of included emotions	Category	Amount of included emotions
Excited pleasant	30	Calm unpleasant	34
Moderate pleasant	53	Moderate unpleasant	61
Calm pleasant	24	Excited unpleasant	46
Calm neutral	14	Excited neutral	20

Subsequently, in the third step, the set was further reduced by eliminating those emotions that are approximately similar to others in the set. Participants ($\underline{N}$ = 40) rated the similarity of the emotions in pairs. With the use of a hierarchical cluster analysis, the set of 69 emotions was reduced to a set of 41 emotions. In a final study, participants ($\underline{N}$ =23) rated all 41 emotions on a five-point scale (from 'very relevant to product experience' to 'not relevant to product experience'). On the basis of the mean scores, the final set of 14 emotions was selected. Although, evidently, products can elicit more than these 14 emotions, these are the ones that can be considered to occur most frequently. Moreover, PrEmo requires a set that can be surveyable. The set of 14 is regarded as a workable balance between comprehensive and surveyable. Note that a detailed report of the selection procedure can be found in Desmet (2002).

3.2 Dynamic cartoon animations

The idea to use expressive portrayals of the 14 emotions was based on the assumption that emotional expressions can be recognized reliably. Ekman (1994) found that facial expressions of basic emotions (e.g. fear and joy) are not only recognised reliably, but also univocally across cultures. As the emotions measured by PrEmo are subtler than the basic emotions, more information than merely the facial expression is needed to portray them reliably.

Figure 3. *Two animation sequences*

Our approach to this problem was to incorporate total body expression, movement, and vocal expression. It was decided to use a cartoon character because these are often particularly efficient in portraying emotions. This efficiency is achieved with abstracting which reduces the emotional expression to its essence. Abstracted portrayals can make the task of recognizing emotional expressions easier because the amount of irrelevant information is reduced (Bernson & Perret 1991). Moreover, with cartoon characters it is possible to amplify (or exaggerate) the expressive cues that differ between emotional expressions (see Calder et al. 1997).

A professional animator designed the character and created the animated expressions. A vocal actor synchronized the vocal expressions. To enable the animator to create clear portrayals, a study with actors was conducted. In this study, four professional actors (two males, two females) were instructed to portray each of the 14 emotions as expressive and precise as they could. These portrayals were recorded on videotape and analysed by the author and the animator. On the basis of this analysis, the animator created the animations. By ways of example, Figure 2 shows the animation sequences of *inspiration* and *disgust*.

3.3 Validity and reliability

The validity of PrEmo, i.e. the degree to which it accurately measures the emotions it was designed to measure, was assessed in a two-step procedure. The first step was to examine the validity of the animations. An important requirement was that PrEmo should be applicable in different cultures or language areas. Therefore, the study included participants from four different countries ($\underline{N}$ = 120; 29 Japanese, 29 United State citizens, 33 Finnish, and 29 Dutch participants). Participants were shown three animations and asked which of these three best portrayed a given emotion. Of the three animations shown, one was designed to portray the given emotion, and the other two portrayed other emotions (yet similar in terms of pleasantness and arousal). The animation that was supposed to portray the given emotion was considered valid when it was selected more often than could be expected by chance. A strict significance level (i.e. $p < .001$) was applied because it was important to identify also slightly inaccurate animations. On the basis of the results, it was concluded that in order to be valid, the animations portraying *desire* and *disappointment* needed further development. These two animations were found to be invalid in Japan and therefore adjusted on the basis of a study with four Japanese actors.

The validity of the instrument was examined in a second study ($\underline{N}$ = 30). In this study, both PrEmo and a verbal scale were used to measure emotions evoked by six chairs. The level of association between the results obtained with PrEmo and those obtained with the verbal scales was analysed. The correlations between emotion scores measured with the two methods were high (r varied from .72 to .99) and all but one (i.e. *amusement*) were significant ($p < .05$). For each emotion a repeated measures MANOVA was performed to examine interaction effects between chair model and instrument (i.e. either verbal scale or PrEmo). None of the analyses found a significant interaction effect between chair and instrument. In agreement with the high correlation, these findings indicate that the participants did not respond differently to each of the chairs as a result of the measurement instrument applied. Based on these results, it was concluded that PrEmo is satisfactory with respect to its convergent validity. Moreover, participants reported in a questionnaire that they preferred using the animations to using words for reporting their emotional responses. The animations were found to be more intuitive in use and, importantly, much more enjoyable.

4. CROSS-CULTURAL APPLICATION

The application possibilities of PrEmo have been explored with a between-culture study in which emotions evoked by six car models (see Figure 3) were measured both in Japan ($\underline{n}$ = 32) and in The Netherlands ($\underline{n}$ = 36). It was decided to use cars because in previous studies we found that car models that vary in appearance can elicit strongly different emotions (see e.g. Desmet, Hekkert, & Jacobs 2000). Participants were matched on gender and age (20-60 years old). In a written introduction, it was explained that the purpose of the experiment was to assess emotional responses to the car designs. After the introduction, participants were shown a thumbnail display that gave an overview of all the models. Subsequently, photos of the six car models were presented in random order. After looking at a photo, participants reported their response with the 14 PrEmo animations.

Figure 4. *Stimuli used in the application study*

In order to obtain a graphical representation of the results a correspondence analysis was performed with two factors: Emotion (14 levels) and Car combined with Culture (12 levels). Correspondence analysis is a technique for describing the relationship between nominal variables, while simultaneously describing the relationship between the categories of each variable. It is an exploratory technique, primarily intended to facilitate the interpretation of the data. Figure 4 shows the two-dimensional solution of the analysis, which explains 90.3 % of the total variance: the 'product & emotion space.'

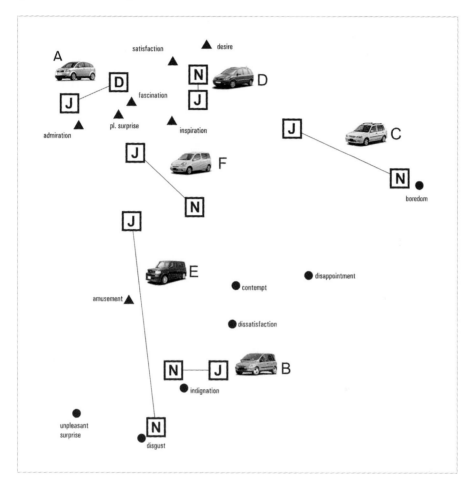

Figure 5. *'Product & emotion space' of Dutch and Japanese participants for six car models*

This product & emotion space visualises the associations between the car models and the reported emotional responses. Pleasant emotions are indicated with a triangle and unpleasant with a circle. The results of the Japanese participants are indicated with a 'J,' and those of the Dutch with an 'N.' The distances between the car models reflect the relationships between them (with similar models plotted close to each other). Similarly, the distances between the car models and the emotions reflect the relationship between them. This means that car models that are plotted close to each other evoked similar emotions, whereas those plotted at a distance from each other evoked different emotions. Cars A and D, for example, evoked similar emotions, whereas Cars A and B evoked noticeably different emotions.

In the product & emotion space some effects catch the eye. Clearly, the degree to which car models differ from each other also varies. The difference between Cars A and D, for example, is smaller than the difference between Cars A and B. Moreover, some car models appear to have elicited mainly pleasant emotions (e.g. Car D), some mainly unpleasant (e.g. Car B), and some both pleasant and unpleasant (e.g. Car F). In addition, two between-culture effects can be observed. First, the degree to which the emotional responses of the cultures differ depends on the car model. The space indicates that cultural differences are greatest for Cars E and C. Cars, A, B, and D, on the other hand, appear to have elicited similar emotions in Japan and in The Netherlands. Secondly, the product & emotion space indicates that the Japanese experienced generally higher ratings on pleasant emotions than the Dutch. The three car models that showed the largest cultural differences elicited more pleasant emotions in Japan than in The Netherlands.

4.1 Between-culture differences

The correspondence analysis is an exploratory technique, primarily intended to facilitate the interpretation of the data. Because it is not appropriate to draw conclusions, the observed between-culture effects have been examined in more depth, with an analysis of variance. For each emotion a two-way repeated measures MANOVA was performed with Car (six levels) as within-participants factor, Culture (two levels) as between-participant factor, and the emotion as dependent variable. Some interesting culture effects have been found. For three emotions, cultural differences independent of car model were found. Japanese participants showed higher mean scores on the following emotions: *admiration, satisfaction*, and *fascination* ($p < .01$). This may point to a cultural difference in how car models are experienced: apparently Japanese people are generally more admiring of, satisfied, and fascinated by car models than the Dutch. Some Car x Culture interaction effects indicated that there are also cultural differences in responses with respect to the particular car models used in the study. Interaction effects were found for *disgust, unpleasant surprise, dissatisfaction, amusement, admiration*, and *satisfaction*. For example, the Dutch participants were not amused by the same car models as the Japanese.

A notable finding was that, contrary to expectations, cultural differences cannot be explained by product-familiarity. For instance, for Car B (Fiat Multipla) no significant cultural differences were found with respect to the emotions it elicited. This was not expected, because the Dutch participants were familiar with this model, and the Japanese were not. These findings confirm the idea that in product development, cultural differences must be recognized, and that these differences are both difficult to predict and to explain. Companies involved in 'global marketing' should be aware of these differences and should perhaps develop various design strategies for different cultures, instead of attempting to market identical products in different countries.

5. DISCUSSION

The unique strength of PrEmo is that it combines two qualities: it measures distinct emotions and it can be used cross-culturally because it does not ask respondents to verbalise their emotions. In addition, it can be used to measure mixed emotions, that is, more than one emotion experienced simultaneously, and the operation requires neither expensive equipment nor technical expertise. And, also important, respondents reported that the measurement task with PrEmo is pleasant or even enjoyable. A limitation for the application in human computer interaction is that the 14 measured emotions represent a cross-section of emotions experienced towards static product design. It is not said that this set also represents emotions that are experienced towards dynamic human product interaction. Some emotions may be over-represented, whereas others may be missing. Before PrEmo is applied for the measurement of emotions evoked by interacting with a computer (or any other product) it must be determined if the 14 emotions are adequate and, if not, the set animations should be adjusted.

What is the point of measuring emotions evoked by products or computer programs? More interesting than discovering *which* particular emotions are evoked by a set of stimuli, is to understand *why* those stimuli evoke these particular emotions. This information can be used in the development of new products, to elicit pre-defined emotion profiles. Hence, the interpretation of PrEmo results requires theoretical propositions about how product emotions are related to the product's appearance and interaction, and the characteristics of the person who experiences the emotions. In cognitive emotion psychology, emotions are regarded as outcomes of appraisal processes. According to Frijda (1986), emotions are elicited when a subject appraises a stimulus as important for the gain of some personal concern. A concern can be any goal, standard, attitude, or motive one has in life, e.g., achieving status, feeling safe, or respecting the environment. In following Arnold (1960), Frijda argues that when we appraise a stimulus as beneficial to our concerns, we will experience positive emotions and try to approach this particular stimulus. Likewise, when we appraise a stimulus as conflicting with our concerns, we will experience negative emotions and try to avoid it. As concerns are personal, different subjects have different concerns. As a result, individual subjects will appraise a given product differently. As different types of emotions are evoked by different kinds of appraisals, appraisals can be used to differentiate emotions (e.g., Ortony, Clore, & Collins 1988). For the 14 emotions measured by PrEmo, Desmet (2002) described the specific appraisal patterns underlying each emotion. Understanding these patterns could guide designers in controlling the emotional responses to their designs.

A second application possibility of PrEmo is to use it as a means to communicate emotional responses to products. The emotional aspects of a design can be difficult to discuss because they are often based on intuition. The 'product & emotion space' that results from a PrEmo experiment makes the intangible emotional responses tangible. In various design workshops, the space has proven to be a valuable support to discuss emotional aspects of design in a design team. In addition, designers found it to be effective when used as a means to communicate, argue, and defend their ideas to non-designers who are also involved in the product development (e.g. marketing, engineering, etcetera).

The decision to design an instrument that measures both pleasant *and* unpleasant emotions was based on the notion that unpleasant responses are as interesting as the pleasant. What are the characteristics that make one product more enjoyable or attractive than another? Some of us find riding a roller coaster fun, whereas others would not want to be found dead in one. Some consider the fear experienced when thrown from a bridge with elastic tied to one's ankles to be fun whereas others prefer to play a game of bridge. Whatever the interpersonal differences in what we find to be fun, it would clearly be incorrect to assume that that fun is related only to pleasant emotions. Frijda and Schram (1995) stated that art often elicits paradoxical emotions, that is, positive and negative emotions simultaneously, and that it is precisely these paradoxical emotions that we seek and enjoy. In the words of Frijda (p. 2) "we enjoy watching tragic miseries, and we pay fair amounts of money to suffer threat and suspense." It may be interesting for designers and design researchers to investigate the possibilities of designing such paradoxical emotions. Eventually, these efforts may result in products that are unique, innovative, rich in their interaction, interesting, and fun to use.

6. ACKNOWLEDGEMENTS

This research was funded by Mitsubishi Motor R&D, Europe GmbH, Trebur, Germany. Paul Hekkert (Delft University), Jan Jacobs, and Kees Overbeeke are acknowledged for their contribution to this research.

7. REFERENCES

Ark, W., Dryer, D.C., & Lu, D.J. (1999). The emotion mouse. *Proceedings of HCI International '99*, Munich Germany, August 1999.

Arnold, M.B. (1960). *Emotion and Personality: vol 1. Psychological aspects.* New York: Colombia University Press.

Bernson, P.J., & Perrett, D.I. (1991). Perception and recognition of photographic quality facial caricatures: implications for the recognition of natural images. *European Journal of Cognitive Psychology, 3,* 105-135.

Cacioppo, J.T., Berntson, G.G., Larsen, J.T., Poehlmann, K.M., & Ito, T.A. (2001). The psychophysiology of emotion. In M. Lewis & J.M. Haviland-Jones (Eds.), *Handbook of Emotions (2nd ed.)* (pp. 173-191). New York: The Guilford Press.

Calder, A.J., Young, A.W., Rowland, D., & Perrett, D.I. (1997). Micro-expressive facial actions as a function of affective stimuli: Replication and extension. *Personality and Social Psychology Bulletin, 18,* 515-526.

Desmet, P.M.A. (2002). *Designing Emotions.* Unpublished doctoral dissertation.

Desmet, P.M.A., & Hekkert, P. (1998). Emotional reactions elicited by car design: A measurement tool for designers. In D. Roller (Ed.), *Automotive Mechatronics Design and Engineering* (pp. 237-244). Düsseldorf, Germany: ISATA.

Desmet, P.M.A., Hekkert, P., & Jacobs, J.J. (2000). When a car makes you smile: Development and application of an instrument to measure product emotions. In: S.J. Hoch & R.J. Meyer (Eds.), *Advances in Consumer Research* (vol. 27, pp. 111-117). Provo, UT: Association for Consumer Research.

Desmet, P.M.A., Overbeeke, C.J., & Tax, S.J.E.T. (2001). Designing products with added emotional value; development and application of an approach for research through design. *The Design Journal, 4(1),* 32-47.

Ekman, P. (1994). Strong evidence for universals in facial expressions: a reply to Russell's mistaken critique. *Psychological Bulletin, 115(2),* 268-287.

Ekman, P., & Friesen, W.V. (1975). *Unmasking the face: A guide to recognizing emotions from facial cues.* Englewood Cliffs, NJ: Prentice-Hall.

Ekman, P., & Friesen, W.V. (1978). *Facial Action Coding System: A technique for the measurement of facial movement.* Palo Alto, CA: Consulting Psychologists Press.

Ettcoff, N.L., & Magee, J.J. (1992). Categorical perception of facial expressions. *Cognition, 44,* 227-240.

Frijda, N.H. (1986). *The emotions.* Cambridge: Cambridge University Press.

Frijda, N. H., & Schram, D. (Eds.). (1995). *Special issue on emotion and cultural products.*

Izard, C.E. (1979). *The Maximally Discriminative Facial Movement Coding System (MAX).* Newark: Instructional Recourses Centre, University of Delaware.

Johnstone, T., & Scherer, K. R. (2001). Vocal communication of emotion. In M. L. J. M. Haviland-Jones (Ed.), *Handbook of Emotions* (Second ed., pp. 220-235). New York: The Guilford Press.

Kaiser, S., & Wehrle, T. (2001). Facial expressions as indicator of appraisal processes. In K. Scherer, A. Schorr, & T. Johnstone (Eds.), *Appraisal processes in emotion* (pp. 285-300). Oxford: Oxford University Press.

Lang, P.J. (1985). *The cognitive psychophysiology of emotion: anxiety and the anxiety disorders.* Hillsdale, NJ: Lawrence Erlbaum.

Ortony, A., Clore, G.L., & Collins, A. (1988). *The cognitive structure of emotions.* Cambridge: Cambridge University Press.

Picard, R. W. (2000). Towards computer that recognize and respond to user emotion. *IBM Systems Journal, 39*(3/4).

Russell, J.A. (1980). A circumplex model of affect. *Journal of Personality and Social Psychology, 39,* 1161-1178.

JOHN KARAT AND CLARE-MARIE KARAT

CHAPTER 10

THAT'S ENTERTAINMENT!

1. INTRODUCTION

1.1 Motivation for the Project

What kind of entertainment do people want from a web site on art and culture? And what is the appropriate context of use for people to enjoy entertainment on the Web? Is this an individual activity or one that that would be most engaging if it occurred in a social context? And would people like to do this in multiple locations, for example, at home, work and on the road? At this time, there really is no Web experience similar to the most common entertainment activity, namely, watching TV (Vogel, 1998). In this chapter, we present our experience in developing an entertainment web site for art and culture where the user-centred design (UCD) process led us to the design of TV-like, streaming, multimedia experiences delivered over the Web and similar to TV documentaries, but enriched by hotlinks enabling user control of the experience and access to extra content. The "less clicking, more watching" design approach that emerged through the research is in contrast to the prevailing notion that entertainment on the Web must be highly interactive and participatory as in the model for video games and chat rooms. Although almost one-half of Internet users spent some time with other members of their household every week (Cole, 2000), there are few online entertainment opportunities appropriate for such group experiences. We explored this possibility by testing individual as well as small group use of the Web entertainment prototypes. The chapter begins with a brief discussion of the entertainment concept, followed by a description of the UCD process through which the design emerged for the initial prototype, discussion of the usability testing of the enriched prototypes, and a discussion of the lessons learned about the research topic and the methods employed to address it.

1.2 Entertainment on the Web

Many traditional forms of entertainment such as talking, reading, listening to music, watching movies and TV, playing sports and games, shopping, cooking, gardening,

Mark A. Blythe, Andrew F. Monk, Kees Overbeeke and Peter C. Wright *(eds.),*
Funology: From Usability to Enjoyment, 125—136
© 2003 *Kluwer Academic Publishers. Printed in the Netherlands.*

eating, drinking, visiting museums, attending cultural events have their counterparts on the web. Talking and gossiping have a forum in electronic chat rooms; reading news on the web is becoming increasingly popular; the previously solitary video-game experience has found new meaning in the networked game era; and shopping has gigantic proportions on the web, newly augmented by the thrills of on-line auction.

As stated previously, our research examines possible web counterparts for a TV-like experience, i.e., web-based "watchable" entertainment experiences provided on the screen of a desktop or laptop computer. Currently, few web sites have experienced success in this arena, and those that have are of limited scope (The Economist, 2000). The best examples are sites featuring animated cartoons, often based on parody, such as Joe Cartoon (www.joecartoon.com); sites that show short films, previews, and commercials such as Atom Films (www.atomfilms.com); and the "web cam" phenomenon.

The three most common explanations for this shortage of options are the lack of bandwidth for video; the inadequacy of the desktop sitting position; and the need of interactivity in web entertainment (The Economist, 2000). However, networked video games have shown that the first two problems are not enough to deter entertainment: pre-downloading and local computer graphics rendering can deal with bandwidth problems, and people seem to sit forever in front of video-games.

So, if interactivity is the defining component of web experiences, then the concept of a "watchable", TV-like web experience is a contradiction in terms. In fact, throughout the development of this project, web designers repeatedly told us that people are entertained by computers only when actively interacting with the content (see also Murray, 1997). This belief is strengthened by the repetitive failures of the traditional entertainment industry to create web entertainment. The first cycle, fuelled by the success of the *"The Spot"* (www.spot.com) and by the MIT Media Lab advocating interactive TV, failed spectacularly in 1997 both for Microsoft and AOL (see Gierland and Sonesh-Kedar, 1999). The dot.com phenomenon of 1999/2000 spurred a new wave of projects that also ended mostly in failure, particularly in the case of Steven Spielberg's www.pop.com, the Digital Entertainment Network, and Pseudo (www.pseudo.com) (Red Herring, 2000; The Economist, 2000). The opposite model, making TV into a web device, has also mostly failed, notably in the case of WebTV (The Economist, 2000).

Does that mean *"...the Internet will not be the main vehicle for electronic entertainment..."* (The Economist, 2000, pg. 32)? Although we do not have a definitive answer to this question, our work in the e-culture project, described in the remainder of this chapter, suggests that people not only want and like to watch TV-like web experiences, but also that those experiences may be significantly different from both traditional TV viewing and web-surfing.

2.   METHOD

2.1 Overview of User Centred Design Approach

What kind of entertainment do people want from a web site on art and culture? To answer this question, we conducted a variety of UCD activities including interviews with curators and cultural programmers, focus groups with a range of participants in different cities in the United States, interviews with visitors to museums in New York City, online surveys of museum web sites, and usability walkthroughs and test sessions with prototypes of the design concept for the art and culture site. The detailed description of all of these UCD activities and results is beyond the scope of this chapter. Please see another publication (Vergo, Karat, Karat, Pinhanez, Cofino, Riecken, Cofino, and Podlaseck, 2001) for details regarding the curator and visitor interviews, web surveys, and focus groups. In this chapter, we will describe the group usability walkthroughs and the individual and small group usability test sessions with target users that informed the design of the prototypes of the web site.

2.2 Users

Based on existing research about internet users, information from the cultural institutions with which we were partnering to develop the web site, and from IBM, we defined our typical user as a person at least 9 years old who spends an average of 10 or more hours a week on a computer, and of that time, five or more hours are spent on the Internet. Our target users attended at least one cultural event in the last 12 months.

2.3 Iteration 1: Usability Design Walkthroughs

Based on the results of the interview and survey data from visitors to museums and online museum sites, the team developed five early design concepts to walkthrough with target users in group settings. The usability design walkthroughs were run in 12 sessions with a total of 70 participants ranging from 9 to 72 years in age who were screened for cultural interest and experience with the web. Participants were first shown "best of breed" excerpts of existing web sites related to culture, and then they were presented mock-ups of new design ideas. Qualitative and quantitative data were collected. The mock-ups of design ideas shown in the second part of the usability walkthroughs encompassed five different design approaches for exploring cultural content:

1.   A filtering system based on direct manipulation of large databases with visual feedback (such as in Alberg & Shneiderman, 1994). Current uses of this visualization design for database information are the display of chronological events in patient medical records, judicial records for juveniles, and inventories of movies.

2. A set of lenses (tools) to manipulate the way content could be viewed (such as in Stone, Fishkin, and Bier, 1994). This approach allows the user to select a lens for "history" or "music" and place it on a visual display of artwork in order to learn about events in history or the music at the time the artwork was created.
3. A chat system where people could talk about a particular art work (such as Viegas and Donalth, 1999). This approach resembles a virtual art exhibit: art objects are distributed around a "room" and the user is represented by a bubble on the screen and can drag their bubble near others in order to chat with them and join their conversation.
4. A notebook system where the user collects and comments on artistic content, and later publishes the notebook for public/private viewing. This approach enables the user to create and keep a personal "scrapbook" of their experience in viewing or hearing artistic content.
5. A multimedia system where the user watches guided multimedia tours, interacting whenever interested in related information. This approach resembles a guided tour in a museum, but is augmented by the ability of the user to take control of course of the tour and see related information or detailed information on the cultural content of the tour.

A major finding of the usability design walkthroughs was that most participants viewed unfavourably web sites involving active interaction with content or other visitors they did not know. They viewed these more interactive design concepts as work-like experiences, not entertainment. They saw little value in interacting with other people who were not acknowledged experts in the cultural area being presented in the tour. The guided tour format was clearly the best received among the design ideas. Participants strongly suggested the replacement of text by audio. We summarized these findings by hypothesizing that in this domain of entertaining web experiences, users wanted *less clicking, more watching*. Users were comfortable with the idea of a streaming web experience that leads them through artistic and cultural artefacts where, unlike television, the stream can be paused, replayed, or interrupted for further exploration. Users have a strong desire for the availability of related information through hypermedia links and in-depth analysis of the works of art. Users were adamant about having a "human voice" behind the multimedia experience, that is, a personal viewpoint and narrative in the exposition of the content.

2.4 Iteration 2: The Design and Evaluation of the Interactive Prototypes

Based on the results of the usability design walkthroughs, we developed a design concept for the cultural web site based on the idea of providing users multimedia tours guided by experts, artists, or celebrities. In our design, a tour presents information to the user continuously, from beginning to end, unless the user chooses to explore related material or to exercise control. To cope with the requirement for a minimum of 56Kbps bandwidth, we decided to explore multimedia experiences primarily based on still pictures and sound with minimal use of video. At 56Kbps, a continuous video stream is of insufficient quality, but at that speed it is possible to download combined audio and images that have reasonable quality. The primary use of still photographs also reduced production costs since shooting video is more expensive than using still pictures accompanied by recorded audio. As a note, because of copyright issues, the web site is for IBM internal use only at this point in time, and is not accessible via the World Wide Web.

In our design, the main multimedia experience, or main tour, is composed of multiple scenes connected linearly that play continuously to tell a story from the tour guide's perspective. The tours resemble a short TV documentary and play within a web browser window. The main tour is enriched by the addition of user controls such as pause/resume, a navigation map to enable scene changes, and by the inclusion of hot spots for two different kinds of related content that we labelled side tours and branches. A side tour is a self-contained multimedia segment focusing in depth on some aspect of the tour. A branch is a static web page with text, pictures, and links to related information on a specific subject. Since side tours were more costly to produce than branches, we produced side tours only for highly desirable related information.

Figure 1 shows a snapshot of a tour with key features enlarged and presented to the right of the main screen. The majority of the screen area is filled with tour content (pictures, text, occasionally very short segments of video). On the bottom left-hand side, a pictorial navigation map gives the user an idea of their position in the tour, the duration of different scenes in the tour, and the proportion of the tour remaining.

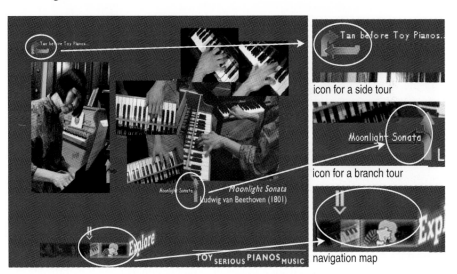

Figure 1. *Typical Scene of a Tour with its Navigation Map, Links to a Side Tour, and Two Branches. Expansions of three user interface components shown on right*

Rolling the mouse over the map presents textual information about each scene, while clicking on the picture of a scene interrupts the current scene and immediately starts the scene corresponding to the clicked image. As the tour progresses, hot spots indicating the availability of side tours and branches appear on the screen. These hot spots remain for a minimum duration of 10 seconds and then fade away. The hot spots appear when the content relates to them and fade away after the related part of the tour has finished. When a side tour is selected, the main tour is interrupted and the side tour is played. When a side tour finishes, the main tour resumes from the point where it was left. A click on a branch pauses the tour and opens a new window on the browser, displaying the web page associated with the branch. To resume the main tour, the user must click on the pause/resume icon above the map.

All the tour content including the scenes from the main tour, side tours, and branches is available from the Explore Page at the end of the tour. Figure 2 depicts the Explore Page for the tour shown in Figure 1. Clicking on the tour map restarts the tour from the beginning of the scene that is clicked. Similarly, clicking on side tours and branches immediately starts them. The user can access the Explore Page at any time during a tour by clicking on the corresponding hot spot on the right of the map.

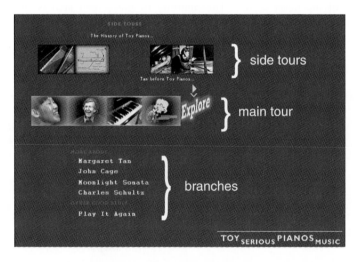

Figure 2. *Exploration Page that Allows Access to the Main Tour, Side Tours, and Branches.*

We developed two prototypes. The first tour featured the work of a toy pianist, Margaret Leng Tan. In the tour, the pianist talks about her involvement with toy pianos, how music is arranged for a toy piano, and her connections to Schröeder, the famous cartoon character created by Charles Schulz. Two side tours describe the history and mechanics of toy pianos and the work of Margaret Leng Tan before becoming a toy pianist. The main tour lasts 4:15 minutes and the side tours take 1:18 minutes and 0:50 minutes, respectively. The tour also includes five branches.

The second tour focused on Ludwig van Beethoven and his Ninth Symphony. Three side tours are provided; one about Beethoven's deafness, and two side tours that enable the user to explore Beethoven's scores and his Heiligenstadt Testament. Beethoven's main tour lasts 10:10 minutes and the first side tour is 2:00 minutes in length. The other side tours, since they incorporate interactive elements, have no fixed duration, although their exploration typically took 1:00 minute each. There are also five branches available for user exploration.

The usability test of the two tours focused on answering the following questions:
1. Can a web tour experience with "less clicking, more watching" be entertaining and engaging?
2. Are users satisfied with the level of interactivity designed in the web tours?
3. Do users who report higher subject matter appeal interact more and/or spend more time on the tour?
4. Do users look for related information during the streaming portion of the tour or from the Explore Page?
5. Does social context (singles or pairs) have an effect on reported levels of our subjective measures?

2.4.1   Usability Test Procedure

Participants in the study were assigned to one of two conditions: they experienced the web sites alone (Singles) or in pairs (Pairs). The experimental procedures were very similar for the two groups. Participants in our study completed three web experiences, based on our two pilot tours. We used the first two experiences as learning trials and only analyzed data from the third. Participants first experienced both the low-interactivity and high-interactivity versions of one tour and then experienced the high-interactivity version of the other tour. Low-interactivity tours had limited play control (only pause and resume) and no side tours or branches. During the third tour, the users were provided a fully interactive tour and were free to interact with it however they desired.

The participants were recruited based on the profile defined in the "Target Users" section above. The age range of the subjects was from 21-55 years old. Eight participants were randomly assigned to the Singles condition, and eight groups of two participants each were randomly assigned to the Pairs condition. Participants in the Pairs condition all knew each other before the session. Participants sat facing a 17-inch personal computer monitor placed on a table with a keyboard (which was not used) and a mouse. The sites that the participants evaluated were presented in a full screen Netscape 4.7 browser window. After participants had filled out a pre-session questionnaire, the experimenter then set the browser to the first site, briefly introduced it, and then left the room to observe the session from the control room. After each tour, participants filled out a post-session questionnaire (PosSQ) describing their experience. Subjects were instructed to spend as much time on each tour as desired and to tell the experimenter when they were done. After all three tours were completed, the experimenter interviewed the subjects using the debrief questionnaire (DQ).

Immediately before the first experience with a high-interactivity tour, participants were directed to take at least one branch and one side tour during the main tour, and also told that they could explore as much of the information as they wanted on the Explore Page. Participants in the Pairs condition were instructed to take turns controlling the mouse and to make sure that each of them take at least one side tour or branch selection. Before the final (high-interactivity) experience, participants were told to interact with the tour as much or as little as they wanted. The main part of the PosSQ was a set of four questions asking the users to rate the level of engagement, entertainment, satisfaction with the level of interactivity and subject matter appeal of each of the tours they experienced, using a seven point Lickert scale.

We analysed the videotapes and logged the user's mouse activity as follows. We counted the number of times the participants moved the mouse pointer so that it was located on an object that could be selected (rollovers), and the number of times an object was actually selected. The objects could have been branches, side tours, or navigation map scenes including the Explore Page. Since the length of the two tours differed, we calculated a "time in exploration" as the total time the participants spent on the tour, minus the base time of the main tour itself (if no branches, pauses or side tours were taken): Time (explore) = Time (total) - Time (base) where, Time (total) was the total time a user spent on the tour, from the moment they started until they announced they were done. Total time included the time spent with the tour, pauses, plus the time spent on all branches and side tours.

3. RESULTS

The data presented are from the PostSQ, the DQ, and user mouse activity that were analyed for the third, high-interactivity experience of each participant or pair of participants.

3.1 User Ratings of Tours

The means for user ratings of the four aspects of the tours (how engaging, entertaining, satisfied with the level of interactivity, and appealing the subject matter was) were all above neutral (4.0), ranging from 4.63 to 5.56 (see Table 1). The Beethoven tour was slightly more positively rated than the Tan tour on all four measures, however, there were no statistically significant differences. Entertainment, engagement, satisfaction with interactivity, and subject matter appeal were all positively inter-correlated, with engagement and entertainment the most highly so. The range of the inter-correlations was 0.59 to 0.89.

We explored the relationship between explore time spent on the tours and the user's subjective ratings of the tours. Participants spent an average of 3:52 minutes of explore time on Beethoven and 6:12 minutes on Tan (p>0.12). There were no statistically significant differences on the amount of time spent on the tours by singles and pairs. Also, there were no significant correlations between the four subjective measures and the explore time spent on the tours. Thus the amount of time participants spent in exploring related information was not a factor in their subjective ratings of the tours.

Table 1. Means for Singles, Pairs and All Users on Engagement, Entertainment, Satisfaction with Interactivity, and Subject Matter Appeal (7-point Likert scale, 1=most negative, 7=most positive).

Means	Singles	Pairs	Total
Engagement	5.56	5.50	5.52
Entertainment	5.00	5.38	5.25
Satisfaction with Interactivity	5.37	4.63	4.87
Subject Matter Appeal	5.12	5.19	5.17

We analysed the videotapes of user mouse activity and the summary data are reported in Table 2 below. The results show that users interacted an average of 16.2 times during each of the tours. Given that the participants spent an average total time of 10:30 to 14 minutes on the tours, this meant that a participant was clicking about once a minute during the experience. The number of interactions before reaching the Explore Page was similar to the number of interactions after reaching the Explore Page, thus our assumption that participants would interact both during and after the tour was supported. There were no statistically significant differences in the types of user activity.

Table 2. *Summary of User Mouse Activity During the Final Tour.*

Type of User Mouse Activity	Mean Actions Before Explore Page	Mean Actions After Explore Page
Branches Taken	1.91	2.33
Side Tours Taken	0.83	1.58
Scene Changes Made	1.75	1.25
Rollovers Made	3.79	2.75
Total Actions Taken	8.29	7.91

We next analysed the relationship between user mouse activity and the user's four subjective ratings of the tours. Results show that user mouse activity was negatively correlated with engagement and entertainment both before and after the Explore Page (see Table 3). Subject matter appeal was negatively correlated with mouse activity after the Explore Page. This means that participants who watched the tours more, and interacted less, were more engaged and entertained, and found the material more appealing. Conversely, those participants who were less entertained and engaged were more likely to interact with the tour. From the DQ, results showed that 18 out of 24 participants said they would like to have the multimedia experiences similar to this again.

Table 3. *Correlations of User Mouse Activity with Engagement, Entertainment, Satisfaction with Interactivity, and Subject Matter Appeal.*

User Mouse Activity	Engagement	Entertainment	Satisfaction with Interaction	Subject Matter Appeal
Total Mouse Activity	-.44*	-.48*	-.44*	-.45*
Mouse Acts Before Explore Page	-.41*	-.35	-.29	-.01
Mouse Acts After Explore Page	-.46*	-.44*	-.19	-.43*

*Correlations significant at the $p < 0.05$ level.

3.2 A Comparison of Singles and Pairs

We analysed our data for differences between single participants and pairs of participants. There were no significant differences between the means for singles and pairs on any of the four subjective measures or on mouse activity of any type. In the debrief questionnaire, 10 out of 16 pair participants reported that they thought the experience was more fun as a pair than it would have been had they experienced it alone. Of the 18 out of 24 total participants who said they would return to the site, 12 said they would want to do it with family and friends rather than alone.

3.3 User Debrief Data

At the end of the sessions, all 24 participants reflected on their experiences and answered a set of open-ended questions from the experimenter. Participants thought that the web experiences flowed well and were entertaining. They stated that the navigation map worked as expected, was valuable, but would be even better if continuous control over the flow of the experiences were provided through rewind, fast forward, and jump capabilities to position the tours anywhere within a scene. When asked about the side tours and branches, participants responded that they were also valuable, worked as expected, and would be even better if they were more in-depth and contained more content. They were adamant that the web experiences should be just one level deep in terms of access to related information. Participants said they liked the integration of the various forms of media with the presentation of the story, and the user control and interactivity choices they had were the best parts of the multimedia experience. Participants said they would like to have these types of experiences at work, home and on the road. They thought it would be a valuable and refreshing break to be able to take 5-10 minutes at work and enjoy a cultural experience like these in the study. They also said they would really enjoy being able to explore the tours with friends and family and said they might preview these cultural experiences alone at first, and then engage others at home and in various mobile computing situations in the communities in which they live to experience the tours with them.

4.   DISCUSSION AND CONCLUSIONS

Is the web an interactive medium? Most certainly yes, but not exclusively, as this research shows that users indicated satisfaction with watchable experiences. We found an interesting design dilemma. Users want to have continuous control over cultural web experiences, however, those who report the highest satisfaction, entertainment, and engagement with the experiences use the controls the least. Both the literature (Laurel, 1993; Murray, 1997) and our informal experience with web-designers during the project suggest a strong disbelief in TV-like experiences on the web. Although our research (and the participants' views) was heavily influenced by the pervasiveness of TV as the primary entertaining experience for people, we do not regard our results as an endorsement of TV as the ultimate entertainment experience. Instead, the results indicate that a major factor in entertainment is who we are entertained by and not the level of audience control over the entertainment experience. It is important to note that our design was defined as much by the idea of *"human voice"* as by the *"less clicking, more watching"* paradigm. In other words, perhaps people have both a remarkable interest in the flow and experience of listening and watching stories, and they are engaged by a storyteller as a respected person with a point of view. In this light, TV can be considered a highly developed and engineered storytelling medium, while the web is still trying to discover how to tell good stories.

Another key point is that this research topic is a complex and multifaceted one. This study reports significant correlations between user behaviour and self-reported entertainment and engagement in the range of .43 to .48. This means that through an examination of the variables in this study, we are able to explain about 20 percent of the variance in user behaviour. This topic is likely one where a user's behaviour is influenced by many factors. The results regarding social and physical context support the notion of designing entertaining experiences for singles and groups in various locations. Participants thought the design of the tours made them wonderful as "refreshing breaks" at work and that they would watch them multiple times with friends and family and explore the links in various ways. The lack of statistical difference in the ratings by singles and pairs confirms the value of the experiences in different social contexts.

Certainly the tour content has an impact on how entertaining users perceive the tours to be. We expected that people who were more interested in a topic would spend more time on a tour by exploring more related information. The results did not support this idea. We found that subject matter appeal was not related to the duration of the experience, but was negatively correlated with the level of interactivity by the users. These surprising results warrant further investigation.

As a methodological note, we found utilizing both small group design walkthroughs and individual evaluation sessions to be highly beneficial. In the small group sessions, we were able to collect data from a large number of people about a large number of design alternatives to filter the data and arrive at a design for individual testing. The individual sessions were time and labor intensive for the team to carry out, however we were rewarded with rich and detailed design information from the participants. We feel that the two methods are appropriate for different stages in the design process, and that they provide complementary information.

The web enables a wide range of entertaining experiences for users, and there is much more to learn about the potential for entertainment on the web. Future research can help to build a framework for understanding this topic through an in-depth investigation of user reactions to web experiences of varying duration, content, with various types of interaction possible, social context, and physical settings.

5.   REFERENCES

Alberg, C. & Shneiderman, B. (1994). Visual information seeking: Tight coupling of dynamic query filters with starfield displays. Proceedings of CHI '94 (Boston MA, April 1994), ACM Press, 313-317.

Cole, J. I. (2000). Surveying the Digital Future. Los Angeles, California.: UCLA Center for Communication Policy.

Geirland, J. and Sonesh-Kedar, E. (1999). *Digital Babylon: How the Geeks, the Suits, and thePonytails Tried to Bring Hollywood to the Internet.* Arcade Publishing, New York, New York.

Laurel, B. (1993). *Computers as Theatre.* Reading, MA: Addison-Wesley.

Murray, J.H. (1997). *Hamlet on the Holodeck: The Future of Narrative in Cyberspace.* New York, NY. The Free Press.

Red Herring. (2000, November 13, 2000.). *The sorry state of digital Hollywood.* Available: http://www.redherring.com/mag/issue85/mag-sorry-85.html.

Skelly, T.C., Fries, K., Linnett, B., Nass, C. & Reeves, B. (1994). Seductive interfaces: Satisfying a mass audience. *CHI '94 Conference Companion* (Boston MA, April 1994), ACM Press, 359-360.

Stone, M., Fishkin, K., & Bier, E. The movable filter as a user interface tool. . *Proceedings of CHI '94* (Boston MA, April 1994), ACM Press, 306-312.

The Economist. (2000). *A survey of E-entertainment* [October 7, 2000]

Vergo, J, Karat, C., Karat, J., Pinhanez, C., Arora, R., Cofino, T., Riecken, D., and Podlaseck, M. (2001). "Less Clicking, More Watching": Results from the user-centered design of a multi-institutional web site for art and culture. In Bearman, D., and Trant, J. (Eds.), *Museum and the Web 2001: Selected Papers from an International Conference*, Archives & Museum Informatics, 23-32.

Viegas, A. and Donath, C. (1999). Chat circles. *Proceedings of CHI '99*, ACM Press, 306-312.

Vogel, H. L. (1998). *Entertainment Industry Economics*, 4th Edition, Cambridge University Press, Cambridge, UK.

Webster, J. & Ho, H. (1997). Audience engagement in multimedia presentations. *The Data Base for Advances in Information Systems*, 28 (2). 63-77.

RANDY J. PAGULAYAN, KEITH R. STEURY,
BILL FULTON, AND RAMON L. ROMERO

CHAPTER 11

DESIGNING FOR FUN: USER-TESTING CASE STUDIES

1. INTRODUCTION

The goal of this chapter is to demonstrate that extending current usability methods and applying good research design based on psychological methods can result in improved entertainment experiences. This chapter will present several case studies where user-centered design methods were implemented on PC and Xbox games at Microsoft Game Studios. The examples were taken from several series of larger studies on Combat Flight Simulator (PC), MechWarrior 4: Vengeance (PC), Halo: Combat Evolved (Xbox), and RalliSport Challenge (Xbox). These examples were chosen to illustrate a variety of user-centered methods and to demonstrate the impact user-centered design principles can have on an entertainment product. Furthermore, these examples are presented in a way that illustrates a progression from addressing usability issues similar to those found in productivity applications, to extending usability methods to address more unique aspects of game design, to using survey methods to address issues related to fun for which standard usability methods do not suffice. For more detailed descriptions of Microsoft Game Studios User-testing methods and laboratory facilities, see Pagulayan, Keeker, Wixon, Romero, and Fuller (2003).

1.1 Methods and Games

The many similarities between productivity applications and games suggest that traditional discount usability methods would be suitable in the entertainment domain. Games have selection screens and menus just like other software applications. Task persistence, performance, ease of use, learnability, and all the potential obstacles to efficiency and productivity are found in games as well. However, it is possible to conceptualize usability in games as including other areas of game design, such as the comprehension of rules and objectives, control of characters, and manipulation of camera (view), to name a few. A game designer must script an experience within a game, so an extension of usability techniques from productivity applications to games becomes clearer. Usability testing in games

Mark A. Blythe, Andrew F. Monk, Kees Overbeeke and Peter C. Wright *(eds.)*,
Funology: From Usability to Enjoyment, 137—150

(and productivity applications for that matter) can be viewed as an experiment designed to assess whether users will interact with a given product in the way the designer intended.

Video games also differ from productivity applications in a variety of ways. For example, productivity applications represent tools as a means to an end, whereas games are designed to be pleasurable for the duration of gameplay. This distinction means that we must ensure that the user has an appropriate level of challenge and engagement while playing a game, rather than focusing on how efficiently they can achieve their goals. Goals are often defined externally in productivity applications, whereas games define their own goals. This implies that goals and objectives in games must not only be clear to the user at all times, but that they must be interesting as well. Another difference between games and productivity applications lies in the number of choices available. While there are relatively few productivity applications designed for a specific purpose, there are many games. Games must compete with other game titles for consumer attention, but they must also compete with different forms of entertainment, such as watching television or reading a book (Pagulayan et al., 2003). The implication is that games that are not immediately enjoyable will be dismissed quite easily in favor of other forms of entertainment.

It is our intent to show that the HCI field has access to methods drawn from current usability methodologies and experimental psychology that can be adapted to address issues in the entertainment industry. Extending current usability methods and utilizing good research design can result in improved entertainment experiences.

2. CASE STUDIES

Below are four examples of user-centered design methods that were used on video and computer games at Microsoft Game Studios. The first case study begins with more traditional usability methods. Subsequent case studies extend the use of current methodologies to situations that demonstrate how one can address some of the unique issues encountered with games.

2.1 Combat Flight Simulator

This case study is an example of a usability issue identified using limited-interactive prototypes. This method is not substantially different from standard usability methods. The focus of the usability test in this case study was on the game shell screens for the PC game, Combat Flight Simulator (CFS). Game shell screens consist of all menus and screens (e.g., Main Menu, Options, etc.) which are used to set the particular desired gaming experience, but not encountered during actual gameplay. For example, in the game shell a user can often change the difficulty level of the game and set other gameplay parameters.

A usability test was performed early in the development cycle of CFS and used a limited-interactive prototype of the game shell screens (i.e., functional screen widgets including radio buttons, check boxes, and toggles). Techniques utilized included user and task observations, scenarios, and thinking aloud protocols (e.g., Nielsen, 1993). Some of the tasks presented to users were exploratory and not performance based. In general, the users' tasks were to explore a particular game shell screens while thinking aloud.

In CFS, parameters users can modify using the game shell include aircraft selection, start location, time of day, weather, number of enemies, and difficulty of enemies. During the exploratory task for the Options screen, a usability problem was detected related to terminology. "AI" is an acronym for artificial intelligence commonly used in the video and computer games industry to refer to the behavior of non-human entities. For example, the cars players drive against could be referred to as "AI" as well as the marines that fight along side of players, providing that in both situations the cars or marines are not actively controlled by a human player. In CFS, "AI" referred to the skill level of computer-controlled enemy pilots, which confused participants in several different ways. Figure 1 represents a portion of an Options screen presented to participants.

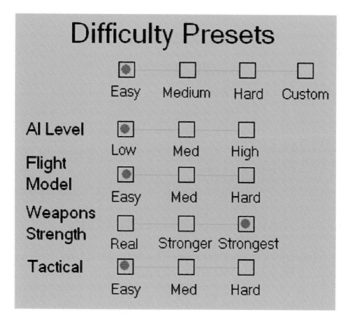

Figure 1. *Portion of Options screen presented to participants*

The term "AI Level" was not well understood by most—in fact, just two of seven understood the intended meaning of the term. In addition, the options presented for AI Level (Low, Med, High) failed to provide helpful context cues. The main problem was with the term "AI". While it is a jargon term for game developers, it is unfamiliar to many gamers. It is worth noting that all participants had experience with computer games, and the majority of them also had experience with flight games. A poor choice of fonts further compounded the problem. The font used was sans serif resulting in participants confusing the uppercase "I" with a lowercase "l", or the numeral "1". This introduced incorrect cues that some participants used as a basis for guessing (e.g., "is it ALtitude"?). These quotes from participants were representative of the problems they encountered.

"A-One-level? I don't know what that means. I have no idea..."

"A. I. uh..this uh...AL level? A.I. level? I don't understand this terminology."

"A-One-level, I'm not sure what that means, or AL level."

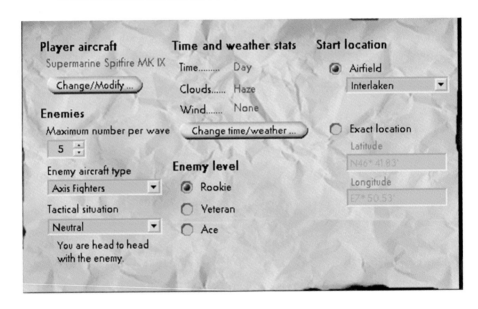

Figure 2. *Final interface for Options screen.*

Figure 2 represents the final solution. The term "AI Level" was replaced with "Enemy Level". The options that were originally "Low," "Medium," and "High" were replaced with "Rookie," "Veteran," and "Ace". Subsequent testing detected no difficulties with these terms, and the options are relatively clear in the context of a WWII fighter pilot game. This terminology has remained consistent through subsequent releases of the Combat Flight Simulator series.

In this example, information obtained from users through current usability practices was used to improve upon the usability of the game shell. This is a case where the user goals for the options screen did not substantially differ from user goals in productivity applications; the tools were a means to an end. Users should be able to set their preferences with maximum learnability and minimum errors.

2.2 MechWarrior 4: Vengeance

The popular MechWarrior series is based in a science fiction future where wars are fought by elite warriors who pilot giant destructive walking tanks called Battlemechs. One of the defining features in MechWarrior games is that they are action-oriented. However, the are also designed as simulations, which are games that attempt to model the complexity of the real world. Mastering the complexity is part of the fun for those who enjoy this type of game. For example, in MechWarrior, all weapons were designed with limitations that could exist in the real world, such as limited ammunition, differential firing rates for different weapons, and the potential for the Battlemech to overheat and shut itself down with the overuse of some weapons. This level of complexity can be quite intimidating for novice users. A simplistic solution to this problem would be to make the game simpler. However, because some of the game's fun stemmed from its complexity, the goal was to help novice users sufficiently master the intricacies of the game in an enjoyable way. In the following case study, user-testing methods helped identify areas of assistance for novices who experienced difficulties controlling their Battlemechs when playing MechWarrior 4: Vengeance (MW4), without sacrificing the complexity that helps define the MechWarrior series.

The development team established a goal of making MW4 as approachable as possible for novice users. In particular, novices needed to be able to use the basic movement and weapon controls with minimal difficulty. The controls in MW4 are complex because Battlemechs are capable of a movement called torso-twisting, where the top part of the Battlemech can rotate to look in a direction different from its movement trajectory, similar to a gun turret on a modern tank. Weapons are placed in the upper part of the torso, so rotating the upper torso is fundamental to aiming weapons while playing the game. To help users coordinate these movements, on-screen aids were included as part of the standard interface.

Figure 3 is a screenshot of the MW4 interface during gameplay. There are two items on the screen that were created to aid users. The green cone-shaped item within the circular radar placed at the bottom-center of the screen represents the user's line of sight, or field-of-view. It is marked Field of Vision. Figure 4 is an enlarged version. In this situation, the torso is rotated slightly to the left relative to the bottom portion of the Battlemech. If the cone funneled out toward the right, the line of sight would be to the right of the Battlemech.

Figure 3. *User interface for MechWarrior 4 during gameplay*

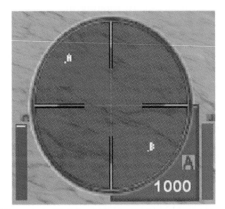

Figure 4. *Field of Vision indicator and Radar*

The second item is a green horizontal scale placed in the center of the screen beneath the targeting reticle where a horizontal bar represents the amount of torso rotation (see Figure 3). This is marked as Torso Twist. This provided users with a graphical cue for torso rotation on the x-axis relative to the bottom part of the Battlemech. For example, if a Battlemech is facing straight forward (i.e., the torso is perfectly aligned with the lower portion of the Battlemech) there is no horizontal bar beneath the reticle. The length of the horizontal green bar is a function of the distance the torso moves away from the center in either direction. In other words, the length of the bar grows as the Battlemech rotates further from perfect alignment of the upper (torso) and lower portions of the Battlemech. In Figure 5, the green bar represents the Battlemech rotated slightly to the left in panel A. In panel B, the Battlemech is rotated much further away from the center toward the left.

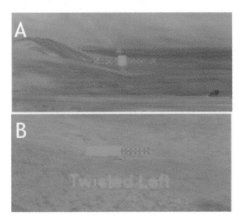

Figure 5. *Torso Twist indicator. A) slightly turned to the left, B) severely turned to the left*

Usability testing of these interface items included common pass/fail and error counting techniques. During this test it was shown that novice users struggled with the basic controls of the game. In particular, they struggled to control the Battlemech's torso, frequently confusing the direction of the upper torso for the direction in which the Battlemech was moving. The fundamental problem was that few people were using the on-screen cues created to avoid this exact problem. Four of seven participants did not notice or use the field of view reference (green cone), and no participants noticed or used the green rotational bar. Only two participants demonstrated a skillful use of torso twisting, but all demonstrated difficulties steering their Battlemech.

It became apparent that torso-twisting with Battlemechs is a skill with a gradual learning curve. Based on these results and other convergent evidence, the development team chose to create a training mission with the primary goal of educating users about the visual cues in the interface while giving them a relatively safe environment to practice the use of torso-twisting. Follow-up testing showed that the training mission decreased the torso-twist problem, but did not eliminate it. In a follow-up study, all participants knew how to use the on-screen visual cues to correct or avoid torso-twisting problems, though they still struggled to control their Battlemechs. The critical difference between the game prior to the addition of the training mission and after is that although users still experienced difficulties learning the controls, they were empowered to fix the problems themselves after completing the training mission.

Educating novice players through training makes the game more accessible to a larger population without alienating the current population of MechWarrior gamers. The training mode gives more time to novice users to adapt to the game's complexity, and for more experienced users, the training mode is optional.

2.3 Halo: Combat Evolved

A skilled game designer can create an experience that people consistently enjoy. However, as with any product, a user may not use it in the way the designer intended. In the case of video games, this may lead to an experience that is less fun for the user. This case study presents an example from the development of Halo: Combat Evolved (Xbox). It presents one of the biggest challenges in game design: making the user feel like they are making interesting decisions while ensuring that they are playing the game in a way that leads to the most fun. This example illustrates how discount usability methods enabled the designers to see how users approached their game, to understand barriers that were preventing users from experiencing the game as intended, and to refine the game so that it drew the user into the optimal experience.

One of the greatest difficulties involved in game design is perfecting the balance between scripting an experience intended by the designer without making the user feel restricted in the choices they can make. For example, a designer may want the user to move the character to a particular location in the virtual world, where an exciting battle awaits them. This could be accomplished by creating a narrow pathway, or by placing barriers in the virtual world restricting the user to only one path, with no other choices. However, such restrictions may be unsatisfying to users because they feel like they have no control over their decision-making. Alternatively, the designer could implicitly control the user's behavior by giving him or her free range of movement, but placing something attractive (e.g., a new weapon) at intermediate points between the user's current location, and the designer's desired location (i.e., the location of the exciting battle). This may draw the user down a certain path, while making him or her feel in control. While tactics such as this are common, there are a number of different variables encountered in game design that interact with one another, making it very difficult to predict exactly how users will play the game.

Different mechanisms affect a user's experience of combat in games. Because Halo is a game about combat, it was very important to the team that combat be compelling. The development team spent a lot of time refining the aiming controls, enemy behavior, weapon variety, and the layout of the environments to make combat as enjoyable as possible. In addition, the designers created a wide variety of combat situations and areas where users could engage in different tactics to succeed. Certain situations were created where a particular strategy would yield the most rewarding and fun experience. The assumption was that if users approached the combat situations as the designers intended, users would have as much fun as the designers did.

The Halo team wanted to see whether the typical user would have fun playing the game, and if not, what issues were blocking them from doing so. To provide this information, eight participants who liked to play console action games were recruited to play the game in a usability test format.

Participants were presented with a mission and asked to play the game as they would at home. For this test, traditional error counts and pass/fail criteria were not used. Instead, the focus was on the tactics that participants used to complete the level in comparison with the 'ideal' tactics created by the designers. Designers were present at all sessions. This was critical because they best understood how they wanted players to respond to their game, and they could also see, first hand, what cues users were not seeing.

The designers had created large, outdoor environments that gave players more freedom to approach situations in a variety of ways. However, the large environments afforded players the ability to see enemies from a long distance. Testing revealed that participants were trying to fight enemies from much further away then the designers intended. During usability sessions, novice players began shooting at the enemy as soon as they could see them, but the designers had wanted the players to first move closer to the enemies, and then fight. While all users were able to successfully complete the missions using these tactics, the game was designed to be most enjoyable when combat was engaged at a much closer distance. At greater distances, the experience was less satisfying. For example, the weapons were not designed to be effective at these longer distances resulting in participants complaining that their weapons were not accurate enough.

From observing the usability sessions, designers quickly identified several solutions. First, they revised subtle cues that they had placed in the aiming reticle. The aiming reticle refers to a graphical indicator in the center of the screen that represents where the user is aiming a weapon. In the original design, at any distance from the enemy, the reticle would turn red when placed over an enemy, informing the user that their weapon was aimed properly at the enemy. The designers modified the reticle behavior so that it turned red when the enemy was targeted, but only at a combat distance intended by the designers. Therefore, when the player aimed at the enemy from a long distance, the reticle would not change color, providing a subtle cue that they were not at an optimal distance, thus encouraging users to move closer. The designers also increased the diameter of the reticle to emphasize its inaccuracy at greater distances. Second, the team modified the enemy behavior. When the user shot at the enemy from a much greater distance, the enemy now would not return fire, but would dodge the shot or move behind a rock or tree, requiring the user to move closer. When the user reached the optimal engagement point, the enemy would step out of cover and engage in battle with the player. At other times, the enemy would approach the player to maintain the intended combat distance.

Subsequent usability testing showed that these changes encouraged the majority of users to engage in combat from the intended distance. Users were able to see more of the interesting components of the game, were more satisfied with the performance of their weapons, and as predicted, enjoyed the game more.

In standard usability practices, the goal of the test is to ensure that the design of product effectively supports what the user is trying to accomplish. In this case study, the perspective of usability test goals has been shifted away from the end user, and toward the designer. In the Halo example, the goal was to ensure that the user experience matched designer intention. These types of situations often require less structure than more common usability methods.

Once we are confident that users are playing the game in the way that designers intended, we can begin to get feedback about subjective preferences on the game's design. Although this may not require direct observation, a larger number of users must be utilized to ensure reliability of participant response, as the next case study illustrates.

2.4 RalliSport Challenge

RalliSport Challenge (RSC) is a racing game on the Xbox console. As in many popular racing titles, the Career Mode is one of the core pieces of this game. In order to understand how user-centered design methods were able to influence the design of this game, one must first understand how the Career Mode functions in RSC.

The Career Mode starts with a limited set of cars available to the user, and a limited set of driving events they can participate in. Depending on the users' performance, new cars and more challenging events are made available to users as they progress through their careers.

Each event consists of several stages (or races). After each stage, users gain points based on a number of factors; top speed, what place they finished (e.g., 1st, 2nd, etc.), lap times, and amount of car damage. Once an event is over, all of the points gained from each stage are added up to obtain the user's total points. The user's goal is to accrue a specified number of points to gain access to the next set of cars and events that are currently unavailable to them. Reaching the specified point total is the only way to progress through the game. This is often referred to as "unlocking" cars and events.

This design is not unique in racing games. It is common to specify a certain performance criterion in order to progress through the game. However, keeping in mind that playing games is a choice (i.e., users are not forced to play), the manner in which this design is implemented could cause frustration for many users. In RSC, the issue revolved around the users' ability to re-race a stage within an event to earn more points.

To better illustrate this issue, consider a scenario where a user has three racing events that are currently available to them, each comprising several stages: Event A (stages A-1 through A-4), Event B (stages B-1 through B-5), and Event C (stages C-1 through C-6). To unlock the next set of events and cars, the user must accumulate a minimum set of points by racing through most (and sometimes all) of the stages in Events A, B, and C. If a user races all Events, but does not earn enough points to unlock new cars and events, what options are they left with? According to the developer's design, their only option would be to re-race an entire Event, including all stages within that Event. If the user selected Event C, all of the previous points earned from each stage (C-1 through C-6) are erased, and the user must then re-race stages C-1 through C-6.

The developers preferred this model because they felt the game would be too easy otherwise, and also because this system is much closer to the actual sport of rally racing. This is a valid argument. Games should not be too easy and must ensure the appropriate level of challenge and success. On the other hand, this strategy potentially puts users in the situation where they lose points on several stages they are already happy with. If the user performed very well on C-1, C-2, C-3, C-5, and C-6, but performed very poorly on C-4, they would lose points on all stages, which could result in extreme frustration.

To address this issue, a series of tests was designed to assess how frustrating this situation may be to users. The goal in designing these tests was to simulate as close as possible a situation where users would actually play through a series of events, but not accrue enough points. Simply asking users about this situation would not suffice; users had to experience it. In addition, data collected from a traditional usability study sample size would not be sufficiently reliable to measure a subjective preference. Therefore, a survey methodology that would allow for a larger sample size and not require direct observation was used.

Working with designers, a mock career mode was created that consisted of three Events, each with a minimum of four stages. Secondly, a profile that described the population of users was created. In this case, nearly thirty users who frequently play racing console games were brought in. To prevent contamination of the data, standard experimental research protocols were implemented. The laboratory was set up so that responses from each user could be collected independently, with no interaction between users.

Participants were instructed to play through the mock career mode as if they were at home. Once they finished the events, they were informed that they did not earn enough points to unlock the next set of cars and events. At this time participants were given the following options, and asked which option they would use for unlocking the next set of events:
a) Re-race any of the previous 3 EVENTS to improve your total point score;
   However, you must race ALL stages within the EVENT(S) you choose;
b) Re-race CERTAIN STAGES in any EVENT of your own choosing to improve your total score;
   Then participants were asked how they felt about the following methods for unlocking the next event.
a) Re-racing an entire event (including all tracks within the event);
b) Re-racing any stage of my own choosing within an event;
   Lastly, users were asked the same question, but presented with a situation where the Events consisted of nine stages (which was representative of some Events in the actual game, although they did not experience this).

The data gathered provided fairly convincing evidence against forcing users to re-race the entire Event. The majority of participants reported a preference for being able to re-race a single stage as opposed to an entire event and this preference became even stronger when presented with the nine stage event. A smaller percentage of users preferred to be able to re-race only entire events, suggesting that they agreed with the developers, who felt that allowing users to re-race stages made the game too easy.

Based on these survey data, the recommendation was to implement multiple difficulty levels, one of which allowed the re-race option (Normal difficulty), but the more advanced levels that did not (Difficult or Advanced difficulty). This solution met the needs of both user preferences, those who want to be able to re-race any stage at any time, and "hard-core" users who prefers more of a challenge and penalty when playing through their career. This was presented to the developer, who in turn implemented the functionality into the design of the final retail product--Normal (no re-race) and Easy (re-race). The developer felt the no re-race option was truer to the sport of rally racing, which is why it was termed Normal. More importantly, the decision to implement multiple difficulty levels was also validated by some reviews from popular gaming magazines and gaming sites after the game was released.

> ...punishingly difficult and repetitive, depending on which of the two available skill levels you choose when you start the game....With no "re-do" button available in Normal mode to simply restart a race if you screw up, some gamers will find themselves angered and frustrated with having to start over from the beginning of the series, while others will embrace the degree of challenge with open arms - Mahood, 2002

> We were also ready to slap the game down for being too hard, until we tried it on the easy difficulty setting. Normal difficulty, as well as giving you some stiff times to beat, doesn't allow you to retry a stage – if you mess up, you have to restart the whole event. Even racing veterans would be well advised to play Easy mode to get to grips with the tracks at first, as this allows you to retry. - Smith, 2002

In this example, the question being addressed (to allow re-racing or not) did not have a clear answer before data were collected, and did not have a specified task-based performance criterion. Finding a solution for this design question was not necessarily related to the learnability of the product, or the efficiency of use, or the number of errors a user would make. The solution was based on what was most fun for users.

3.   CONCLUSION

There are a variety of approaches that can be taken from existing HCI-related methods to address the unique aspects of user-centered design issues found in games. Although the case studies discussed above focus on specific issues, they should also be viewed as a broad representation of some methods currently being utilized by the User-Testing Group at Microsoft Game Studios. Each of these examples is part of a larger series of tests performed throughout the development cycle of each of the games. It is not sufficient to run a single test for one game. As in any HCI-related field, to be maximally beneficial, user-testing must be integrated into the development process from the very beginning.

Each of the methods presented in the case studies has limitations, and should only be used when appropriate. A good user-testing engineer must understand the points in the development cycle at which certain methods should be used to address particular problems, and convince development teams of the general value of data collected through user testing.

In general, standard usability methods are not appropriate when assessing subjective preferences, due to the small sample size that accompany typical usability studies. With fewer participants, reliability of the results comes into question. However, usability methods used in conjunction with more open-ended tasks provide rich information about how a user interacts with a product which can provide a designer with greater understanding of how a user approaches and plays their game.

Larger sample methods are good for assessing subjective preferences, but they are limited because they rely on self-report. Usability studies, which typically focus on a user's actions, are better for obtaining in-depth, behavioral information. Just as in traditional usability testing, it is also impossible to look to the user to tell you how to design a game. Users can only evaluate aspects of the game ("this is fun", "that is not"). From there, it is up to the user-testing engineer and designer to work together to define the root causes of issues and create compelling solutions.

Unfortunately, there is no set formula for how the pieces fit together. The variability in the process through which games are developed must be reflected in the methods used for addressing user-testing issues.

Furthermore, there are many challenges with obtaining feedback on all areas of the user experience when playing games. For example, the survey methods that we utilized in testing adults proved to be problematic when trying to obtain feedback from children on child-oriented games. Additionally, testing multiplayer portions of a game (when two or more people play the same game together) presents further difficulties. Interactions bettween participants do not allow us to assume that the observations are independent, which makes it difficult to know the extent to which the results (i.e., subjective ratings) are influenced by the players' social interactions within the game, or pre-existing social relationships between them.

Finally, most of our research focuses on the initial experience of a game. Information based on this stage of the user's experience is critical because designers and developers are so immersed in the game that they often forget what the initial experience is like for someone who has never played their game. While many development teams would also like to obtain detailed feedback about gameplay that occurs beyond the initial experience, doing so with current development practices has many practical constraints. As such, these issues need to be explored further to provide cost-efficient user-testing methods to obtain feedback on all these areas of the user experience.

For more in-depth case studies, see Pagulayan et al., (2003) (MechCommander 2, Oddworld: Munch's Oddysee, and Blood Wake) and Medlock et al., (2002) (Age of Empires II).

4. ACKNOWLEDGMENTS

Special thanks to the development teams on CFS, MW4, Halo, and RSC and Digital Illusions. In particular, we'd like to express our gratitude to Christina Chen, TJ Wagner, David Luehmann, Jaime Griesemer, John Howard, Hamilton Chu, and Peter Wong for permitting us to use the actual games in our examples. We'd also like to thank the Microsoft Game Studios User-Testing Group, in particular, Lance Davis, Kyle Drexel, Kevin Goebel, David Quiroz, Bruce Phillips, John Davis, and Kevin Keeker.

5. REFERENCES

Mahood, A. (2002). RalliSport Challenge. *Official Xbox Magazine*, April 2002. Brisbane, CA: Imagine Media, Inc.

Medlock, M. A., Wixon, D., Terrano, M., Romero, R. L., & Fulton, B. (2002). Using the RITE Method to improve products; a definition and a case study. *Humanizing Design, Usability Professional's Association 2002 Annual Conference*; 2002 July 8 - July 12; Orlando, Florida: Chicago, IL: Usability Professionals' Association, 2002.

Nielsen, J. (1993). *Usability Engineering*. New York: Morgan Kaufmann.

Pagulayan, R. J., Keeker, K., Wixon, D., Romero, R. L., Fuller, T. (2003). User-Centered Design in Games. In J. Jacko & A. Sears (Eds.), *The Human-Computer Interaction Handbook: Fundamentals, Evolving Technologies and Emerging Applications* (pp. 883-906). Mahwah, NJ: Lawrence Erlbaum Associates.

Smith, M. (2002). Reviews: RalliSport Challenge. *British Telecommunications plc*.

KRISTINA ANDERSEN, MARGOT JACOBS AND
LAURA POLAZZI

CHAPTER 12

PLAYING GAMES IN THE EMOTIONAL SPACE

1. INTRODUCTION

The nature of user studies is changing, reflecting changing visions of both *what* is relevant to study and *how* to study it in order to understand the user. The focus has progressively moved from the task to the activity including an analysis of not only people's actions but the social, cultural, and economic factors that influence their behaviour. Now, with the so-called ubiquitous technologies moving out of the office and pervading people's personal sphere, designers must examine different facets of the user; in order for a product to be good (and successful), it should be both satisfying and pleasurable in the private life of the individuals. From a methodological point of view this raises new challenges: How do we ensure that an application is pleasurable for a given audience? How do we collect data pertaining to the personal sphere and useful in understanding the experiences of people and their emotions? How do we interpret this data in order to inform the design process?

The work of Gaver et al. (1999) suggests that methodologies inspired by artistic or creative techniques can be successfully applied to user studies. Using tools that are both provocative and aesthetically pleasant to involve people in engaging experiences is a possible way of accessing their intimate sphere and collecting revealing data. We believe that these kinds of surveys are particularly useful as preliminary studies in the design of enjoyable applications. Although the results they produce are not scientific in a traditional sense, they can be applied in a rigorous manner. While designing for pleasure, the information we receive may not always be measurable and must be interpreted using alternate methods.

This paper presents the approach we used during the FARAWAY project. The aim of the project was to explore how new technologies might support remote communication between people in affectionate relationships, decreasing the perception of distance; an additional objective became investigating the means with which to access and study peoples' experiences inside this domain. As a result of our investigations, we propose considering fun and pleasure as qualities of both the products we design and the methodology we adopt to involve users in the design

151

Mark A. Blythe, Andrew F. Monk, Kees Overbeeke and Peter C. Wright *(eds.)*,
Funology: From Usability to Enjoyment, 151—163
© 2003 *Kluwer Academic Publishers. Printed in the Netherlands.*

process. Creating enjoyable experiences for the users we want to understand can provide revealing insights for the development of enjoyable applications.

Our approach is based on the concept of game play. Fun, enjoyment, and emotions are spontaneous aspects of human life, difficult to isolate, observe or measure. However, they can be provoked. Like narrative and poetry, games are valuable instruments that can trigger sincere emotional response in artificial situations. Designing games also means designing a framework for experiences, which is the final objective of designing applications for fun or pleasure. And designing games could prove to be a way to understand and influence the design of interactions. Our study shows that using games results in a high level of spontaneous participation from users, increasing both their degree of involvement in the design process as well as the value of their contribution. Hence, evaluating the level of participation and enjoyment for a game can be a way to test the validity of a solution.

2. FARAWAY

The FARAWAY project starts from the sense of privation experienced by people that are emotionally close but physically distant. In order to mitigate this sense of loss, loved ones seek alternative means of communicating. Linguistic studies demonstrate that for people in an intimate relationship the very objective of mediated communication is to feel each other's presence. Telecommunication is used primarily by loved ones '*to express a wish to be together*' (Channel 1997: 144) as opposed to any actual exchange of verbal content.

Existing media only partially supports these kinds of interactions. Real-time communication creates a sense of each other's presence by virtue of the simultaneity of the exchange, yet current media offer a narrow channel for people who are communicating in order to do affective work. One disadvantage in distance communication with respect to face-to-face interaction concerns the lack of sensorial richness in current technological artefacts. A series of design and research projects like 'LumiTouch' (Chang et al, 2001), 'The Bed' (Dodge, 1997), 'Kiss communicator' (Buchenau & Fulton 2000) and 'Feather, Scent and Shaker' (Strong & Gaver, 1996) have already experimented with the use of non-verbal languages and sensorial modalities to exchange emotional content over distance; in these projects interaction modalities like blowing, touching and squeezing have been successfully incorporated into concepts and prototypes for sending and receiving messages remotely.

However sensorial weakness is not the only limitation of existing artefacts. Most of the effort in the telecommunication industry goes towards increasing the bandwidth of the channels, the miniaturisation of the technology, and the ubiquity of the services. Yet, as Taylor and Harper (2002) assert in their study of mobile phone usage amongst teenagers, designing communication technology requires a more articulated and profound understanding of the user's practices and their capacity to build and share meaning. In the context of FARAWAY and from an interaction design perspective, we explored new ways of conveying presence and emotions over distance focusing more on people's experiences and desires than on the technology itself. Understanding how this kind of communication works was, for us, a starting point to imagine how interaction design might support and enrich it.

One of our main routes of investigation involves symbolic objects and their power to embed presence and affective meaning. Thanks to specific, yet diverse rules, human beings are able to transform items into virtual 'traces' and tokens of affection for something or someone that is not present. In other words, these objects become symbolic surrogates of presence. Religious objects like the Eucharist and symbols of love like wedding rings or friendship bracelets are examples of this process. How does symbolic investment work in affectionate relationships? How can these mechanisms be utilised to design an artefact? These types of issues are dependent on cultural factors and even idiosyncratic values and attitudes. As designers, we felt the need to study the latter empirically, exploring and testing our ideas through a user survey. But the private nature of this type of communication is an serious constraint; how could we access the desires and behaviours of people inside their affective relationships? Instead of observing, we chose to create experiences that provoked response from the users. The core idea being to gradually shift from the existing to the new by creating, collecting and interpreting individual experiences within the defined design space.

In order to create meaningful experiences we had to create a meaningful context. Generally, people enter the emotional sphere by virtue of their relationship with a loved one. In our case we had to artificially trigger this process, simultaneously keeping the natural qualities of the emotional experience. The IF ONLY games are the method we developed for this purpose.

3.   ANOTHER REALITY

The idea of using games was influenced by game theory and techniques of arts movements. A game is a way to create another reality and allow people to enter that reality. According to Mataes (2001), games, like poetry and movies, demand what Coleridge calls a 'suspension of disbelief' (Coleridge 1817: Vol. I., chapter 14); when participants are immersed in this kind of experiences, they are willing to accept the internal logic of the experience, even though this logic deviates from the logic of the real world. Murray (1998) goes further and suggests that creators of games need to not only suspend disbelief but 'actively create belief' by allowing players to manipulate objects and engage in enactment rather than processing descriptions.

The same kind of principles is evident in the artistic methods of the surrealist movement. Through playful procedures and methodologies of the fantastic, surrealist games (Gooding, 1995) lead to out of the ordinary situations where the player is allowed to express her or himself in a more spontaneous and intuitive way. In other words, these methods stimulate the players to suspend their disbelief and access a 'surrealist' realm of creation. For example, in one of the more direct surrealist techniques, automatic writing, participants are encouraged to write whatever comes to mind, in a *stream of consciousness* style where nothing is corrected or rewritten. The unexpected material produced by this free associative writing game reveals unconscious thoughts and desires that may not otherwise be accessed.

The IF ONLY games refer to game theory and surrealism on two levels. On one level we created a 'surrealist' situation that allowed our players to produce and contribute emotionally truthful content and on another level we allowed them to experiment with non-conventional methods and use their creativity in order to investigate and express that content in new ways.

4.   DESIGNING THE GAMES

When they are in an intimate relationship, people usually develop a universe of specific codes, languages and references that identify their private mode of communication. These elements become the constituents of an alternative space, or 'emotional space', that people enter while communicating with their loved ones. The IF ONLY games aim at re-producing this emotional space as a framework for the players to experience different kinds of emotional communication. Each game invites the players to experiment with a new and unusual way of communicating presence and emotions within the emotional space created by an affective relationship: by creating objects, by wearing particular clothes, by sharing physiological information, etc. In order to trigger expressive responses and allow players to provide real emotional content, the games have been designed using specific procedures, language and graphics.

The Interaction Design Institute Ivrea, where the project was initiated, is full of people from different countries who are away from home and who participate in long distance communication with loved ones on a daily basis. We chose students, researchers, and staff of the Institute as our players. The same group was maintained throughout the experience. The players were invited to play through 'invitation cards' (figure 1) containing instructions or recipes. The invitation cards were in some cases complemented with a 'comment card' or with a 'questionnaire' card containing specific questions about the experience created by the game. During one week the game cards 'appeared' on the desks of the players each morning. The players would then leave the results on their desks the following morning from where they would 'disappear,' thus making the exchange of cards and results a game in itself. At the end of the first week the 'mystery' was revealed during a collective meeting where we presented the project and lead a discussion about the overall experience and the specific games. The following games used the same modality, but with a smaller set of people.

5.   THE IF ONLY GAMES

The IF ONLY games consist of 13 games played by up to 44 players. The games as a method are still being developed towards a point where they can be used to fully involve users' desires and dreams not only in an initial information gathering process, but for use during the entire span of a design process. In this sense the following games and the context they were played in can be seen as an initial proposal and a pilot study. In the following we take examples from three of the games and the responses of the players.

5.1   *This is how I feel*

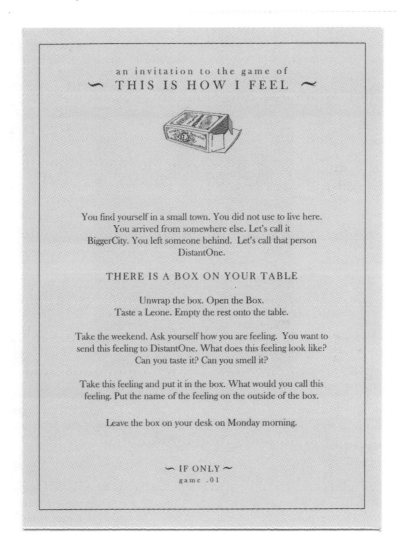

an invitation to the game of
◝ THIS IS HOW I FEEL ◜

You find yourself in a small town. You did not use to live here.
You arrived from somewhere else. Let's call it
BiggerCity. You left someone behind. Let's call that person
DistantOne.

THERE IS A BOX ON YOUR TABLE

Unwrap the box. Open the Box.
Taste a Leone. Empty the rest onto the table.

Take the weekend. Ask yourself how you are feeling. You want to
send this feeling to DistantOne. What does this feeling look like?
Can you taste it? Can you smell it?

Take this feeling and put it in the box. What would you call this
feeling. Put the name of the feeling on the outside of the box.

Leave the box on your desk on Monday morning.

◝ IF ONLY ◜
game .01

Figure 1. *Game card of the game 'This is how I feel'*

This game initiates the IF ONLY series, inviting the player to participate. The overall objective is to introduce and establish an emotional connection between the individual players and IF ONLY, and to test the player's willingness to play as well as generate an index of representations of emotions. The focus is on the modalities of expression of emotional content and the related levels of earnestness and intimacy.

The card (figure 1) sets the context and mood and invites the players to the first game. DistantOne is introduced as the loved person with whom the player wants to communicate. The player is asked to express an experienced emotion within the three-dimensional space of a candy box. By collecting and analysing these communications instead of actually allowing them to be exchanged, the results are a series of one-way messages from the player.

Figure 2. *'I can hear you' is an example of response where the player used an object to create an emotional experience for the loved person. The seashell contained in the candy box is an invitation for the receiver to listen to a sound that is emotionally charged for the sender.*

The task takes a complex concept, an emotion, which is by definition impossible to express fully and suggests to represent it though an 'impossible' medium, the limited three dimensional space inside a given box. The underlying idea is to counter an impossibility with another impossibility. Within the scope of the games this logical contradiction is meant to liberate the player from the difficulty of the undertaking and encourage lateral thinking

The game generated a large variety of responses. The players put written texts, colours, textures, images, objects, combinations of objects, etc. in their boxes. Many of them tried to communicate physical sensations like warmth and coldness, light or shining by using objects with particular sensorial properties (e.g. metal for cold); others (figure 2) created a suggestive experience for their DistantOnes by providing them with tools to interact with. Surprisingly, a task people found difficult was generating a verbal description for the represented emotion.

> I got a little frustrated trying to resolve the complexity of it in a single word. (C.)

> I found choosing a word to describe what I felt was very standard, I mean, it was impossible. (A.)

Words are normally considered as a natural and effective way to communicate to someone else how or what we feel. This game suggests how other media can be powerful in translating our inner states into a message.

5.2 Here I am/Take me with you

This game is played in two parts. The first part is an exercise in self portraits, asking the players to manifest their identity in a small object, 'LittleYou.' In this sense the task is to wilfully transfer ones own presence into an object. The objective of this game is to explore different modalities and styles in creating a symbolic self-representation. How do the players perceive their own presence and how do they translate this perception in something physical?

The second part is testing whether this transfer has been successful by letting someone else relate to the object and look for levels of identification, care and affection. The players are asked to exchange and take care of each other's self-representations, 'LittleOther' (figure 3). The couples of players exchanging objects are created randomly. At the end of the game each player is given a questionnaire to compile. The objective of this game is to test the ability of the 'LittleYou's' to convey the presence of their creators, looking for levels of personification in the objects, the transfer of emotional meaning from the creator to the care-taker and the degree of ownership with both players.

Figure 3. *One player with her 'LittleOther'*

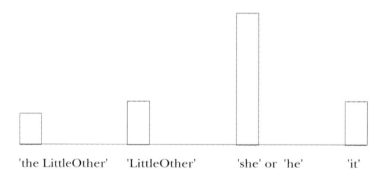

'the LittleOther'   'LittleOther'   'she' or 'he'   'it'

Figure 4. *How the players refer to their 'LittleOther' in the questionnaires*

This game revealed the nature and qualities of the objects as conveyers of presence. The results from part 2 show a high level of personification in the way the players refer to the 'LittleOther'. Besides the use of 'her or him' (see figure 4), this attitude is generally reflected in the answers to the questionnaires and in the later debriefing discussion. The 'LittleOthers' are perceived as live entities and in many cases the players explicitly project the qualities of their creators onto them.

> He's fragile so I feel very protective of him (K.)

> [LittleOther is] shy like the creator but I like it for this reason. (S.)

This process of projection strongly interacts with the relationship between the caretaker and the creator of the object. In the above case the 'power' of the 'LittleOther' even went beyond the purposes of the games, by mediating an interesting social interaction between the two players during both the day of the testing and at the later group discussion.

> How you made it? Very fast, I think. And like wrapped it from the heart and that's not the way you normally work. I would like to encourage you to do it more because I was immediately taken away by the way you did it. (M.)

Other interesting aspects concern the level of attachment to the 'LittleOthers' and its relationship with the emotional and personal effort employed by the creators in building the 'LittleYou'. According to the questionnaires, 13 players out of 17 did not want to part with their 'LittleOther'. In these cases, the other person's representation ('LittleOther') was much more important than their own ('LittleYou') and the separation at the end of the day was perceived as a loss.

> If it's possible to keep her that would be perfect (F.)

> I was more attached to the LittleOther than LittleMe. I just made my LittleMe and then spent the day with LittleOther. I actually forgot about LittleMe (M.)

In conclusion, the game confirmed the power of the objects as vessels for presence and pointed out a series of mechanisms in the processes of personification and emotional attachment. At a general level the objects created during part 1 were successful in provoking emotional reactions and interactions in part 2.The crucial role in the presence attribution seems to be played by the ritual of the exchange itself; it is this ritual that allows the object to acquire an emotional and symbolic meaning. As one player pointed out, the 'LittleOther' itself becomes live because 'it comes from a live person', once given its symbolic meaning the object continues to transmit the presence of the other.

5.3 You Gave Me This

This game further explores the potential of a ritual gift exchange. 'You gave me this' is entirely based on the concept of symbol; the purpose is to determine how the ritual of exchange and symbolic investment can relay the presence of another person. It is based on the results of the previous games but differs in that we have designed and produced a game piece, a 'bean', through which the game is conducted. This game also introduces a new element by letting the players connect and play with their actual 'DistantOne'.

The bean is a padded object sewn in white fabric (figure 5). It is activated and invested with symbolic meaning by the sender (player 1) and then given to the receiver (player 2) who will have it in a fixed state (on). As the input modality the first players are given the opportunity to put artefacts of their choice inside the bean. These secret artefacts are attributed to the bean in order to symbolically invest it with the presence of player 1. The beans are then sent to DistantOne (player 2), who takes care of the bean for one week.. Although player 2 is unaware of what is inside of the bean, they do know that player 1 has placed a secret object inside.

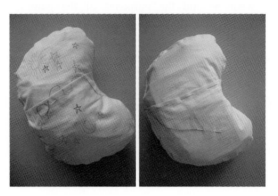

Figure 5. *A bean 'activated' by player 1. The player put an object of his choice into the pocket of the bean and sew the pocket. The bean is then sent to the player's DistantOne.*

The results are gathered through a questionnaire for the sender and a diary for the receiver. Results from this game are still being collected at the time of writing but it is possible to see some tentative directions already. An important tendency is that the senders are generally happy to express themselves through the piece, even if the mode of interaction and the media itself is strictly predefined.

How did you feel during this game?

Introspective and happy (C)

What were you trying to express?

To share sensual experiences of subtle parts of life (L)

The biggest question in relation to the beans is if they are successful in conveying the presence of the distant loved one, decreasing the perception of distance. The diaries of the receivers provide us with important clues in this sense. On one side, the bean seemed to encourage a process of personification, with many receivers giving the bean a name.

This bean should have a name P. Bean - P for short. P is a significant name between the sender and myself. (C)

The bean is definitely a girl and its name is 'beany'. (M)

I decided to call the bean 'Human bean'. (F)

Similarly, emotions are attributed to the bean itself along with actual character traits.

I think it is quite a sad bean, maybe not sad but definitely suffers from a little melancholia now and then. And it seems lonely - lost. (L)

She always makes me smile whenever I look at her - she is so cute and happy. (M)

However, the qualities of these emotional states seem to be reflections of the nature and state of the relationship between the sender and the receiver, with a love relationship having a higher tendency to attribute feelings of loneliness to the bean. Very often the correlation between the bean and the sender is explicitly mentioned in the diaries of the receivers and the symbolic object is recognized as a powerful substitute of the loved person.

It makes me miss her less because I feel like we are together somehow. (M)

Beany is my substitute for the time being and that kind of works out for me. (M)

The beans seem to inspire very different levels of care and responsibility; several players jokingly blame themselves for forgetting the bean for a short time while in few cases the bean is neglected for several days.

I am a bad person. Today I forgot to bring 'Beany' with me to Copenhagen to watch football. (M)

Several days have gone by and I have completely forgotten about the bean. (L)

However, the desire expressed by most of the players to keep the bean after the experiment can be considered as a sign of emotional attachment to the object. A more difficult element to decipher is the role played by the secret inside. The most common response is to not look inside, yet the behaviours vary from player to player. Someone identifies the content of the pocket with the heart of the bean, confirming its role as a vessel of presence, while, in the most extreme example, a player looses interest in the bean after deciphering its content.

In conclusion, the mechanism of investing the object with a symbolic act and the ritual of exchange were successful in triggering emotional response and in some cases affective attachment in the receiver. The diaries of several players also seemed to confirm a process of projection of the loved person's presence into the bean.

6.   CONCLUSIONS

From the experiences conducted so far with the IF ONLY methodology it is possible to draw two kinds of conclusions. One kind concerns the method itself and its suitability for obtaining responses from the users. In this light, the first general observation to make is that the players genuinely enjoyed playing the games. They are very busy people and discovering that so many of them not only participated but also had a good time doing so, was a positive surprise for us. This also made it possible for us to collect a wide and diverse collection of content. The level of participation was especially high considering that we didn't make any agreement with the players beforehand or put any pressure on them to continue to play. We estimated that about 38 people of the 44 that we invited, played at least one of the games. It was evident that playing was fun just by observing people during the different experiences or talking with them informally. Yet, more explicit confirmations came from the comments expressed by the players in a collective meeting at the end of the first set of games and in the comment cards of the players. Examples of feedback from these two sources are:

> Everything was beautiful and cool! (M.)

> The first day I was a bit nervous, I was like 'oh no, nothing that takes any time, I'm so stressed' and then I was 'I like that it takes some time' because the time it took was as much as I gave it and I needed to give it so much time. (L.)

Another important element is the emotional participation that we obtained from the players. Coherently with our objectives, the games were successful in making people 'suspend their disbelief', 'enter the emotional space' and actively act and react within it. This emotional participation was high and progressively augmented throughout the games. Already in the first game many of the responses contained strong and revealing content. As time went by, the IF ONLY style became more and more familiar for the players and the immersion became more complete. Evidence of this process is in the way in which the language of the games is appropriated; for example in the 'Here I am' game, the words 'LittleYou' and 'LittleOther' are recurrently used both in the 'comment cards' and in the informal conversations between the players. 'LittleYou' and 'LittleOther' rapidly became recognised characters of a common imaginary world.

> The LittleOther is with me for dinner, We will be back soon. Don't worry. (M)

The second type of conclusion concerns the success of the methodology in generating knowledge valid to inform the design of technological applications in this field. The games provided useful insights about what people value in emotional communication, what might allow them to sense the presence of a distant loved person and how emotional content can be creatively expressed. The whole set of results suggested a wide range of directions that interaction design might take in order to enrich existing communication practices; some of them, particularly related to the examples described here, can be summarised as follows.

The first concerns the transmission of emotional content over distance. The games (see 'This is how I feel') indicate that one of the most powerful ways to express emotions is exchanging sensorial information like texture or colours, and creating an experience for the receiver. Both these modalities of expression might easily be supported by existing or upcoming technology and open interesting opportunities for interaction design. Simple sensorial information might be used to enrich existing objects (wearables, pieces of furniture, linens) with new functionalities or completely new products could be invented. More complex solutions might be created allowing users to actively modify their environment or design aural, visual and tactile experiences for the receiver.

Another source of inspiration is the observed process of symbolic investment. The results of the games suggest various ways in which technology might enhance this process; providing people with ways to augment objects with simple behaviours or digital traces that would hold their presence for another user. A potential design direction is represented by the concepts of ritual and exchange. The rules incorporated into the games seem to have been successful in supporting the processes of coding and decoding symbolic meaning. It would be interesting to experiment with how those or similar rules could be incorporated into various systems of communication mediated by technology.

From our experience we learnt that, in order to be successful, these methods need to be applied iteratively. Although the games played so far have allowed us to investigate general ideas and test some low-tech artefacts, further iterations are required in order to move towards real technological solutions. The next step of the FARAWAY project is to design new games incorporating the use of working technological prototypes. Each prototype will be a tool to explore a concept from the first game series in more detail and to investigate which input and output modalities, rules of interaction and technological solutions might support the communication process. These games will be played with people in real long distance relationships using similar rules and the game structure of the previous phase.

The 'if only' method has already provided us with valuable information about sharing emotion over distance as well as ideas about presence and symbolic investment. We believe that further games will generate additional useful data that could be used in order to transform these interaction elements into viable products or services.

7.   REFERENCES

Buchenau, M. & Fulton, J. (2000). Experience Prototyping. In *Proceedings of DIS '00*, ACM Press, pp. 424-433.

Chang, A., Koerner, B., Resner, B. & Wang, X. (2001). Lumitouch: An Emotional Communication Device. In *Extended Abstracts of CHI '01*, ACM Press, pp. 313-314.

Channel, J. (1997). 'I Just Called to Say I Love You': Love and Desire on the Telephone. In K. Harvey & C. Shalom (Eds.), *Language and Desire*. London: Routledge

Coleridge, S. T. (1817). *Biographia Literaria; or Biographical Sketches of my Literary Life and Opinions*. London: Rest Fenner.

Dodge, C. (1997). The Bed: A Medium for Intimate Communication. In *Extended Abstracts of CHI '97*, ACM Press, pp. 371-372.

Gaver, B., Dunne, T., Pacenti, E. (1999). Cultural Probes. *Interactions*, 6 (1), pp. 21-29.

Gooding, M. (Ed.). (1995). *A Book of Surrealist Games*. Boston, MA: Shambhala Redstone Editions.

Mateas, M. (2001). A Preliminary Poetics for Interactive Drama and Games. In *Proceedings of SIGGRAPH '01, Art Gallery, Art and Culture Papers*, pp. 51-58.

Murray, J. (1998). *Hamlet on the Holodeck*. Cambridge, MA: MIT Press.

Strong, R., Gaver, B. (1996). Feather, Scent, Shaker: Supporting Simple Intimacy. In *Videos, Demonstrations, and Short Papers of CSCW'96*, ACM Press, pp. 29-30.

Taylor, A., Harper, R. (2002). Age-old Practices in the 'New World': A study of gift-giving between teenage mobile phone users.

ALAN DIX

CHAPTER 13

DECONSTRUCTING EXPERIENCE: PULLING CRACKERS APART

1.   WORDS

the cursed animosity of inanimate objects (Ruskin)

I was recently shown the above quotation. It was quoted in a book by Madeleine L'Engle (L'Engle, 1980, p. 11). She does not just quote this, but says "What I remember from Ruskin is ...". It is not just a quote from Ruskin, but for her it is THE quote. The significance was not only personal for her, the reason it was shown me was because it made an impression on my wife and the reason I quote it here was because it also made an instant impression on me. What about you?

So why is it such a powerful phrase?

First it is something instantly recognisable with which we can all resonate. L'Engle talks about tangled coat hangers, but I am sure we all have stories about doors that won't lock or unlock, drawers that get stuck, cars that start every morning except the morning of that job interview.

But if it were just the sentiment L'Engle probably would have not remembered the exact words.

Let's look closer.

I think it is instantly obvious that the phrase turns on the two words "animosity" and "inanimate". Structurally in the sentence they sit opposite one another, but furthermore the two words have a similar look "...anim..." and sound[1]. Resonance in speech brings the words together in our minds – a frequent 'trick' of poets and orators.

But then the words tease us. They sound very similar, but one has the prefix "in". So the sentence appears to say: "the X of non-X". There is a dissonance, an apparent contradiction within the surface form of the utterance. Digging a little deeper, as soon as one thinks about the meaning of the individual words, this dissonance evaporates. The word "animosity" is about enmity whereas "animate" is about life. So at a semantic level there is no contradiction. However think yet deeper and again we are struck by the dissonance of ideas – "animosity" presupposes intent and

Mark A. Blythe, Andrew F. Monk, Kees Overbeeke and Peter C. Wright *(eds.),*
Funology: From Usability to Enjoyment, 165—178

personality, attributes of the living not the inanimate. Dissonance resurfaces in pragmatics.

Yet the sentence, however paradoxical, is also familiar. Resonance and dissonance in form and meaning.

~ ~ ~

The idea of "deconstructing experience" can sound alien – somehow wanting to take apart something integral and personal. By understanding and rationalising experience don't we devalue it? However, the process of analysing and deconstructing[2] aesthetic experience is well established in literary, graphic and musical art.

This analysis and deconstruction is not just an academic exercise for the critic or interested observer. Instead the artist is aware and using this knowledge of form and technique to guide and support the creative process.[3]

Let's look again at some of the things we have learnt from Ruskin's quote:

a) the use of similar sounds to bring words into contrast
b) the use of sentence form to do the same
c) the use of parallels between surface form and deep meaning
d) the use of paradox (also seen in oxymoron)

Understanding these it is possible to start to use them oneself. Let's take the second and try to make something using them:

She fans the glowing embers while ice gathers on the sill

Not great poetry, but note by pivoting the sentence on the conjunction "while", the two words "embers" and "ice" are in some way brought together, and in their contrast focus the contrast of the two clauses.

And even in writing this section I've deliberately used the rest of the techniques. Notice the repeated use of the words "resonance" and "dissonance". The words sound similar (they rhyme!) and hence call themselves together, yet they are opposites. But furthermore as words they are opposites at two levels. We use them for ideas and concepts – hence we could say that the idea of enmity of a non-living thing is in some way dissonant and yet that the idea itself somehow resonates with our personal experiences. However, the words can also be used about sound – the surface form – and indeed that is their origin: things that sound good together and those that don't. So opposites have been brought together by sound and meaning - the surface reflects the deeper meaning.

This is the power of analytic deconstruction – it gives us tools for thought and the means for construction of something new.

2. PICTURES

So we have seen how deconstructing a paradigmatic example can uncover techniques that can be used to construct new things. This deconstruction to understand is the very stuff of science and academic enquiry giving rise to theory, the language of generalisation. The application of this theory to guide the construction of new things is the essence of design.

However, when the topic of deconstruction is human experience and aesthetics, we do not expect a theory that, like physical theory, completely explains and allows us to predict the exact form of future things. Instead, these humane theories are potential pathways, more like worn tracks on grassland than signposts on roads.

In the example we found techniques that can be taken away and applied again and again. However, this process of deconstruction and reconstruction can be applied in a more situated and contextual fashion in order to understand a particular artefact and redesign it for a slightly different setting or for a different media. It is the latter – the changing of media – that will be the main focus of the rest of this chapter.

~ ~ ~

Graphic designers have faced a rapid change in their discipline over recent years. After a century or more of growing understanding of print media in magazines, books and posters, the computer has completely upturned patterns of work. For many the drawing board has all but been replaced with the workstation and tablet. Effects such as feathering of images, morphing and layering, that would have in the past required great expertise in draughtsmanship, painting and photographic manipulation, have become possible in a few clicks in Photoshop.

But as well as changing the tools to produce images on traditional media, they have increasingly been called upon to design for new electronic and often interactive media – initially CD-ROM delivered content and increasingly the web.

It took cinema more than a generation to move from a filming of theatre to a creative discipline in its own right with its own vocabulary, reference works, and rich genres. Graphic design has been expected to make a greater transition largely within the last 10 years.

There are two major ways in which we, as humans, make old experience available to new situations. One we have already discussed – theory and abstraction. The other is perhaps more grounded – examples and analogy. The latter is probably the major way in which a lot of visual design works, allowing incremental progress through reapplication of the familiar. But analogy does not promote more fundamental leaps.

This entrapment by the incremental has been a problem especially with web pages, where designs that look good on paper or even on screen fail when transferred to the web. Sometimes the only way in which the design could be rendered was as a single large bitmap, or collection of bitmaps leading to slow download times and often strange alignment problems as formatting differed between web browsers.

The problem is that the web appears at first to be a medium just like a computer screen – after all that is where a web page appears. However, the internal structure of web pages and dynamics gives it different properties. To design for the web one needs to understand those properties.

the golden rule of design
understand your materials

One example of this are images rather like those in figure 1.i. A strong frame (the box) with some element, usually a curve or angled line crossing the frame. Although this is drawn more iconically, this may be the design for the page as a whole with text and further graphics within and around the frame.

(i)　　　　　　　　　　　　　　　　(ii)

Figure 1. *Breaking boundaries*

This sort of design is very common, but translates badly to the web environment. This is because of the crossing highlighted in figure 1.ii. This requires either that the whole image is a bitmap, or that different parts are very precisely aligned. However, the slightly different formatting on different browsers means that attempts to fragment the image lead to unexpected spaces or poor alignment.

This has got better recently as more recent versions of browsers have allowed more precise positioning, but the difficulty of achieving this type of effect (and others) is one reason why designers often turn to Flash splash screens even for fairly static content.

However, if we dig more closely and ask *why* the image is the way it is more solutions become apparent. The use of a strong element breaking a boundary is used because it gives a sense of dynamism. We know that web pages can render rectangular frames very easily. We also know that precise positioning is possible, but we would like to convey the idea of the strong image crossing the boundary.

Look at figure 2.i. Although the lines do not actually cross the boundary, our visual gestalt 'fills in' the gap and the lines still appear to cross. Note the use of several smaller lines rather than one big one, this means that precise alignment is not critical.

(i)   (ii)

Figure 2. *Gestalt flow*

Note here we are deconstructing and reconstructing in two senses. First we are taking surface elements: the box, the angled lines, and re-placing in the new image. However, more important we are also looking at the underlying effects of those visual elements: the breaking of boundaries, the dynamism, and how to achieve these experienced effects in a different medium. Some of the precise visual features are lost in the redesign: the actual crossing, the single line is changed to several lines, but the underlying feelings are reproduced (table 1).

Table 1. *Deconstruction and reconstruction of the image*

original image (figure 1.i)	new image (figure 2.i)
surface elements	
strong box	strong box
single thick diagonal	several thin diagonals
actual crossing	not present
experienced effects	
breaking boundaries	gestalt feeling of boundary crossing
dynamism by crossing	dynamism by gestalt crossing plus multiple lines suggest movement

Of course this does not create a solution, these are just sketches, a particular design would require more detailed work, but the deconstruction and reconstruction opens up the design space. If the constraints were different we would need to look for different solutions. For example if the image were in fact a company logo that we needed to preserve in appearance we could not take the liberties we did in figure 2.i. Instead we might use a toned down version as a background image, or perhaps use a small version with large elements that emphasise key visual features as in figure 2.ii.

The general lesson is that as we move between media we need to deconstruct the effects that make the experienced image and reconstruct those not the surface image. This will typically include preserving certain surface features, especially if these are themselves evocative, but we can move away from reproduction to reconstruction.

3.   CRACKERS

Now those of you who do not come from Britain or Anglicised parts of the world probably do not know what a cracker is. Crackers are tubes of paper pinched in near each end to make a tubular 'package' in the middle (see below). Two people pull the cracker, one holding each end. Inside the cracker is a tiny amount of gunpowder so that when the cracker eventually pulls apart it also makes a loud bang. Then, from inside usually fall three things: a motto or joke (usually a very bad joke), a paper hat and a small plastic toy.

It was nearing Christmas 1999 and aQtive, a start-up company I was involved with, wanted something to send to friends and contacts ... and perhaps spread a little the brand name! There were numerous electronic card sites, this was passé – couldn't a hi-tech company do better. Then, one day whilst driving on the motorway the idea came – why not an electronic cracker?

Of course, it is not as easy as that. Real greetings cards are flat, largely printed, arrive in the post. Although different in electronic form than on cardboard, there is not a great gulf. In contrast, real crackers are solid (well not flat), are used together with someone else, not just looked at, but pulled and things found inside. It is not clear that any electronic version could work – because the experience would be too different and too impoverished.

In fact, Virtual Christmas Crackers were a great success and many of those who received them from aQtive sent them on to others. Sadly their life time is short (about 3 weeks leading up to Christmas), so they are not a major year-round product, but each year since they have been equally successful and attract frequent 'fan mail' to TorQil the cracker elf.

> *I love this site!!!!! Thank you, thank you, thank you!!!*
> *And Merry Christmas to everyone involved!!*
>
> cracker feedback

Virtual Crackers were successful because they did not simply try to emulate real crackers, but in some way captured aspects of the essence of the experience – deconstructing the experience of real crackers made of paper and gunpowder and reconstructing it in the very different medium of the web.

We'll look briefly at how virtual crackers work for the sender and receiver and then examine more deeply this process of deconstruction and reconstruction.

The sender's interface starts off very much like any electronic greeting card. There is a web page where you fill in your email address and name, the recipient's email and name and a short message to be delivered with the cracker (figure 3, step ①). Again, rather like an electronic greeting card, you get to choose a general cracker theme (Christmas, Valentines, New Year) and a design for the outside of the cracker.

When the sender is satisfied the form is submitted and an email is sent to the recipient (step ②). The email contains a URL where the cracker can be found, again like most electronic greetings cards. However, clicking the email does not lead to the full cracker contents, but instead to a "closed cracker" page with the outside of the cracker and button to press (step ③). When this button is clicked the cracker pulls apart, but very very slowly – almost painfully so (step ④). When the cracker image has pulled apart the web page is replaced with an "open cracker" page and a 'bang' sound (step ⑤). Only then can the recipient see the joke and links to further pages with a 'web toy' (an animated GIF or applet game) and a mask. The mask is on a page of its own and is big enough that if you print it out you could cut out the mask and wear it.

The sender also has a URL both on a confirmation web page and in an email sent at the same time as the recipient's email. The sender's web page only shows the outside of the cracker until the recipient has opened it (step ⑥). So the sender can't peek ahead of the recipient!

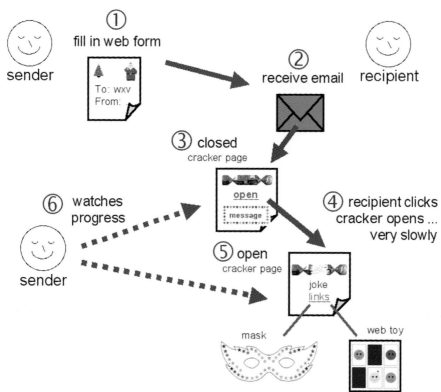

Figure 3. *The process of sending a virtual cracker*

Table 2. *The crackers experience*

	real cracker	virtual cracker
surface elements		
design	cheap and cheerful	simple page/graphics
play	plastic toy and joke	web toy and joke
dressing up	paper hat	mask to cut out
experienced effects		
shared	offered to another	sent by email, message
co-experience	pulled together	sender can't see content until opened by recipient
excitement	cultural connotations	recruited expectation
hiddenness	contents inside	first page - no contents
suspense	pulling cracker	slow ... page change
surprise	bang (when it works)	WAV file (when it works)

4.   EXPERIENCE

The operation of the virtual crackers sounds a bit like a mixture of electronic greetings cards, a direct translation of some aspects of physical crackers, and some ad hoc additions. In fact, looking more closely we can see that the virtual crackers are a reconstruction of a deconstruction of the real cracker 'experience'. Virtual crackers succeed not because they replicate real crackers, but because they capture the essence of the experience: an experience that is interactive and multi-party.

We'll look at some of the facets of this deconstructed experience in turn (summary in table 2). The table classifies these facets into surface features and experienced effects as in table 1. However, this distinction is a little arbitrary; for example, it was not clear how to classify 'surprise' (due to bang). This is natural as the surface features of course give rise to the experienced effects.

> *I think your crackers are fantastic!!*
> *These are very cool! Well done!*
>
> cracker feedback

Design: Although there are expensive crackers for high class dinners, on the whole crackers are a cheap and cheerful part of Christmas celebrations – crepe paper, simple designs, plastic toys, looking good for a while and then torn apart. The web pages reflect this, simple bold graphics and page design. Furthermore, the cheap materials of crackers means that sometimes the 'bang' doesn't work, etc. The virtual crackers use dynamic effects that tend to be flaky and browser dependent. Even with great care in construction dynamic web material tends to be less than perfect. This becomes 'forgivable' because it merely picks up existing qualities of the real crackers! If instead one wanted a virtual Fabergé egg things would be different. The experience would be one of opulence and would require meticulous design – quirky, unreliable, even minutely imperfect web pages would be unacceptable.

Play: Real crackers contain a joke (usually a very bad joke) and some sort of toy: plastic ring or figure, tiny game, etc. This was the easiest aspect to translate to the virtual experience except that the toy becomes an electronic toy: either an animated image or a small web game.

Dressing up: The other thing inside a real cracker is a paper hat. The first thought for this was to show a 'smilie' face with a hat on it. This would have been fun and pretty, but hardly captured the essence of a paper hat. A paper hat is something you can put on – dress up in. The next thought was to have a separate page with a hat that you could print out and cut out. However, this would need at least one glued joint and some quick measuring of head circumferences showed it would need to be in two parts. The solution eventually adopted was a cut out mask. This fits on an A4 or US letter paper and is a different way to 'dress up'. Often people do not put on the hats from the crackers, but they would be upset if the hat was not there. With virtual crackers we do not expect that many people actually print and cut out the masks, but the fact that you *could* leads to an apparent tangible experience.

Shared: With real crackers, each place setting typically has a cracker and the person will offer their cracker to pull together. It is a shared experience. Because the virtual crackers are offered, albeit by email and not in person, they also have aspects of this sharedness. The mail to the recipient and the cracker web pages all emphasise who the cracker has come from, so the sharedness is re-enforced throughout.

> *your virtual crackers are the bomb!*
> *they are too cool to be kept to myself*
>
> cracker feedback

Co-experience: A harder aspect of the cracker experience is the physical pulling. This is clearly very tactile, and pressing a mouse button hardly compares! The fact that the sender cannot see the inside of the cracker until the recipient has opened it does add a little to this sense of co-experience, but it is perhaps one of the weaker aspects. If combined with an instant messaging technology, perhaps it would be stronger.

Excitement: Real crackers are pulled in the middle of a party or celebration meal. Although they are just made of paper and plastic there is a real excitement about pulling them. This is partly because of the situation, but partly because of the cultural connotations that go with them: childhood Christmases, family celebration. Virtual crackers are able to recruit some of this excitement, because people associate them with the real thing. Often feedback to TorQil has mentioned this sense of nostalgia. Although the focus is on the deeper aspects of experience, it is the surface visual characteristics that give the instant familiarity. Recall the Ruskin quote. It is often the nature of aesthetic experiences that they rely on a confluence of surface attributes and deeper meaning.

> *Thank you for putting a smile on my face and bringing back some funny memories! My mother is from England and I grew up pulling the "real" crackers during the holidays.*
>
> cracker feedback
>
> *This is such a great idea! As an ex-pat Brit' I have missed Christmas crackers all the years that I have lived in the USA*
>
> cracker feedback

Hiddenness: the contents of a real cracker are hidden until the cracker is pulled apart. Similarly with virtual crackers, the first page the recipient sees when the cracker URL is followed does not show the joke etc. Only when the cracker is 'opened' does the recipient (or sender) see inside.

Suspense: Although crackers are made out of paper they are surprisingly difficult to pull apart. There is a sense of growing suspense as you start to pull and pull. Sometimes even frustration when the paper never seems as if it is going to break. In fact, for children I've occasionally had to make a small tear in the paper to make it break for them at all. Virtual crackers are, of course, not physically pulled, but the slow (painfully slow) movement of the halves of the cracker when the 'pull' button is pressed and the long wait until the contents are revealed adds to the sense of suspense.

Surprise: The pulling of the real cracker ends in the explosion as the cracker bursts open with a bang! Well, usually with a bang, sometimes they just come apart and the bang never comes. The opened virtual cracker also produces a 'bang' albeit simply a .wav file, and just like real crackers this 'bang' sometimes fails depending on browser capabilities!

~ ~ ~

Before moving on, I guess I should note that this analysis of the deconstruction and reconstruction of the crackers experience is itself partly a rational reconstruction of the process we went through in producing the final design. Virtual crackers succeeded partly because when faced with problems we explicitly tried to look for the underlying issues and aspects of real crackers in order to be able to recreate a similar experience in virtual crackers. But also there were times when we did not do this explicitly, but looking back we can see that virtual crackers succeeded because we unconsciously or perhaps even accidentally reproduced aspects of the deeper essence of the experience.

The above analysis should be read therefore rather like the analysis of the Ruskin quote. It may be that Ruskin was explicitly aware of the techniques he was using, as he was clearly reflective on the nature of art. But he was also a very practised, skilled and inspired writer, so it may be that these techniques were unconscious and unplanned. Or it may even be an accident and the fact that this quote is remembered was because it just happened to embody the right features. Whichever is true about that quote it is certainly the case that, for those of us without Ruskin's genius, more structured methods and heuristics can help us achieve more robust and effective prose.

Similarly, we know that the virtual crackers in some way 'worked' and in unpacking this we can perhaps move towards 'designing in' that success.

5. REFLECTION

Rather than starting with a 'method' and then applying it to examples to demonstrate utility, this chapter has progressed by successive revelation as we examined increasingly more complex examples of deconstruction and reconstruction of experience.

As previously noted, the process of deconstruction lies at the heart of science and academic study. The main use is to allow us to unpack the generic issues that underlie a particular instance in order to understand related phenomena elsewhere. All the points (a)-(d) we uncovered in section 1 are of this form. Generic properties or facets of the Ruskin quote that we could use in other literary works. This is the sort of thinking that is common in detailed low-level literary analysis.

In fact, several of these points can clearly be generalised across media. For example, point (c) parallels between surface form and deep meaning can be seen as a version of Louis Sullivan's "form follows function" (About 2002; Miller 2000). Also point (a) says that things with similar surface characteristics are somehow 'brought' together by that. This is also a principle of visual perception used frequently in information visualisation, graphic design and fine art.

In other chapters of this book we can also see this process at work, in particular throughout most of the first part of this book insight from various related areas is being translated into general design advice and understanding. For example, Wright et al's identification of their four aspects of experience, or Reed's use of the existing sociology of play and playfulness. In the normal course of the academic process, these all attempt to produce generic universal principles and heuristics that can be applied to new problems and situations.

However, the graphic design example and even more the deconstruction of the crackers experience point to a more situated use of deconstruction that enables the reconstruction of the *same* experience in a different medium. Of course, I am using the word 'same' here cautiously – it is by no means an identical experience either encountering virtual crackers after real ones, or even the variants of the simple line and rectangle graphic. However, the essence of the experience is in some way captured.

In the case of the graphic design there are also general lessons like those from the literary analysis. For example, the principle of breaking boundaries to give dynamism can be deliberately used where a sense of dynamic is required. This is the sort of generic heuristic that can be found in more analytic discussions about design. This synthesis of new designs from a 'bag' of heuristics and guidelines that have been distilled from previous experience, this construction of the new based on the deconstruction of the old, this is the heart of more systematic design and engineering.

However, the new graphics in figures 2.i and ii are not synthesised from scratch but instead borrow the precise set of deep characteristics found in the original graphic (figure 1.i) and do so by embodying it in features that follow as closely as possible the surface features of the original. So, figure 2.i is not just a different graphic that expresses dynamism, it does so by using the more particular technique of breaking boundaries. Not only this, but it uses a rectangle and an angled line. So, the final graphic is in some way recognisably consonant with the original and recognisable as being 'the same' in a different way.

Similarly with virtual crackers, if we had dug to the deepest level of the experience and then *only* asked "can we reproduce these", then we might have produced a totally new (and possibly successful) 'fun' and 'party-like' artefact, but it would not have deserved the name 'virtual cracker'. Blindly recreating surface features (like the image of the hat) in a different medium may NOT recreate the same experienced emotions and effects. So reconstruction in a new medium is not reproduction in that medium. However, equally we try to stay close to the original surface form in order to be 'the same' as the original.

It is interesting to note that the excitement of the virtual crackers borrows from the cultural nuances of the original, which are themselves evoked by similarity in surface features.

Looking at the deconstructed crackers experience, we could go on to abstract these to find some general principles to aid the design of experience in other domains. However, the most important lesson from this is not the particular deconstructed facets, but the process of deconstruction and reconstruction itself.

6.   DISTILLATION

Deconstruction of instances and analysis to form abstractions is the essence of science. Construction of new artefacts by the synthesis of these abstractions in new contexts is the essence of design. These can be applied to experience as in other domains. Of course, as we are dealing with human emotions the abstractions, like those in literature and art, are guidance and heuristics, not hard rules.

However, in the successive examples in this chapter, leading to the rich crackers experience, we have seen a movement from general principles to a more situated use of deconstruction and reconstruction as a process of analysing a particular experience in order to translate it to a new medium.

In Janson's History of Art (Janson 1977, p. 14), he shows how Manet's famous painting *Le Déjeuner sur l'Herbe* reproduces aspects of a previous engraving after Raphael and that engraving itself is based on older Roman sculptures. This process of inspiration across media clearly occurs naturally over time. However, the rate of change of digital media exceeds any previous times when reconceptualisation occurred between media. A more systematic approach to dealing with this transition is not just an academic luxury, but essential if design is to keep up with technical change.

This chapter offers one part of a systematic armoury for the design and remediating of experience.

http://www.hcibook.com/alan/papers/deconstruct2003

7.   ACKNOWLEDGEMENTS

Virtual crackers are an online product of vfridge limited and can be seen (and experienced!) at: http://www.vfridge.com/crackers/

The first version of virtual crackers was produced by aQtive limited in conjunction with Birmingham University Telematics Centre. Thanks especially to Ben Stone who produced the first cracker implementation. Since then they have evolved through comments from numerous people.

An early version of the analysis in this chapter was presented at the 2001 Computers and Fun conference (Dix, 2001), where I received many helpful comments.

This is part of a wider study of the nature of technological creativity and innovation (see http://www.hcibook.com/alan/topics/creativity/) and this has benefited from discussions and input from many people and especially recent support from the EPSRC funded EQUATOR and CASCO projects.

8.   NOTES

1. In fact the two words "animosity" and "inanimate" come from a group of related Latin words derived from "anima" – breath, soul or life and "animus" – spirit or mind.
2. Note I am not using "deconstruction" here in the recent traditions of post-modern criticism, but in a broader looser sense of just taking apart, teasing out the strands that make something what it is ... and, in this context, especially those that make something 'work' as an experience or as a designed artefact.
3. The vocabulary of literary and other artistic criticism is large and rich. For example, the Penguin Dictionary of Literary Terms and Literary Theory (Cudden 1998) contains over 4500 terms. Poets and artists are amongst those expanding and using this language. For example, Gerard Manley Hopkins coined the term "sprung rhythm" to describe a metrical form of his own verse, which was also found in far earlier writing, and in so doing both reinforced his own style and influenced later poets (Hopkins 1918).

9. REFERENCES

About.com. (2002). *Master Architect – Louis Sullivan*.
  http://architecture.about.com/library/bl-sullivan.htm
Cudden, J. A. (1998). *The Penguin Dictionary of Literary Terms and Literary Theory*. (Fourth
  ed.). London: Penguin.
Dix, A. (2001). *Absolutely crackers*. Paper presented at Computers and Fun 4, York, U.K.
  http://www.hcibook.com/alan/papers/crackers2001/
L'Engle, M. (1980) *Walking on Water*. Lion Publishing, Tring, UK. ISBN 0 86760 341 0
Hopkins, G.M. (1918). *Preface* to *Poems*. (quoted in [[C98]] pp. 854–855).
Janson, H. W. (1977). *A History of Art: A Survey of the Visual Arts from the Dawn of History
  to the Present Day*. London: Thames and Hudson.
Miller, C. (2000) *Lieber-Meister – Louis Sullivan: The Architect and his Work*.
  http://www.geocities.com/SoHo/1469/sullivan.html

RICHARD HULL AND JO REID

CHAPTER 14

DESIGNING ENGAGING EXPERIENCES WITH CHILDREN AND ARTISTS

1. INTRODUCTION

Product (and service) designers have long been concerned with the user's direct experience of their offerings, with ease-of-use often the primary design goal. However, we believe that the indirect experiences evoked by a product are at least as important to many users. For example, a comfortable bicycle seat is valued by most cyclists but the fun of speeding through the open country with good friends is more likely to motivate the purchase of a bicycle in the first place.

The 4D Experience project at Hewlett-Packard Laboratories is concerned with exploring experiences of this second kind, particularly in the context of ubiquitous and wearable computing. We ask two key questions:

- What constitutes a compelling consumer experience?

- How can we deliver such experiences through emerging computer technologies?

Our research methodology combines technology development, experimental prototype deployments, and user research. In this chapter, we will sketch three attempts to develop systems that evoke engaging experiences in their users, review those exercises in the light of an underlying model of experience, and discuss the positive involvement of users and artists in the design process.

2. ZAP SCAN

Our first exercise involved the development of an exhibit for the Explore@Bristol hands-on science museum (Explore, 2002) intended to demonstrate that engaging, fun experiences can be made from everyday office technology. The resulting exhibit, Zap Scan, allows users to draw a picture with supplied paper and crayons, scan that picture (or anything else) through a one-button interface, and see the scanned image appear on digital picture frames on either side of a vertical screen. Separately, if they wish, they can move to a nearby print station, select their image on a touchscreen, enter their name, insert a pound coin, and produce a glossy greetings card with their

Mark A. Blythe, Andrew F. Monk, Kees Overbeeke and Peter C. Wright *(eds.)*,
Funology: From Usability to Enjoyment, 179—187

image on the front and their name on the back. Figure 1 shows Zap Scan in place at Explore.

Figure 1. *Zap Scan deployed at Explore@Bristol*

Zap Scan was targeted at children aged between 3 and12, many of whom were recruited in a multi-stage, participatory design process as users, testers, and informants (Druin, 2002; Winograd, 1996). At the outset of the project, we visited Explore to understand the environment, observe visitors, and review operational matters with staff. Based on these early observations and our previous research in image sharing, we chose a concept and value proposition – electronic display of scanned drawings – that would appeal to children in this age range. Then at various stages of development, we solicited input from the potential users as follows (see figure 2):

- Pre-school children at a local play scheme helped to test the concept using a standard display, scanner and printer

- Older children at a local primary school explored user interaction, flow and timing issues with an integrated prototype

- Children at a local junior school provided feedback on the overall system behaviour and appeal.

The completed exhibit was deployed in April 2001. Despite (or because of) its deliberately simple functionality, Zap Scan turned out to be very popular. For example, nearly thirty thousand images were scanned between April and October 2001, and between 17 and 37 cards were printed each day of the summer holidays. Users often spend a considerable time working on their drawings. Parents sit beside their children watching them draw or joining in themselves. Friends sit together and share in the excitement of seeing each other's drawings on the digital picture frames. Young children nudge their friends and point excitedly when a picture appears. Children also gaze in anticipation into the printer and watch the cards appear bit by bit.

Figure 2. *Testing the Zap Scan concept and prototypes*

So, lots of people, usually children, had lots of fun using a computer-based exhibit that actually did very little. What they seemed to enjoy was the act of drawing, social interaction, the joy of seeing their creative work on public display, and the attractive cards. In the later discussion, we will begin to explore why this might be so.

3.   A WALK IN THE WIRED WOODS

A Walk in the Wired Woods is an art installation in which an exhibition of woodland photographs is augmented by a digital soundscape. Equipped with headphones connected to a small shoulder bag, visitors typically spend around twenty minutes wandering around the exhibition, viewing the photographs and listening to audio pieces chosen to enhance the images (see figure 3). The particular sounds heard by a visitor at any point are determined automatically by a small computer system in the bag that monitors the visitor's location within the exhibition space (Hull and Reid, 2002; Randell and Muller, 2001). For example, when standing close to certain photographs, a visitor might hear atmospheric music fitting the scenes depicted. As she moves on to other images, the music might be replaced by natural woodland sounds, or by a spoken fragment of woodland mythology. The overall effect is of a situated soundscape that might be characterized as "what you hear is where you are".

Figure 3. *Images of A Walk in the Wired Woods*

The content for the installation was developed in parallel with the underlying wearable computing technology with the deliberate intention of allowing each to influence the other. We formed a multi-disciplinary design team with artist Liz Milner and musician Armin Elsaesser to explore both *what* might be done with this new technology and *how* it might be achieved. This resulted in a number of possible technology enhancements, some of which were incorporated into the installation.

For example, as it became clear that different soundscapes would require different audio characteristics such as mixing, looping, and fading with distance, we developed a HTML-like mark up language for specifying the behaviour of the visitor's wearable client with respect to particular content (Hull and Reid, 2002)

The completed installation, incorporating around thirty pieces of situated audio, was deployed in the atrium of the Hewlett-Packard Laboratories building in Bristol in the early part of 2002 (Mobile, 2002). During it's residency it was visited by several hundred people from a variety of backgrounds whose responses were overwhelmingly positive. Of course, the high quality of the photographs and music contributed significantly to this outcome, However, most visitors reported that the extra dimension added by the contextual juxtaposition of the two media adds significant further value. A simple ranking exercise revealed that more visitors likened the exhibition to a walk in the woods (something that it attempts to evoke but really is not) than to a museum tour (something that it really is) (Hull and Reid, 2002). This reinforces our belief that it is possible to create a convincing and compelling experience with the kind of mobile technology that we can expect to become pervasive over the next ten years. Moreover, our own experience of the design process confirms our belief in the power of collaboration with artists to drive innovation in both technology and content.

4.   SOUNDSCAPE WORKSHOPS

In the Zap Scan exercise, children played the roles of user, tester, and informant, while the Walk in the Wired Woods explored the use of creative practitioners as full partners in the design process. Recently, we put those two elements together in a pair of workshops in which children were invited to take on the lead design role in the creation of digital soundscapes. The participants were 11 to 12 year old children drawn from two local secondary schools.

The first workshop involved ten pupils from John Cabot Technology College in Bristol and ran over two consecutive days. Pupils were first introduced to the technology, the idea of the soundscapes, the authoring tools, and the process of production. Then they were divided into working pairs and let loose. Each pair was assigned an adult enabler who encouraged, helped and observed but did not interfere with the creative process. At the end of the workshop, the pairs had produced five diverse soundscapes:

- a trip to the beach that starts with sounds of the car journey and ends with the sounds of sea surf and happy play

- a tiger cub riddle where audio clues were distributed along a visually marked path

- music from different parts of the world

- a walk-around radio station with different kinds of music in different areas

- a game to match flags from different nations to the appropriate music and sounds of that country.

Though these did not have the depth of professional works, they were a lot of fun and showed creativity, technical proficiency and hard work. One interesting aspect was that all five pairs had to use the same physical space for their soundscapes, leading to negotiations over physical props or visual signs that were used to anchor pieces of audio (see figure 4). It also forced the technical team to provide mechanisms for navigating between multiple digital soundscapes occupying a given space.

Figure 4. *Pupils from John Cabot creating a soundscape*

The second workshop, involving pupils from St Gregory's school in Bath followed a similar structure except that the two days of the workshop were separated by a week to allow time to explore design ideas and prepare materials. In particular, the participants spent two afternoons in school working with an artist in residence. The result was a single design based on a haunted house that involved hand painted props, a tent and a video loop (see figure 5). The second day of the workshop was spent implementing as much of the design as possible in the time available. Again, the end result was imaginative and rich with content, and the workshop as a whole was considered a success by the participants and visiting staff.

The workshops confirmed that children are capable of adapting quickly to new technologies and creating novel and engaging applications. They are able to respond to the responsibility of the design partner role with ingenuity, creativity, and enthusiasm. On the other hand, both groups tended to produce soundscapes that had echoes of the examples that had been used to introduce them to the technology, though this may simply reflect the severe time pressure under which they worked. The pupils seemed very engaged in the design process and very satisfied with what they produced.

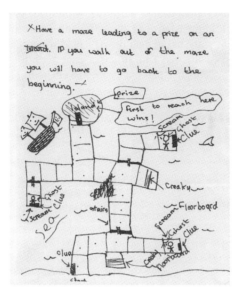

Figure 5. Plan of the St Gregory's soundscape

5. DISCUSSION

The exercises described demonstrate that it is possible to deliver engaging experiences through systems with fairly simple functionality. We can begin to explain the positive responses of users to the resulting systems through the model of experience shown in figure 6.

The model is one of the outcomes of a study at the Explore@Bristol science museum in which we observed visitors interacting with the exhibits and explored their responses through discussion groups, interviews and questionnaires (Kid, 2003). It attempts to unpack the nature of engaging experiences by identifying three key dimensions that are likely to play a role in those experiences:

- Challenge, achievement and self-expression

- Social interaction, including bonding, sharing and competing with others

- Drama and sensation, including stimulating sights, smells and sounds, and other cues that trigger the imagination

The model is inevitably partial and provisional, but we can begin to use it to interpret the success of our prototypes in terms of the elements that they provide. Our hypothesis is that experiences that contain some mix of these dimensions *will* be engaging. For example, Zap Scan scores highly on the social dimension as users congregate around the drawing area and display, and also provides an opportunity for self expression. In contrast, the Walk in the Woods emphasizes the Drama/Sensation dimension by stimulating the visitor's senses and imagination through music, sounds, images and narrative. Moreover, the exercises suggest that emphasizing a single dimension may be sufficient to engender a good experience, although some recent work based on a desert island soundscape suggests that adding a second dimension (challenge) to an experience with a strong single dimension (sensation) can further enhance that experience (Nethercott, 2002).

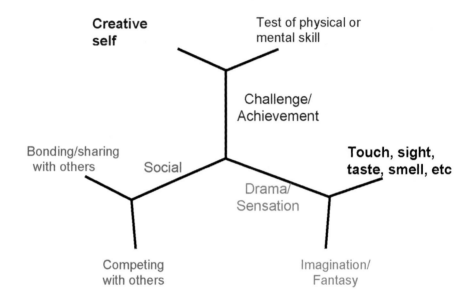

Figure 6. *A provisional model of consumer experience*

The exercises also illustrate different types of user participation in the design process. Zap Scan is the most conventional example, with primary and pre-school age children playing the roles of user, tester and informant (Druin, 2002). Their input helped to reinforce our belief in the value proposition of the system, and refine its presentation and operation. Overall, we consider that Zap Scan confirms the value of participatory design as espoused by many over the last two decades. Furthermore, one of the children was responsible for the exhibit's cool name, which was far better than any of the technical team's suggestions!

The Walk in the Wired Woods exercise was motivated by a desire to discover what artists would make of *and* with wearable computing technology. We work with artists because they tend to be imaginative, creative, demanding, meticulous, and extreme users of technology who are used to asking what-if questions. Given this perspective, we encouraged the artists to act as full design partners of both the experience *and* the underlying technology. Naturally, the artists tended to have more influence on the content, and the technical team on the technology, but both elements of the design clearly benefited from the collaboration. The participation of the artists ensured that the resulting installation was fascinating and that the technology evolved appropriately.

The children's workshops enrolled secondary school age children as full design partners, again to see what they would make of and with new technology. In this case, we provided prototype wearable computing technology, tools and training but left the experience design activity completely to the children. Naturally, the resulting experiences lacked some of the depth of more experienced practitioners, but the systems they managed to produce in a few hours were a great testimony to their creativity and application. The main result from our perspective is that it does seem possible that users will be able to create their own contexts for experiences using this technology much as people create their own websites today. This is crucial if the emerging technology is to be rapidly adopted and shaped towards its eventual meaning and value.

In conclusion, then, we believe that the exercises show that engaging consumer experiences can be evoked through applications of computing technology, that it is possible to model experiences in such a way as to inform their development, and that the involvement of users and creative practitioners in the design process greatly increases the likelihood of success.

6.   REFERENCES

Druin, A., (2002). The role of children in the design of new technology. *Behaviour & Information Technology, 21*(1), 1-25.

Explore (2002) Explore@Bristol http//www.at-bristol.co.uk/explore

Hull, R. and J. Reid, (2002). Creating Experiences with Wearable Computing. *IEEE Pervasive Computing, 1*(4), Oct-Dec, 2002.

Kidd, A., (2003). *Technology Experiences: What Makes Them Compelling?* Hewlett-Packard Laboratories.

Mobile (2002). *Mobile Bristol Conference* http:/www.hpl.hp.com/hosted/mbristol

Nethercott, J., (2002). An Experimental Comparison of Two Soundscapes Based on Two Theories of Motivation: Implications for the Design of Compelling Experiences, MSc Dissertation, Department of Computer Science. University of Bath.

Randell, C. and Muller, H., (2001). Low Cost Indoor Positioning System. in *UbiComp 2001*. Atlanta: ACM.

Winograd, T. (1996). *Bringing Design to Software*. ACM Press.

ANTONIO RIZZO, PATRIZIA MARTI, FRANÇOISE DECORTIS
JOB RUTGERS, AND PAUL THURSFIELD

CHAPTER 15

BUILDING NARRATIVE EXPERIENCES FOR CHILDREN THROUGH
REAL TIME MEDIA MANIPULATION: POGO WORLD

1.   INTRODUCTION

POGO world is an information technology environment to support the development of narrative competence in children. When we first started our user study for the design of POGO world we were conscious that the development of educational technologies calls for new interaction design approaches to overcome the limitations of current personal computer-based metaphors and paradigms. To help understand the limits and constraints of computer based technology for mediating educational activities and to have sound empirical evidence to share within our multidisciplinary design team, we carried out a longitudinal study in two European schools; one located in Siena, Italy the other in Brussels, Belgium. In this study, we observed and described more then 30 narrative activities, and we discovered that even though in one of the schools advanced digital technologies were available, and although there were several activities that included the use of computers, none of the narrative practices involving such equipment were perceived by the teachers as successful. Moreover, the teachers considered the introduction of computers into the activities that were successful a potentially disruptive factor that would prevent cooperation. The teachers supported their claim with evidence drawn from their own experience (UniSi & UniLi, 1999). Thus one of the main challenges we faced in designing a new system for interactive story building was to envision a new form of interaction that encourages creativity and cooperation and that did not jeopardise successful pedagogical activities currently used in the schools.

   In the following we describe a general model of successful narrative activities that we developed from the field study in the two schools. We then present the POGO tools in some detail in order to briefly illustrate how the proposed tools embody the concept of *situated editing* as a metaphor to mediate interaction between children and the POGO world. Finally we present a summary of the tests carried out in the schools with the last version of the POGO world prototype. This provides some empirical evidence to show that POGO world does not jeopardize successful narrative practices, but empowers it.

Mark A. Blythe, Andrew F. Monk, Kees Overbeeke and Peter C. Wright *(eds.),*
Funology: From Usability to Enjoyment, 189—199
© 2003 *Kluwer Academic Publishers. Printed in the Netherlands.*

2. NARRATIVE ACTIVITY IN CLASSROOM

Through our observation of narrative activities in the classroom, we found that the cycle of creative imagination proposed by Vygotsky (1998) as a psychological process to account for the creation of knowledge occurring in the zone of proximal development, could be used to represent the different chronological and structural phases of a narrative activity. The cycle of creative imagination has four phases namely, *exploration, inspiration, production* and *sharing* and describes how the individual experiences the external world, elaborates the impressions received, assembles them in a novel way and shares this production with others. The narrative activities at school included a focus on all of these phases, often in linear sequences, sometimes with small loops or repetition, sometimes with a leap.

Exploration. This consists of the interactions with the real world, which can be either direct or mediated by social relations. All narrative activities that we observed are rooted in the child's experience. The narratives represent things the child has seen, heard, touched or encountered in the museum, the forest, the seashore or even in the classroom but with the support of objects, instruments and people that create an event. This means that the teacher initially focuses on the sensory experiences of the child, which subsequently constitute the starting point for the theme and for the ideas. At this stage, the child uses instruments appropriate for exploration (e.g. dip net, shovel, microscope, points of view, etc.) and handles various materials (e.g. earth, shells, sand, photos, objects, etc.).

Inspiration. This is a phase of reflection and analysis on the experience had during the exploration. The child is encouraged to think about the previous experience, discuss it and sort out the elements they gathered. The teacher supports the child in the analytic process and in the discussion of choices. Individual writing, drawing or group discussion usually supports this phase. In any case there is a moment when their ideas and thoughts are externalised in more or less lasting way.

Production. This corresponds to the recombination of the elements dissociated and transformed during the previous phase. In other words, production is the moment where children, based on selections and choices of elements made previously, produce new content usually through a great variety of media. During this phase, the teacher's role is to supervise the organization of narrative content, as well as to ensure conformity with standard rules of story construction. The teacher also makes sure that the text is coherent and sufficiently rich. During this phase, the children mainly use their notebooks, pens and pencils for illustrations, cardboards, puppets, posters and bricolage sets.

Sharing. This is the phase in which children's externalised productions start to exist in their social world. Children present the result of their production and verify the effects of this production on the others (e.g., children, teachers, parents). We observed that to conclude the activity, the teachers propose a moment of exchange and sharing of the narratives produced. In conventional activities, this is the phase when the teacher concentrates on the presentation of the final product created by the child. The most important document in this phase of the activity is the Story Notebook, which contains the final product: text and drawing. In other cases the sharing phase is a full-scale performance of groups of children or of the whole class.

The pedagogical activities observed in the schools were modelled as Narrative Activity Models (NAM) and were used in order to define the users' requirements and to relate them to the POGO concept and enabling technologies. A set of requirements were produced both to assess and refine the design concepts proposed by the industrial designer of Domus Academy and Philips Design and to foster further concepts to be expressed in mock-ups. One of the key concepts for the interaction design was the one of situated editing supported by "invisible computing" (Norman, 1998), that is, to allow a seamless integration of the physical and virtual world through intuitive interaction modalities.

3. POGO WORLD

From the NAM it was clear that in the school environment children use a number of tools to construct narratives. In referring to the phases that constitute the activity, we ascertained that the Exploration phase is usually carried out in groups. Afterwards each child independently carries out the process of creating the narrative. The graphic illustration of the story is also done individually, during or after the verbal description. In other words, in conventional activities story making is mainly an individual undertaking. Nevertheless, we also observed several activities where all the children of the class or of sub-groups worked together to create a single story. The patterns of cooperation vary on a case by case basis, but generally the phases of group activity (choice of story subject and story line, etc.) alternate with individual creation (drawing, inventing dialogs, etc.), where each child makes his/her personal contribution to the construction of the story and the same tools are used to support both individual and group activities in a seamless way.

Most of the personal computer technology available in the school does not fit with this articulated way of carrying out narrative activities; the technology is just out of the loop.

3.1 The POGO Tools

The POGO environment can be thought of as a virtual story world, accessible through a number of interactive physical tools distributed in the environment. The active tools are the main interface to the narrative process. The functionality of the tools spans many areas from gestural (live performances), visual (manipulation of images and drawings) and aural (sounds and atmospheres), to manipulative (physical feedback, kinematics) and material (surface and texture, weight etc.). Although the system is computer-based, the standard computer interface of keyboard, screen and mouse has been replaced with a far more intuitive one. The interaction is very simple so that children can begin to play with no need for instruction.

The system has a number of tools that support the process we call situated editing. Raw non-digital media elements (e.g. drawings, sounds) can be converted into digital assets using tools for rich asset creation. These digital assets are stored on physical media carriers and can be used in tools that support story telling. With these tools assets come alive on a big projection screen, sound system, paper cardboard, paper sticks etc. The system provides tools to capture the creative end-results and share it with others using the internet in movies or in digital or paper based storyboards. POGO has been developed in a modular way allowing parts of the system to be re-used and combined for different purposes. The following tools compose the POGO World:

The *Beamer* is a threshold tool that connects the real and the virtual environment by allowing the passage of physical things into the virtual story world. The Beamer captures new story elements such as real world objects (including the children) or live video. It has a base unit integrating a horizontal LCD screen with a pressure sensitive touch panel, a video camera, a Card reader, and a composition area (Figure 1). Drawings and objects can be positioned in the composition area, and collages can be created there. The captured image can also be edited in the same composition area. The camera can be used to capture these elements and also as a simple, live video mode where the images are directly projected onto the walls.

Figure 1. *The Beamer*

The *Cards* are media for exchanging story elements such as sounds, pictures and video clips. They are a 'memory' for story elements that can be associated to real-world objects by physically attaching the card on drawings, clay models or toys. cards contain a unique ID tag and are used as physical pointers to Virtual Story World elements. Whenever the card is activated (e.g. inserted in the silver mat) it displays the corresponding image or sound. When the children pop a story card in the slot on the table and press the record button, the pictures are stored on the card. If a child places a card in one of the pockets on the side of the silver mat, the pictures on the card are displayed as a background. If a child puts the story card into one of the Mumbos, whatever is on the card is shown on the mat in front of the background.

The *Mumbos* are tools to control foreground elements on the screen. Through the Mumbos, images can be animated (moved) and modified. For example, if the

Mumbo is rolled, the image stored in the card contained in the Mumbo moves in the direction of the roll.

The **Camera** tool allows to record live video which can be stored in cards and displayed together with the other elements and characters. A controller allows the image size on the screen to be adjusted and photos to be taken which can then be inserted in the background (Figure 2).

Figure 2. *Mumbo and camera tools*

The ***Settings***, comprise a silver mat surrounded by leather cushions and various tools. The mat is a screen on which to project images. However, it is also possible to project images anywhere in the physical environment, including onto the children's body (Figure 3). The Background Composer is inserted into the Setting. This allows up to three cards to be inserted to create a hierarchical background. Dropping cards into the Background Composer activates background images and/or related sounds in mixed media combinations. Background images can be created by the children (e.g., drawings, collages, composition of elements picked from the real world) or they can be selected from a database. The Background Composer provides a continuous output, so even if there is no Card in it, a live video image is shown as background. In a sense, the live image allows children to "perform" a story in the real world on a virtual background.

The ***Colour Wheel*** is located in the setting and is used to set the background colour for the screen. It uses four joystick buttons for controlling the colour value, and the effect will be visible directly.

Figure 3. *Silver mat*

The **Sound Twister** allows activating sounds by inserting a sound card into the mat (Figure 4). The Sound Twister Tool is used to playback sounds that are stored on cards. The tool consists of a number of pads. The sounds stored on a card are assigned to these pads and are played if a pad is pressed. Sounds generated in this way are mixed so that multiple sounds can be played at the same time.

Figure 4. *The Sound Twister*

The **Sound Mumbo** is used for sound playback using effects such as pitch shifting and echo. An effect can be selected by tilting the tool in the X-Y plane. The sound source can be real-time using an embedded microphone for input, or can originate from sounds stored on asset cards.

The **Voice tool** allows users to insert their voices into the story. A controller allows recording and modifying these voices. Children can speak in strange voices and can add echoes and noises.

The **POGO VCR** tool (Figure 5) is used to capture everything that is played in the POGO System. It can record video and audio streams that are generated with the Play PC and convert them into a movie file. The Recorder/Reader records and displays story scenes.

Figure 5. *POGO VCR*

When a card is inserted in one side of the Recorder/Reader, the scene is recorded in real time. When it is inserted in the opposite side, the recorded scene is displayed.

4.   THE EVALUATION OF POGO

Rather than performing formative and summative evaluation sessions, we decided to constantly assess the outputs of our design process with teachers, children and colleagues. Thus in a sense, we renounced formal evaluations in favour of a longer term qualitative assessment of the project outcomes. In particular, testing of the final prototype attempted to understand if and how the designed technology had fulfilled the pedagogical goals, how the transition from current pedagogical praxis had been embodied into the praxis of the POGO design solution, and how the POGO environment could mediate the narrative cycle in various activity settings.

In the following, we report the evaluation activity performed at school on the final prototype with children aged from 6 to 8 years. All activities were designed, set up and co-ordinated by the teachers according to their pedagogical objectives. Different kinds of activities were proposed by the teachers ranging from free activities that were selected and coordinated by the children who were responsible for creating the narrative as they wished, to more structured activities proposed and coordinated by the teacher who decided timing, rules, content and dynamics.

All narrative sessions were videotaped and the dialogues transcribed. The resulting narrative productions were analysed and used as basis for debriefing sessions with teachers to analyse and interpret results. The results are described below.

4.1   Impact on the narrative activity phases

Exploration. POGO seems to integrate smoothly with the current practices of collecting story elements: children can bring personal objects, intimate memories, photographs etc. into the POGO environment and evolve them into elements of the narration. The POGO environment supports the transition from everyday life experiences to the fantastic world of narration by affording the collection of different media such physical objects, sound and noises and transforming them into virtual objects thus creating a rich repository of elements useful for the story. In particular the Beamer, which enables the user to import a virtual version of any sort of object, stimulates children to store an experience represented by the object itself.

During the testing, the teachers encouraged the children to explore potential story elements by using the Beamer, projecting images of seashells gathered on the beach and mushrooms picked in the woods and so on. In traditional activities, they could only reproduce them in the form of a drawing, a kind of activity that is sometimes so time consuming as to prohibit a further elaboration of the drawings into story elements. With POGO, it is possible to immediately import an object, to draw and transform it in a virtual element of the story, so that the exploration phase is not conceptually separated from other phases of narrative activity. We consider this a clear added value over traditional ways of supporting the exploration phase.

Inspiration. As happens with traditional activities, during the inspiration phase POGO can be used to encourage children to rethink an experience, to analyse its constituent parts and to express it orally or by drawing. The change with POGO is in the resources available to stimulate thought and decision-making. In comparison with traditional practices, the POGO tools seem to offer greater support to the children. The possibility of combining and recombining elements on the Beamer table, and of displaying the result on the screen in real time, facilitates experimentation and comparison of different solutions. In addition, screen displays have an amplifying effect that facilitates perception and information sharing. The tools support personal reflection, collective comparison and meaning negotiation. This was particularly evident in one activity "Mushroom Development", where the children spent nearly all the class in the Inspiration Phase. They placed themselves around the Beamer and the teacher encouraged them to use the material available to reconstruct the developmental phases of the mushroom. The Beamer acted as a support for handling the material, and for producing drawings. The teacher encouraged each child, in turn, to suggest ideas by modifying the material on the Beamer table. The screen enabled them to monitor their own production, as well as the productions of other children, providing a basis for further discussion. Intermediate products were stored in different cards recording individual as well as collective contributions.

Production. Narrative activity in the school is very rich, rewarding and successful. In designing POGO, we learnt from the most successful existing practices and tried to amplify them in the learning process through the use of the POGO technology. The testing confirmed that we achieved this objective, and the production phase was one of the most surprising in terms of creative constructions made by the children. They made new connections among contents just by manipulating the tools. They explored the flexibility of the tools in representing and structuring the narration. Furthermore, the POGO tools allowed teacher and children to take clear roles, from guidance to content direction, technical direction, and performance. In general we assisted an interesting process of role diversification. We observed a division of labour during the creation of scenes between 'producers of content', responsible for arranging into acts and scenes, and 'technicians', responsible for producing elements of the story like backgrounds, characters, sounds, etc. (Figure 6). The first group created the story, and the second was focused on realising them. The new role of 'technician' enabled shy children who generally do not participate enough in conventional activities, to be more involved, doing something that allowed them to join the negotiation process through their actions and not their words. The distribution of the tools and their location in space helped the diversification of roles: the Beamer was the area to create contents (for technicians), other tools served to memorize (cards) or reproduce (screen) the results (the work of content producers).

Figure 6. *Production with POGO: Distribution of roles*

During the test, we witnessed a process of scaffolding and fading that was perfectly realised through the tools. When the teacher provided less guidance (fading), the children produced their story with greater independence – as occurred in two activities -"Castle invaded by witches" and "Story of sound" – where the puppet show metaphor was employed. During these activities, the children spontaneously sat behind the Beamer, facing the settings. As soon as the activity began, the children started moving the silhouettes on the glass plate of the Beamer and kept track of the results projected on the settings. Their characters were animated against background scenery, like a Chinese shadow puppet show. The teacher then suggested improvised dialogues, giving voice to the characters, rather than describing the action, as they did in other activities.

The example reveals how role taking with POGO can be extremely varied and imaginative. Children can be actors during the performance, or spectators when looking at the screen.

Sharing. The POGO tools can be used to amplify and enhance collective sharing of the children's production. Children can share both the creative process and the product of the narrative activity. This meta level of sharing stimulates meta-cognition and meaning construction and negotiation.

This effect is demonstrated by the fact that children insisted on 'redoing' the story many times, and presenting it to other children who had not participated in the production. This need for sharing can be explained by the fact that during the creative process the children concentrated mainly on creating a scene, but at the same time they were exposed to the global view of the narration. With POGO they learnt to change point of view and acquire a different perspective on the story, from local events to coherent plots. This effect is difficult to obtain with conventional tools like paper and pencil where al elements of the story are located on one or two pages of a notebook. With POGO the contents are stored in different tools distributed in the space and represented by different media at the same time (Figure 7).

Figure 7. *Sharing with POGO: distributed activity in the space over different media tools*

5. CONCLUSIONS

POGO's challenge was to design innovative technologies for children that should be equally attractive, fun, long lasting and yet offering sound pedagogical learning opportunities to be seamlessly integrated in the current context of European schools. The results so far have been very encouraging. The POGO world does not replace any of the current tools that the teachers successfully use in their teaching practice, instead it empowers these tools and integrates them with new opportunities.

But the most important achievement of our research was the development of an educational tool that supports the entire cycle of creative imagination, letting it evolve as a never-ending creative process.

Indeed the POGO tools allow a rich sensorial interaction where physical and virtual elements of children's reality can be explored, analysed, decomposed, and recombined in new ways. The existing objects or the new one produced working with the different POGO tools can be captured by children and edited in real time. What a child builds or brings as a part of the personal experience can be combined with the products of other children in a continuous negotiation process where the evolution of transformations of the objects is recorded and the movement along this process of meaning construction can be used as a way to understand the other's points of view.

Moreover the physical objects that are produced in this iterative and combinatory activity remain live features of the process and can be used as the physical address for the articulated production of future creative activity.

The POGO project advocated a design that was focused on children and teachers' activities and grounded in thorough research into those activities. Its purpose was to provide a sustainable solution that can help children create and enjoy intellectually interesting activities.

POGO presents a new 'type' of system, an open system. It is a kind of 'personality', capable of intelligent responses. Depending on how it is used POGO it is a camera, a video recorder, a microphone, a display screen. POGO reacts to the user and adjusts its behaviour accordingly. It is open to change. And, while at the moment it supports children in building stories together, POGO offers many avenues of exploration. It proposes new ways of looking at interaction design, of handling knowledge management systems, of enhancing electronic learning for children of all ages. It points into new directions for collaborative working in the office and collaborative, creative activities in the home.

6.   ACKNOWLEDGEMENTS

This research was funded by the European Commission within the I3-Experimental School Environment Programme. We owe particular gratitude to the Hamaïde and Tozzi School's children and teachers for their enthusiastic and generous participation to the project. A special thanks goes to Laura Polazzi, Berthe Saudelli, Claudia Fusai, Gabriele Molari, and Barbara Castelli for the effort spent on the POGO project, in particular working with teachers and children. Our thanks go also to the peer reviewers and to the editors who give us support and very helpful comments.

7.   REFERENCES

Bruner, J.S. (1996). *The culture of education.* Cambridge MA: Harvard University Press
Norman, D.A. (1998). *The invisible computer.* Cambridge MA: MIT Press.
UniSiena & UniLiegi (1999). *Narrative and learning: School studies.* POGO deliverable n°
      00001/v.1
Vygotsky, L. S. (1998). Imagination and creativity in childhood. In R. W. Rieber (Ed.), *The
      Collected Works of L.S. Vygotsky* . New York: Plenum.

SECTION THREE: CASE STUDIES IN DESIGN

INTRODUCTION TO SECTION 3

The first section of this book offered a range of theories and concepts of use in the consideration of enjoyment in human computer interactions. The second section outlined a number of possible methods for research and development ranging from adaptations of standard usability techniques to more innovative approaches. This section is a collection of case studies concerned with the development of particular applications. They are instances of designers and researchers taking up the challenges of designing for enjoyment as outlined throughout the book.

The first three case studies are concerned with making traditionally serious endeavours, telephony, public information displays and programming, more enjoyable. In **The Joy of Telephony,** *Hohl* et al describe the "EasyCom" interface for telephone call management software. Calls are transferred or activated with drag and drop icons and addresses can be personalised with "fun" nicknames and graphics. Users not only enjoyed using this innovative interface but also initiated more complex calls than usual. The EasyCom interface has been marketed as a unique selling point and the authors argue that the "fun of use" can boost productivity and also sales. **From Usable to Enjoyable Information Displays,** is concerned with an innovative form of public information display. *Ljungblad et al* describe an "informational art" display, based on the work of Piet Mondrian, that presents a weather forecast with squares and colours changing as temperature and conditions vary. A prototype was tested at a University campus and was generally received with enthusiasm. The authors conclude that while such informational art would be inappropriate to display train times or other information where accuracy and readability were graver concerns than aesthetics, there are a range of possible applications for this kind of engaging display. In **Fun for All,** *Rosson and Carroll* explore the use of simulations to promote collaboration and community across generations. The authors consider not only ways of making cross-generational programming more enjoyable but also identify the aspects of the simulations which the participants enjoyed most. They found that the boys were most likely to enjoy the game-like elements of simulations and speculate that gender may predict the enjoyment of different simulations better than age. Creating simulations that are enjoyable but do not trivialise community issues remains an ongoing design challenge.

The next three case studies are all, in one way or another, concerned with narrative and, to an extent, the supernatural. In **Storytelling and Conversation to Improve the Fun factor in Software Applications,** *Norbert Braun* draws on models of conversation and a literary analysis of the structure of folk tales in the development of a story telling engine and a conversational interface. These applications were used to tell entertaining interactive ghost stories at the castle of Heidelberg. In **Deconstructing Ghosts,** *Sykes and Wiseman* consider the "fun of fear" and report findings from two experiments that attempted to find out what was scary about the allegedly haunted vaults of Edinburgh. They created a computer-generated representation of the vaults and compared the experiences of test

203

Mark A. Blythe, Andrew F. Monk, Kees Overbeeke and Peter C. Wright *(eds.),*
Funology: From Usability to Enjoyment, 203—204.
© 2003 *Kluwer Academic Publishers. Printed in the Netherlands.*

participants in the real and virtual spaces with fascinating results. By deconstructing the space in this way they suggest aspects of the visual scene and associated narratives that produce effects of fear with clear implications for designers of video games. In **Interfacing the Narrative Experience,** *Jennica Falk* considers the elements of live action narrative game play that have yet to be captured in virtual gaming environments. Falk's work is concerned with extending virtual game space into the physical world and she illustrates this idea with real world tangible interfaces for multi user domain adventure games. By contrasting on and off-line role play gaming she produces a set of design implications for producing more compelling and immersive virtual environments.

The next three case studies focus on engaging users in interactive experiences. In **Whose Line is it Anyway,** *Blankinship and Esara* describe "talkTV" an ingenious piece of software that allows users to search the text embedded in TV programmes to provide subtitles for the hard of hearing. The particular application of this search engine allowed Star Trek fans to locate and cut and paste scenes from the series in order to construct their own mini-films. The authors took a prototype to a Star Trek convention and found that the "trekkies" who used it had "hard fun" with it. In **The Interactive Installation ISH,** *Hummels et al* introduce the concept of resonance - the extent to which a product resonates with the user by connecting to cognitive and emotional skills, personal history and aesthetic sensibilities. They then describe their Interactive Sound Handling (ISH) installation featuring a number of innovative image and sound handling devices. The chapter ends with an evaluation of the products based on user testing which support claims for the importance of rich interactions. And finally **Fun with Your Alarm Clock,** is an engaging piece of writing about an engaging technology. *Wensveen and Overbeeke* describe an alarm clock that gauges and responds to the mood of the user. The design problem and the solution are illustrated with character driven scenarios in which the authors attempt to make getting out of bed a little easier for their long suffering heroine Sophie. We thought it appropriate to end the book with this design for making everyday life a little more enjoyable.

HUBERTUS HOHL, KLAUS WISSMANN AND
MANFRED BURGER

CHAPTER 16

THE JOY OF TELEPHONY: DESIGNING APPEALING INTERACTIONS

1. TELEPHONY – EASY AND FUN TO USE?

In this chapter, we want to highlight the importance of incorporating fun and emotion in user interface design targeted at an application domain that is generally considered to be deadly serious: business telephony and communications. Although telephones are a ubiquitous means for simple everyday communication, they are not always simple to use. In business settings, enhanced convenience phones offer dozens of sophisticated features, such as call swapping, call transfer, call forwarding or conferencing. User experience shows that the more supplementary features are supported the more difficult these phones are to operate. By integrating voice and data communication functions into a single PC-based user interface, there is great potential for increasing the efficiency of employee workflows as they go about their day-to-day business tasks. This is particularly true for users such as teleworkers, telemarketers, call centre agents and inside sales people, who spend most of their time interacting with telephony and PC applications.

2. EASYCOM – TELEPHONY MADE EASY

To this end, we have designed and implemented a novel user interface paradigm for enriched computer-mediated communication (see Figure 1). EasyCom's conceptual model is based on the "communication circle" (Grundel, & Schneider-Hufschmidt, 1999). The user is placed in the center of a graphical circle. Calls are initiated by dragging and dropping communication partners from address books, speed-dial buttons, call journals, etc. into the circle. By directly manipulating the partners involved in a communication situation, even complex telephony functions, such as setting up a conference or alternating between active and held calls can be handled easily with little or no end-user training needed. Data communication is tightly integrated into this interaction concept: by dropping notes or files into the circle, the user can send emails to communication partners or share documents with them (Hohl, & Burger, 2001).

Mark A. Blythe, Andrew F. Monk, Kees Overbeeke and Peter C. Wright *(eds.)*,
Funology: From Usability to Enjoyment, 205—211.
© 2003 *Kluwer Academic Publishers. Printed in the Netherlands.*

When designing EasyCom, our initial objective was to improve the handling of complex synchronous communication processes by striving for ease of use. However, after introducing EasyCom to the marketplace, we realized that designing for fun and emotion has become an equally important success factor and a unique selling point for our product. In the following, we will try to identify and explain the reasons for these unexpected insights. Our observations are based on user feedback collected in internal and external field trials as well as interviews with customers and sales people.

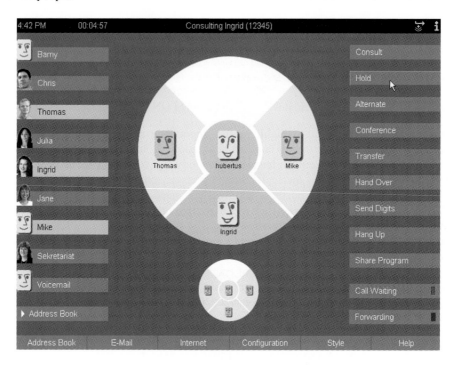

Figure 1. *The EasyCom user interface*

3.   FUN OF USE BOOSTS PRODUCTIVITY AND SALES

Originally, our interaction concept was designed to increase the efficiency of personal communication flows by ease of use. However, we soon realized that our design helped to reduce anxiety. For example, users reported that in particular the appealing drag-and-drop interactions motivated and encouraged them to initiate complex call procedures they never dared to manage with their conventional phones for fear of failure. This behaviour is well known in office telephony, e.g., people often hesitate to make consultation calls or transfer calls, because they are not sure they can successfully reproduce and complete these infrequently used actions.

Additionally, people reported that monotonous and routine telephony tasks were just made more fun by attractive interactions.

The hedonic quality (Hassenzahl, Platz, Burmester, & Lehner 2000) of the EasyCom user interface has an important influence on the system's appeal in the marketplace. The originality of the approach perceived by the customers heavily influenced the marketing strategy. The innovative EasyCom client is marketed as a unique selling point for a whole family of Siemens Voice-over-IP based telecommunication products.

4. REAL GRAPHICAL INTERFACES MAKE MORE FUN

Novel user interfaces that make heavy use of graphics and custom look-and-feel are often valued as more attractive and innovative than standard WIMP user interfaces. This is not only true for game applications, EasyCom also uses graphical means to improve the visual awareness of communication processes. Inside the communication circle, animated characters – so-called Talking Heads – symbolize the communication state and activity of partners, i.e., mouth opened and looking at each other when the call is active, mouth closed when the call is held (see Figure 2). Such characters can also act as emotional avatars or personal assistants representing specific information about the communication partners. Thus, Talking Heads serve two complementary purposes: making telephony applications more enjoyable and more comprehensible (see also (Tractinsky, Katz, & Ikar 2000)). Hence, fun is not designed into the system to distract from the main feature telephony, but to improve interaction and avoid non-transparent situations.

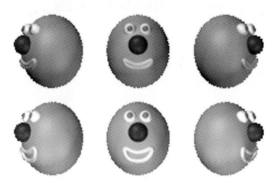

Figure 2. *Talking Heads with communication states of partners*

This approach corresponds to Norman's (2002) findings: beauty in a product has to be more than skin deep. Aesthetic visualizations should always fulfil a useful function, work well, and be usable and understandable. Overbeeke also emphasizes that the beauty of an interface should not be a glued on quality. The focus should "shift from a beautiful appearance to beautiful and engaging interaction" (Overbeeke et al, in this book).

5.   USERS ARE INDIVIDUALS

Customer feedback has shown that EasyCom users want to be empowered to tailor the user interface to their personal needs and preferences. On the one hand, users should be able to adapt the telephony client to their personal context of use (office, secretary, conference room, etc.), on the other hand people also ask for the means to personalize the visual impression of the system. We introduced end-user customization by offering (1) a predefined set of alternative visual design variants, and (2) allowing users to associate individual photos or icons with communication partners. Interestingly, new users spend a lot of time customizing their user interface. The first task they try to accomplish with EasyCom is to configure personal speed dial buttons attaching individual pictures and icons to frequently called communication partners, and to choose their favorite design theme (cf. Figure 3 and 4).

Figure 3. *Emotions expressed in speed dial buttons*

Certainly, the beauty of a visual design is primarily a matter of taste. In fact people use different visual designs to document the social environment which they belong to and at the same time try to differentiate themselves from other social environments (Degen, 2000). Because of the highly different user base of a telephony software and the inherent graphical nature of EasyCom's user interface there can't be one single design which fits every social milieu of our user base. EasyCom therefore offers various visual themes according to the following combinations of emotion and color: serious – inviting, rational – calm, emotional – warm, lively – fresh.

However, people often ask to go further by adding individual image backgrounds to the user interface, using non-rectangular shaped windows or even redefining whole design themes. We plan to integrate an interactive user interface design tool that enables end users to rapidly add their personal touch to the user interface without programming. Thereupon, users could easily modify existing or create new graphic designs by configuring design properties such as colors, fonts, icons, images, etc.

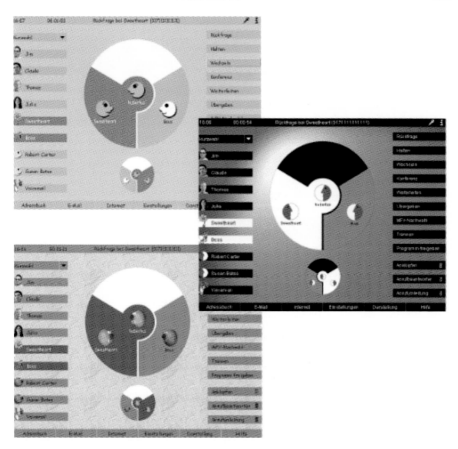

Figure 4. *Some EasyCom design themes*

We have developed an alternative view on EasyCom's user interface which is based on separate windows – so called EasyBlocks – to enable the user to tailor the amount of information and interaction components displayed on screen to his or her personal needs and preferences. To support the user in effectively manipulating a user interface based on multiple windows EasyBlocks can be glued together and subsequently moved and resized simultaneously. Observations have shown that people were having a lot of fun moving EasyBlocks around and glueing them together in every possible way while constructing their preferred arrangement of EasyBlocks (cf. Figure 5).

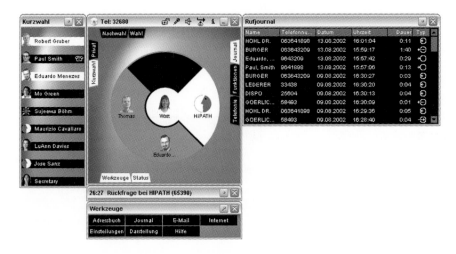

Figure 5. *An individual EasyBlocks arrangement*

6.   TELEPHONY – LIKE PLAYING A GAME

In a sense, EasyCom provides a game-like user interface: interactions are performed by direct manipulation gestures in a graphics-oriented "playing ground". Complex communication processes are handled playfully, fostering learning by doing.

We have also developed a simulation version of EasyCom intended for use by sales people to demonstrate features and present the system to potential customers. The simulator provides the very same GUI and functionality as the real client. We observed that people have a lot of fun using the simulator to set up complex telephony interactions. Managing multiple simultaneous calls and conferences is just like game-playing for them.

7.   CONCLUSIONS

While developing EasyCom, we learned that stimulating fun and pleasure is a noteworthy factor to be considered as an integral part of the conceptual design as early as possible to achieve "designs that engage and empower users [to] increase their enjoyment and encourage them to explore" (Nielsen, 2002). We hope, our observations produce further evidence for the thesis that fun and enjoyment is an important issue even for software products mainly used professionally. With the widespread use of mobile devices and services, the clearcut distinction between business and recreational tasks increasingly becomes blurred. People will use the same tools and applications in different usage contexts and environments. Thus, designing for both workable and enjoyable user interfaces will be a vital challenge in the near future. Have fun!

8. REFERENCES

Degen, H. (2000). Performance Model for Market-Oriented Design of Software Products. *International Journal of Human-Computer Interaction, Volume 12, Numbers 3&4*, 2000 (pp. 285-307).

Grundel, C., & Schneider-Hufschmidt, M. (1999). A direct manipulation user interface for the control of communication processes – making call handling manageable. *Proceedings of HCI International 1999: Vol. 2* (pp. 8-13).

Hassenzahl, M., Platz A., Burmester. M., & Lehner, K. (2000). Hedonic and ergonomic quality aspects determine a software's appeal. *Proceedings of the CHI 2000* (pp. 201-208).

Hohl, H., & Burger, M. (2001). EasyCom: Designing an intuitive and personalized interface for unified realtime communication and collaboration. *Proceedings of HCI International 2001, Vol. 1* (pp. 307-311).

Nielsen, J. (2002, July). User Empowerment and the Fun Factor. *Jakob Nielsen's Alertbox, July 7, 2002.* Retrieved from http://www.useit.com/alertbox/20020707.html.

Norman, D. (2002). Emotion & Design, Attractive things work better, *Interactions, Volume IX.4, August 2002* (pp. 36-42).

Tractinsky, T., Katz, A. S., & Ikar, D. (2000). What is beautiful is usable. *Interacting with Computers*, Vol. 13, Issue 2, December 2000 (pp. 127-145).

SARA LJUNGBLAD, TOBIAS SKOG AND LARS ERIK
HOLMQUIST

CHAPTER 17

FROM USABLE TO ENJOYABLE INFORMATION DISPLAYS

1. INTRODUCTION

When computer screens act as public information displays, they are usually designed
to present information as efficiently as possible. This is appropriate considering the
traditional view of usability, where you wish to achieve optimal readability. Think
of timetables for buses and trains, lists of arrivals and departures at airports, parking
meters, clocks, etc. They are all efficient in the sense that they successfully
communicate the information they are supposed to, but they rarely feel exciting or
aesthetically pleasing (see Figure 1). At the same time, in the same places, you will
find all kinds of adornments, placed there with the sole intent to entertain and
stimulate the people spending time in these places. In a similar way, we decorate our
homes and offices with posters, paintings and other decorative objects to create an
environment that appeals to our senses.

Figure 1. *Electronic timetables for public transportation are seldom attractive,
designed to be usable rather than enjoyable.*

If people like to surround themselves with decorative objects like posters and
paintings and at the same time there is a need for information presentation in the
human environment, why not incorporate the enjoyment factor into the design of
information displays?

213
Mark A. Blythe, Andrew F. Monk, Kees Overbeeke and Peter C. Wright *(eds.),*
Funology: From Usability to Enjoyment, 213—221.
© 2003 *Kluwer Academic Publishers. Printed in the Netherlands.*

This need for beautification is an issue that has been identified by other people, and attempts are sometimes made to make existing information displays more enjoyable. For example, at the central train station in Göteborg, Sweden, a little wooden tower holds a computer screen listing current arrival and departure times (see Figure 2). Despite the designer's effort to make the display more enjoyable by incorporating it in a decorative object, the dull appearance of what is presented on the screen makes it stick out rather than blend in. A more sensible way of designing a decorative information display might be to use people's aesthetic preferences as a starting point when developing information displays that are intended to be enjoyable rather than just usable. Imagine, for example, a weather forecast presented in the style of a painting of a well-known artist such as Piet Mondrian, displayed on a flat panel screen on your living room wall.

Figure 2. *At the central station in Göteborg a computer screen is built into a tower to make the display more esthetically pleasing.*

This is a scenario that might be more feasible than one may think. Plasma and LCD screens are already advertised for hanging on the wall like paintings (T3, 2002). They are intended for viewing TV, video and DVD, but could also become part of spaces where we socialize, read and relax, e.g. displaying a decorative picture. In this case, the computer screen works fairly well as an adornment, but the possibilities that advanced technology offer are much greater. This is especially obvious if you consider that in the near future, things like curtains, walls, lamps and tables could be augmented to present real-time information. Computer technologies are becoming more affordable and unobtrusive every year and new technologies such as "electronic inks" and electro-luminescent materials may soon allow flexible materials such as paper and fabrics to become computer displays. If people are to have various objects in their everyday environments constantly presenting information, it is necessary to make the presentation blend into the surroundings.

Pictures are often used as decoration and considered enjoyable. A picture that presents complex information can be beautiful, and at the same time be a very effective way to describe, explore and summarize a set of numbers (Tufte, 1984). Information visualization uses the possibilities given by computers to present overviews and manipulate large data sets or complex data. In this way, pictures make it possible to show information that would otherwise be hidden or hard to interpret (Card et al, 1999). Furthermore, advances in computer graphics are making it possible to dynamically transform pictures, e.g. with painterly rendering and color transformations, such as those found inAdobe® Photoshop® filters.

Informative Art is a playful combination of traditional wall decorations (such as posters and paintings) and dynamic computer displays (Redstrom et al, 2000). A piece of informative art looks like a piece of abstract art, but instead of providing a static image its visual appearance is continuously updated to reflect some dynamically changing information. The resulting visualization is then shown on a wall-mounted display to give the impression of an ordinary painting. Installations of informative art have previously been displayed in conference settings, such as SIGGRAPH Emerging Technologies (Skog et al, 2001).

1.1   An Example of Informative Art

To illustrate the concept of informative art, we will now describe the display seen in figure 3. The projected image is reminiscent of a Mondrian painting and provides a visual display of e-mail traffic for a group of people working in an office. The visualization has six colored fields, each of them reflecting the e-mail traffic one person has been involved in during the last 24 hours. The more e-mail a person sends and receives the larger the field representing that person gets.

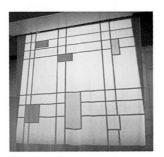

Figure 3. *Informative art: A visualization of e-mail traffic inspired by the Dutch artist Piet Mondrian*

The colors of the fields indicate how much time has passed since a person last sent an e-mail. A field can be of any of the three primary colors Mondrian used for his compositions, i.e. red, yellow and blue. In our visualization, red indicates that a person is "hot", i.e. that she recently sent an e-mail. As time passes without this person sending an e-mail, the color "cools down" to yellow and finally, if the person has not sent an e-mail in a long time, the field turns blue.

The result is a "calm" display, inspired by Mark Weiser's idea of ubiquitous computing (Weiser & Brown, 1996) that is running in an office environment, constantly providing a group of people working there with updated information on their e-mail traffic.

2.   A CASE STUDY OF INFORMATIVE ART

In what sense would a piece of informative art be enjoyable? Would people actually be able to read it? To find out, we conducted a study of informative art in use. We wanted to get perceptions and opinions from as many people as possible, to explore if it would work in an everyday setting. The IT University in Göteborg, Sweden, where about 150 students are present everyday, was chosen as the setting for our study.

Before designing the piece, we conducted a pre-study involving 31 students, to develop ideas that would generate interesting data. Several suggestions were made, including timetables for public transportations, available classrooms, current news, etc. As one of the most common suggestions was a weather forecast, we chose to design a local weather forecast of Göteborg. How the information would be presented was not brought up in the pre-study, except that it would use graphical shapes rather than text. After the pre-study, the simple yet appealing structure of Mondrian's compositions was chosen as inspiration for the piece, as it had previously been designed and was considered suitable for presenting information that was both readable and enjoyable in conference settings (Skog et al, 2001).

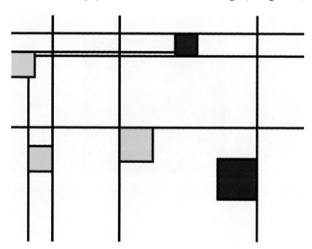

Figure 4. *A weather forecast of the Göteborg area, presented in the style of Mondrian.*

The resulting piece is similar to the Mondrian inspired visualization described earlier. This time, however, instead of a person's mailbox, each colored square on the display represents the weather for one day (See Figure 4). The display is read western style, left-to-right, top-to-bottom. The first square (top-left) represents today's weather, the next top one tomorrow and so on. This gives a four-day weather forecast in the following way:

The size of each square reflects the temperature for that day. The warmer it is that day, the larger the square becomes.

The colors of a square show the weather condition of that day: yellow represents a sunny day, blue represents a rainy day and the remaining primary color, red, represents clouds.

The piece is implemented as a java application that retrieves the weather information from the "Yahoo!" online weather service (http://weather.yahoo.com). The application reflects the information on the Web dynamically and is updated every five minutes to mirror any changes. In this way, the resulting image reflects the current weather and a four-day weather forecast, while still being reminiscent of a painting in the style of Mondrian.

The visualization was shown for a week on a large flat-panel screen in an open public space at the University. We conducted two studies during this testing period, one of them being preceded by a brief explanation of the piece to a group of students. During the briefing about 30 students were told about the overall concept of informative art as well as how to read the piece. The two studies resulted in a total of 40 questionnaires, of which 15 came from students who had attended the briefing.

2.1 Comments from Students Who Attended the Briefing

When provided with a brief introduction, a majority of the students indicated that they could read the visualization, that they enjoyed it, and that it naturally blended into the background. Two students made the following comments:

> "I think it is good because the information is transmitted in a simple way. I don't find the display annoying either, which is positive."

> "Very good. Easy to learn and it immediately blended into the background and consciousness. Actually, I don't want it to be taken away."

However, it turned out that misinterpretations and misreadings did occur, even for students who had been to the briefing. One person made the following comment:

> "An interesting and different way to show an uninteresting weather forecast. The question is how interesting it is to show a forecast with graphics. It would be more informative if it was the actual weather that was being presented."

In fact the piece was designed so that the interpretation of the coming four days temperature would be guided by the current weather, which together with its representation on the display, would serve as a frame of reference. Other people also seemed to have mistaken the display for showing a weather forecast for the coming five days, rather than today's weather and the coming four days.

One student suggested that blue could be associated with a blue sky rather than rain. Another subject found it hard to map the days to the position of the squares as they had different sizes and did not follow a line. This person also mentioned that she associated blue with cold and red with heat.

As we wanted a decorative image to become an information display, we suspected that some might find it hard to read. We also expected that people would be skeptical about this way of presenting information. Despite our fears, the comments were generally positive as the majority actually said that they liked it. One person appeared to be excited by the novelty and surprise introduced by the concept, commenting that it was:

> "Fun and sensational!"

2.2 Comments from Students Who Did Not Attend the Briefing

Those who did not attend the briefing were usually not even aware that the piece was a weather display, let alone how to read it. As the piece only changed its visual appearance rarely, some students believed that it was a static image. One person made the following comment:

> "...this is fairly useless as a painting. The machine is meant for animated images, right?"

This was not the only person who seemed to believe that the display showed desktop wallpaper or a temporary image rather than information:

> "I don't know what it is but it looks like art."

> "A bad paraphrase of a painting made by Piet Mondrian"

> "Some digital art"

When we designed the piece we did not want it to be annoying or attention grabbing. Thus, instead of having gradual transitions or animations that would attract attention, the changes appeared instantly. Many who did not know that it visualized information commented that they had not noticed any changes. The fact that they did not perceive changes might have been affected by the fact that they neither expected it to reveal information, nor to change its visual appearance.

Some people clearly sensed that it probably was displaying some information, without knowing exactly what:

> "It is hard to see if the pattern has changed. Whatever it shows is hard to read"

> "I don't understand the content, but with some information about the context..."

Without any given context, it seems very hard, if not impossible to know that informative art visualizes information, regardless of what it is.

Some students had their very own suggestion on what was visualized. For instance, one student believed that the piece was a map, showing cold and warm fronts. Another student had a more peculiar explanation (especially considering the University was located in Göteborg!):

"It is a network visualization, part of the subway in Stockholm."

Those who did not understand the information could still appreciate the piece as a decorative item, which some seemed to do, considering the following comments on the piece:

"Inspiring!"

"Pretty, however I think that it may be different (the attitude) depending on what kind of art you like."

Figure 5. *The local weather forecast presented as informative art at the IT University in Göteborg.*

2.3 Discussion

Based on the results gathered from the students who had not attended the briefing, we see that it is hard if not impossible to figure out what the information is without an explanation. The fact that "we see things through the eyes, but we understand things with the mind" (Solso, 1999) is literally inevitable with informative art. Whereas many information displays provide the context along with the information, with informative art you need to know what to look for, in order to interpret it correctly. Thus, you will only be able to read the information if you know how to "decode" the visualization.

The majority of the students who had attended the briefing expressed in their answers that they liked the piece; some indicated that the display was both enjoyable and readable:

"It is a nice and easy way to get weather information"

"I got an explanation right away, and then I understood what it visualized, I thought it was nice."

Perhaps an even more important result that this particular piece was enjoyable and readable by some was that it suggested other applications. A student emphasized that not only did she find it inspiring, but also that the piece raised ideas on how other information could be presented.

3.   CONCLUSION

Informative art is not designed to display information in the most efficient way, but rather in a fashion that appeals to people's sense of aesthetics. In general, it does not provide the viewer with exact information, but instead gives an overview or summary of some data, e.g. that the temperature will rise in the coming days, or an overview of the e-mail activity in a group.

It is possible, however, that people could eventually learn how to extract more detailed information from a piece of informative art so that in some cases, it could replace a numerically precise presentation. For instance, in the case of the Mondrian weather display, people might after some time learn to associate the size of a square with a certain temperature, rather than just get a sense of whether it will be colder or warmer in the next few days.

People who are not aware of the informative nature of a piece are likely to perceive informative art as pure decoration. Without an explanation it is extremely hard, perhaps even impossible, to know what a certain piece represents. This suggests the possibility of showing private information in a place where other people also spend time. For example, a piece of informative art could be placed in someone's office to give a daily update about her stock portfolio, or show the time elapsed in different projects. Visitors would look at the decoration, but not be able to read the information.

Is informative art the solution for getting rid of the boring information screens displaying arrivals and departures at airports, parking meters etc. in public places? Probably not; these information displays are designed with efficiency and readability as the most important design criteria. As they display information that has a need for exactness, this field of application is probably not the best one for something that has as a primary aim to be enjoyable. If the same information is presented for a group of people who read the timetables everyday, the time left until the next bus could indeed be presented with informative art.

In the future, informative art could give us a continuously updated overview of complex information and provide opportunities to expose and visualize information that is otherwise hidden or hard to interpret. For instance, context-related information, such as the amount of people in a building or the activity in a workplace could be visualized with graphical shapes and patterns. Such displays would be constantly running in the background in everyday environments, and could ultimately provide a form of natural or "calm" technology, combining an informative function with the aesthetic and visual appeal of traditional art.

4.   REFERENCES

Card, S., Mackinlay, J., Schneiderman, B. (1999). *Readings in Information Visualization Using Vision to Think,* Morgan Kaufmann Publishers Inc, San Francisco, California.

Redström, J., Skog, T., and Hallnäs, L., (2000). Informative Art: Using Amplified Artworks as Information Displays. In Proceedings of Designing Augmented Reality Environments (DARE) 2000, ACM Press.

Skog, T., Holmquist, L.E., Redström, J. and Hallnäs, L. (2001). Informative Art. SIGGRAPH 2001 Conference Abstracts and Applications (Emerging Technologies exhibition).

Solso R. (1999). Cognition and the visual arts The MIT Press, Massachusetts.

T3, September 2002, Future Publishing LTD, London, UK.

Tufte, E., R. (1984). *The visual display of quantitative information,* Graphics Press, Chesire Conneticut.

Weiser, M. & Seely Brown, J. (1996). Designing Calm Technology. In: PowerGrid Journal 1.01.
    Available at: http://www.powergrid.com/1.01/calmtech.html

Yahoo weather service: http://weather.yahoo.com/

MARY BETH ROSSON AND JOHN M. CARROLL

CHAPTER 18

FUN FOR ALL: PROMOTING ENGAGEMENT AND PARTICIPATION IN COMMUNITY PROGRAMMING PROJECTS

1. INTRODUCTION

1.1 Programming as a community activity

The increasing pervasiveness of community networks has opened new channels for community interaction (Carroll & Rosson, 2001). Residents may email questions or suggestions to town officials or leaders of other organizations (Cohill & Kavanaugh, 1997); parents may contact public school teachers online, and track their children's weekly activities through regular email bulletins; community elders may share their memories and wisdom with community youth (Carroll et al., 1999; Ellis & Bruckman, 2001). However, such activities are discretionary: residents must first believe that the new opportunities will be rewarding, if they are to take the time to investigate and participate (Rosson et al., 2002a).

We are exploring the motivational characteristics of community-oriented collaboration in the CommunitySims project, where diverse members of our local community cooperatively design and build visual simulations that raise or illustrate community issues (Rosson et al., 2002). Participants plan, share, and discuss their projects via a Web site [communitySims.cs.vt.edu]. Our initial studies have centred on interactions between middle school children and community elders. Prior work has shown that children of this age are able and motivated to work with visual simulations (Rader, Brand, & Lewis, 1997); elders may be less likely to become simulation programmers, but several studies have demonstrated their willingness and availability for youth-mentoring activities (Ellis & Bruckman, 2001; Oneill & Gomez, 1998; Wissmann, 2002).

Our earlier papers have described the problems experienced by students and elderly residents learning to use Stagecast Creator (Seals et al., 2002; Wissmann, 2002), the participatory design of community simulations (Rosson et al, 2002a; Lewis et al., 2002), and the nature of cross-generational collaboration (Rosson et al., 2002b). In this brief case study, we focus more specifically on participants' subjective reactions to the community-oriented simulations and to the process of simulation programming.

223

Mark A. Blythe, Andrew F. Monk, Kees Overbeeke and Peter C. Wright *(eds.),*
Funology: From Usability to Enjoyment, 223—232.
© 2003 *Kluwer Academic Publishers. Printed in the Netherlands.*

2.   THE COMMUNITYSIMS PROJECT

2.1 The Stagecast Creator environment

CommunitySims projects are constructed with Stagecast Creator, a visual programming environment designed to allow children and other nonprogrammers to build simulations by example (Smith & Cypher, 1999). Users construct simulations by creating a "stage" (a rectangular grid) of animated characters. Each character is given one or more visual appearances, along with a set of rules enabling them to move, change appearance, create or delete other characters, and so on.

Figure 1 shows a CommunitySims project—a schoolyard fight. The students and the teacher are characters, as is the door. The visual *before-after rule* in the lower part of the figure illustrates the visual programming paradigm: if the "before" condition for a rule is met (the visual state of the world and the conditions specified on the left of the rule), the "after" actions are performed (in this case, each of the actions changes the character's appearance). The starting condition always specifies a visual context (here, the two boys next to each other, facing forward), though it may also specify values for variables defined globally or for each character. A key challenge in Creator programming is to map simulation objects and behaviours onto visual effects (Rosson et al., 2002; Seals et al., 2002). For instance, in the schoolyard fight, changes in "tension" cause the boys to begin pushing and hitting each other.

2.2 Cross-generational programming workshops

To study the collaborations between students and adult residents, we organized two community simulation programming workshops: three women and four boys came to the first workshop; one woman and three girls to the second. Two additional elderly women were scheduled to participate in the second workshop, but last-minute personal problems prevented them from attending. Attendees were recruited through email messages or phone calls; each individual was offered a small stipend ($30) as a thank-you for participating in the one-day event.

We wanted the workshops to be a friendly and supportive environment in which middle school students and elderly women could meet and learn about one another, and collaborate on programming projects. Although most of the students knew each other in advance from school, and several of the women knew one another from other community activities, the students and women had never met; an important side goal of the workshop was to introduce them to each other.

Our research team was available to coach and answer questions as needed, so that participants did not feel that they were being "tested"; instead we encouraged them to try out the visual programming examples and tools, and to explore their own ideas for community simulations. Although we planned to characterize the workshop activities for research purposes, we also hoped to initiate and facilitate a small set of informed and motivated community members who could participate in future CommunitySims activities.

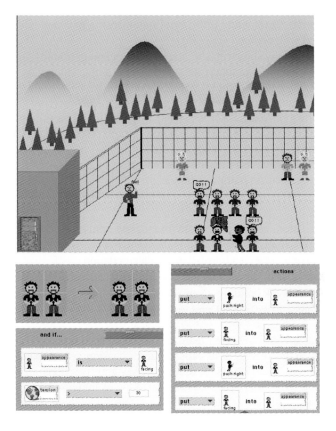

Figure 1. *Stagecast creator sample simulation and code.*

All of the participants had previously been introduced to the Creator programming. The women received their training as part of an experiment comparing the efficacy of two different tutorials (Wissman, 2002); the students were trained during a study of collaborative learning with a minimalist tutorial (Seals et al., 2002). We limited the adult participation to women because our earlier work had suggested that elderly women have more intrinsic interest in the visual programming supported by Stagecast Creator than their male counterparts (Wissman, 2002).

The students (ranging in age from 12-14) reported greater experience with computing than the women (all over 70 years of age). For example, students have had more years of computer use and describe a greater variety of computer-based activities, than the women. An important specific difference is the relative experience with "programming" activities, such as the creation of spreadsheets and Web pages. The students also reported experience with graphics or drawing tools; none of the women had used such tools.

Both workshops followed the same schedule and provided participants with the same materials and activities:

- Introduction to Community Sims; brief statements of personal interests and background with computing.
- Use of CommunitySims web site; logging on, opening, running, and commenting on the example simulations. The example simulations were *Smoking Kids* (two kids smoke, get sick, collapse); *Schoolyard Fight* (kids argue, yell, fight until teacher arrives); *Flirting or Hurting* (cute guy harasses girls in hallway); *Noise Pollution* (noisy neighbourhood party); *Smart Road* (weather affects road conditions); *Cliques* (groups form on playground); and *Classroom Bully* (a boy beats up on other kids).
- Survey of subjective reactions to the example simulations, as well as on a larger set of hypothetical simulation features.
- Refresher tutorial on Creator; review of basic skills as well as more advanced techniques.
- Group formation, with each woman joining one or more students; due to absent participants, two girls were paired with researchers.
- Collaborative work extending 1-2 example simulations.
- Collaborative work generating and elaborating ideas for 1-2 new simulations.
- Collaborative work building a new simulation.
- Survey of general reflections and project goals.

Throughout the day, research team members assisted attendees and took notes. We used two digital recorders to capture the discussion among participants. In the following section, we discuss participants' general reactions to the workshop activities, along with more specific reactions to the example simulations and to a set of hypothetical simulation features. A more extensive analysis of the collaboration episodes between the students and women can be found in Rosson et al. (2002b).

3.   PARTICIPANT REACTIONS

3.1 General reactions to workshop activities

At the end of each workshop, participants completed a survey that included questions about how easy it had been to extend or build new simulations, and what might be done to facilitate their shared programming with partners. The group was moderately positive about the overall collaboration experience (averaging 3.73 on a 5-point scale). During the workshop, we noted many cases in which students were advising one another, observing each other's progress, and in general promoting a sense of activity and excitement in the projects underway. However, several participants voiced concerns about the difference in ages:

W2: "I was overwhelmed and could not keep up with teenagers."

W3: "The young folks are so aggressive with the computer."

G1: "Just make sure that your partner is someone of around the same age so you will agree on more things."

These comments caused us to speculate that real-time collaborative programming may not be the most effective way to establish cross-generational interaction. Our future research will focus on asynchronous collaboration where community elders suggest topics and guide students toward community issues; pair or small-group synchronous collaboration on programming projects will be limited to same-age participants.

Participants also rated their interest in future work with CommunitySims activities. Figure 2 graphs responses to four questions: the extent to which Creator simulations help to build community; whether participants want to build, or to refine simulations; and how well they know the Creator tool[1]. Whereas the students were moderately positive in these final ratings, the women's ratings suggest more uncertainty about future activities. Notably, the average student rating of Creator understanding was 4.0 whereas the women's average was 2.5. However, the women seem to have accepted our community education goals more than the students; the women's agreement that Creator simulations can help to build community was 3.25, compared to a rating of 2.71 for the students.

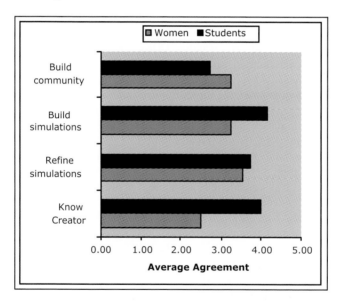

Figure 2. *Final ratings women (N=4) and students (N=7) regarding future work with CommunitySims.*

Participants' open-ended comments reinforced the patterns seen in the rating data. All 11 participants answered "yes" to a question asking if they wanted to continue in the CommunitySims project. But the nature of participants' future plans varied: three of the four boys tied their interest to game development (B1: "I'd like to make games out of existing sims"), whereas all four of the girls conveyed more general positive reactions (G3: "Yeah, I though it was really fun when we got to make our own world and that kinda stuff"). Although the women also answered affirmatively, each was careful to qualify her future involvement (W4: "Yes, but I need to have more knowledge about creating a Community Sims project").

3.2 Reactions to the example simulations

A specific research goal of the CommunitySims workshops was to study the features of simulations that make them more or less appealing to the middle school students and the women. One source of relevant data comes from participants' use of and reactions to the seven example simulations. These simulations were explored during the initial use of the CommunitySims web site, and were also used during the "refresher" training provided in the first few hours of the workshop.

During exploration of the example simulations, participants were encouraged to leave comments; across all seven examples, 22 comments were made by students, 4 by women. When we examined these comments, we found that the women commented on the community issue the simulation had been built to raise. For instance, W2 reacted to Noise Pollution: "I agree that courtesy demands speaking to the neighbours first before calling police. Also, where is a responsible adult?" In contrast, the students focused on simulation usability or realism problems (e.g., "OK…I don't see what is happening here. This one is too short to understand."). We speculate that the women took the topics of our example simulations more seriously, and that they were more motivated to initiate community-oriented discussion. This is consistent with their somewhat stronger agreement that Creator simulations can help to promote community discussion (recall Figure 2).

After exploring the CommunitySims web site, participants were asked to choose the example simulation that they thought was most *fun* to use, most *educational*, and *least useful*. There was considerable agreement about what was most educational (Smoking Kids, 7/11) and least useful (Smart Road, 8/11). There was less agreement about what was most fun, although 4/7 students chose Classroom Bully because "it was funny". In general, participants reported that they preferred simulations that had a clear message, or that "did" something. It is difficult to visualize the impact of a smart road (it measures changes in a car's movements) or a noisy neighbourhood party, whereas it is very obvious that a bully has hit someone, or that a kid has collapsed after smoking for a while.

3.3 Ratings of hypothetical simulation characteristics

Also after exploring the sample simulations, participants completed 21 scales rating the extent to which a hypothetical simulation characteristic would make it more "fun". We created the list of possible characteristics by reviewing the simulations we had built or viewed, and by brainstorming characteristics we felt might be attractive.

We included concepts we expected to be appealing to middle school students (e.g., cute, silly), but also "serious" characteristics that we thought might increase enjoyment by adults (e.g., educational, matching the real world).

Many of the features produced fairly neutral responses, and did not evoke different responses from the boys, girls, and women. However, a few features produced more interesting patterns (Figure 3). For example, the highest "fun" rating overall (4.27) was given to "The different actions and movements of the characters"; this rating also produced considerable agreement across the boys, girls, and women. This finding has a simple interpretation—the participants complained that several of the example simulations were boring or had too little action, so it is possible that frustration with these simulations caused action to be highly valued.

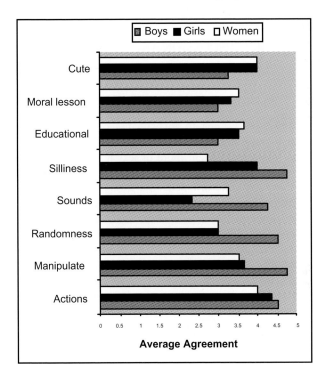

Figure 3. *Ratings of hypothetical simulation characteristics, for boys (N=4), girls (N=3), and women (N=4). The scales rated agreement (1=Strongly Disagree; 5=Strongly Agree) that the given feature would make a simulation more fun.*

At the same time, Figure 3 suggests that not all of the characteristics evoked the same ratings from the different subgroups. For instance, the boys were more positive than the women or girls about simulations that could be manipulated, or that included random behaviour or sounds. Although both the boys and girls gave "silliness" a relatively high rating, the boys tended to have less favourable reactions to educational themes, moral lessons, or "cuteness" in a simulation. Surprisingly, across all 21 ratings, the girls' reactions were more similar to those of the women (r=.37) than to the boys' (r=.03). This leads us to speculate that gender-related concerns or biases may better predict enjoyment of different simulations than age.

A simple interpretation of the boys' ratings is that they believe they will have more fun with simulations that appear and behave like computer games (randomness, manipulation, sounds). This interpretation is consistent with the general observation that all of the boys attempted to add game-like features to the example simulations (e.g., a flying bird that "bombs" other birds). In general, our results suggest a new requirement for the ongoing work of generating and refining community-related simulations—namely how to raise or provoke a real world community issue while also making the simulation interactive and game-like.

4. DISCUSSION AND FUTURE WORK

4.1 Summary of workshops and reactions

We conducted two workshops to investigate community residents' reactions to cross-generational programming, and to explore features of community-oriented simulations that might make them more or less intrinsically interesting to different user groups. Despite the small group size, we identified several interesting patterns in reactions to the community-oriented simulations.

All of the users agreed that the best simulations are those where the characters "do" something. However, the boys clearly viewed Creator programming as more of a computer game than did the girls or women. We observed that the boys spent considerable time making the example simulations more game-like. With respect to hypothetical features, the boys felt that features such as character manipulation, silliness, sounds, and randomness would make simulations more fun—the same features that would cause the simulations to be more like computer games. At the end of the day, several of the boys expressed an interest in converting CommunitySims projects into games.

4.2 Promoting engagement and participation in community programming

Our long-term goal is to promote the development and discussion of community simulations that are intrinsically interesting to all segments of the population. Given the findings of these workshops, we are beginning to explore techniques for making a simulation seem more like a game, but still express community issues. For example, the Noise Pollution simulation has been enhanced to include greater variety in the sounds it uses, to enable viewers to "summon" the police, and to send off the party-goers when the police arrive. Our design challenge is to find a way to make the programming fun without trivializing the underlying community issues.

As expected, the women seemed to take our vision of community interaction and education more seriously than the students. During their work with the students, they helped to ensure that projects contained community-specific content. They also contributed issue-oriented comments to the example simulations, and at the end of the day were more likely to agree that simulations could provoke community discussion. Student contributions tended to be more individualistic and game-oriented, emphasizing the importance of modelling by adult community members.

The differing expectations and reactions of our workshop participants has led to a more refined view of community participation in the CommunitySims project. We plan to recruit adult participants by emphasizing the importance of community discussion, pointing to the programming projects as a way of attracting youth to the topics. Where possible, we will join older residents with students willing to take an idea for a project and build it. At the same time, we will recruit students by trying to give the projects more of a game-like character, or perhaps challenging the students to make the projects game-like but still related to community concerns.

Community networks leverage and develop local resources through online collective endeavour. One of the most precious resources any community has is its elders. This has always been true, but today it may be more true. Our elders have been called the civic generation because of their lifelong commitment to community issues and institutions (Putnam, 2000). CommunitySims is only a first step, but its goal is to leverage and develop this precious resource through mutually-engaging, cross-generational, collaborative learning.

5. ACKNOWLEDGEMENTS

This work was supported by the National Science Foundation (NSF ITR EIA-0081102). We thank Cheryl Seals, Justin Gortner, Tracy Lewis, Jason Snook, and Erik Dooley for their help in planning and conducting the workshops.

6. REFERENCES

Carroll, J. M., & Rosson, M. B. (2001). Better home shopping or new democracy? Evaluating community network outcomes. In *Proceedings of CHI 2001* (pp. 372-379). New York: ACM.
Carroll, J. M., Rosson, M. B., VanMetre, C. A., Kengeri, R., & Darshani, M. (1999). Blacksburg Nostalgia: A community history archive. In M.A. Sasse & C. Johnson (Eds.), *Proceedings of INTERACT 99* (pp. 637-647). Amsterdam: IFIP.
Cohill, A. M., & Kavanaugh, A. L. (1997). *Community networks: Lessons from Blacksburg, Virginia.* Artech House.
Ellis, J. B., & Bruckman, A. S. (2001). Designing Palaver Tree online: Supporting social roles in a community of oral history. *Proceedings of CHI'01* (pp.474-481). New York: ACM.
Oneill, D. K., & Gomez, L. M. (1998). Sustaining mentoring relationships online. *Proceedings of CSCW'98* (pp. 325-334). New York: ACM.
Putnam, R. (2000). *Bowling alone: The collapse and revival of American community.* New York: Simon & Schuster.
Rader, C., Brand, C., Lewis, C. (1997). Degree of comprehension: Children understanding visual programming environment. *Proceedings of CHI 97* (pp. 351-358). New York, ACM.

Rosson, M. B., Carroll, J. M., Seals, C. D., & Lewis, T. L. (2002a). Community design of community simulations. *Proceedings of DIS 2002* (pp. 74-83). New York: ACM.

Rosson, M. B., Seals, C. D., Carroll, J. M., & Gortner, J. (2002b). *Cross-generational learning and collaboration in simulation programming.* Unpublished manuscript, Center for Human-Computer Interaction, Virginia Tech, Blacksburg, VA, 24061.

Smith, D. C., & Cypher. A. (1999). Making programming easier for children. In A. Druin (Ed.), *The design of children's technology* (pp. 201-222). San Francisco: Morgan Kaufmann.

Seals, C., Rosson, M. B., Carroll, J. M., Lewis, T. L. (2002). Fun learning Stagecast Creator: An exercise in minimalism and collaboration. *Proceedings of HCC '02* (pp. 177-186). New York: IEEE.

Wissmann, J. (2002). *Examining minimalism in training older adults in a software environment.* Unpublished Masters Thesis, Department of Industrial and Systems Engineering. Blacksburg, VA: Virginia Tech.

NORBERT BRAUN

CHAPTER 19

STORYTELLING & CONVERSATION TO IMPROVE THE FUN FACTOR IN SOFTWARE APPLICATIONS

1. INTRODUCTION

In this chapter, we describe the general structure of an approach to the design of enjoyable storytelling applications and describe its usage with a project example. First, we give an overview (with a view on related work) of our two level approach, using storytelling (as one level) and conversation (as a second level) to provide a dramatic experience for the user. The two levels are separate modules and each can be used on their own. Used together, they build the basis of dramatic conversational interactions between users and virtual characters - the story level to provide a general dramatic structure, the conversation level to provide a human-like interaction metaphor for the story.

Then we give a project example: We used the approach to prototype a ghost story within an augmented reality environment at the castle of Heidelberg, Germany.

The example explains how the two levels, the storytelling level (to automatically provide a dramatic structure), and the conversation level (to let the user experience the several sub-pieces of a interactive drama in a conversational way) are used to involve the user in a dramatic story. The story itself is played by virtual characters (ghosts). These characters interact with the user in a conversational way (by talking, gesturing, miming) and play a story that is alterable by the user.

As our basic goal is fun for the user, we start with an explanation of our two level approach and its relation to user enjoyment.

2. CONVERSATION AND NARRATION AS HUMAN-CENTRED STRUCTURES OF INFORMATION

We distinguish between two forms of user satisfaction with an application - short term and medium term.

For short-term satisfaction, we suggest a human-centred user interface. Human-centred means that for every task to be performed with the application, there is a task-optimised interface. Depending on the task and the difficulty of the problem,

Mark A. Blythe, Andrew F. Monk, Kees Overbeeke and Peter C. Wright *(eds.),*
Funology: From Usability to Enjoyment, 233—241.

the applications utilize different interface approaches. A conversation metaphor is useful for the organization of discourses between computer and user, as it is oriented to interpersonal communication.

Medium-term satisfaction is determined by the meaning and sense of the application and eludes in this context a universal definition. But, even in this case, its possible to define structures that organize content in ways that are found enjoyable by people. Throughout history stories have been used to organize information in a way that is comprehensible and enjoyable. The use of story to provide information gives the user an easy structure with which to remember information – much easier than a simple database interface that forces the users to build their own information structure among the queried data.

The following sections focus on the abstract modelling of stories and conversation; the rendering of characters is referenced in separate literature.

3. CONVERSATION MODELLING IN USER INTERFACES

Conversations used as a metaphor in user interfaces simulate a human-like means of communication between system and user. The term "humanlike" needs an explanation - as there are a variety of meanings to it. In the case of communication, it means the simulation of natural conversation between at least two individuals (humans). The interchange is not necessarily done by words and sentences. It can be done using any kind of media. For us, a conversation is determined by the following abstract factors:

- Conversation requires at least two communication partners / participants.
- Conversation takes place within an information context that every participant is used to. Often, the context is not made explicit, but the conversation refers to it.
- Conversation means alternating talk, listening and understanding.
- Conversations have social and emotional components.
- Conversations, as well as their sub-parts, have a chronological order; they have a middle, beginning and end. Conversations are therefore continuous within a time interval.

Approaches to the modelling of conversations have been developed by researchers of artificial intelligence - (Harris, 1985) - particularly with regard to the generation and understanding of natural language and speech. The AI community comes from speech and adds aspects of conversation like behaviour (Crangle, 1997). A disadvantage of this approach is the absence of a symbolic notation of behaviour, as well as the absence of an explicit behaviour model. Symbolic and explicit notation is demanded in our approach.

Cassel et al. 1999 demand the usage of multi modal components within conversation models and suggests a separation between propositional- (content elated) and discourse-related (for example the management of turn taking between conversation participants) components. Our approach also involves separating the components in these two categories.

Our approach, models the following features as the basis of a conversation:

- Social and emotional factors using hierarchies and relationships.

- Story: dramaturgical content sequences, modelled as asynchronous data.
- Immersion: the possibility of disturbance, e.g. in case of assistance of the user by the application.
- Focus (perceptual) The actual focus of the user – is the user looking at some virtual character or somewhere else.
- Meta information on the content provided by the application (propositional): Does the application try to deliver a question, an answer or just a simple statement, what are the relations between the single content units. Another aspect is the urgency / priority and importance, as well as an emotional rating of the content – is it positive or negative news to the user.
- Navigational aspects like opening, changing or closing of conversation discourses, getting or giving turns.

The conversational features are abstract and symbolic with a minimized relation to the type of content to be presented, but with a maximized knowledge of the general behaviour of humans or humanlike conversation participants. Thus far, the aspects are without a modality (the 'rendering')- the modal characteristics (like facial expressions, gestures, speech possibilities) are added in specialized input and output modules as described by the author in Braun (2002b). Conversations are modelled and processed on the basis of an AI rule system running on this knowledge base.

4.   INTERACTIVE STORYTELLING FOR PROVIDING INFORMATION

Having described our approach to short term enjoyment, let us now introduce our approach to medium term enjoyment. Medium term enjoyment is attained by the modelling and narration of an interactive story.

We start this paragraph with an introduction to stories and storytelling. As fun is, in a way, related to game play, we will contrast stories and games as well. Then we will focus on our own approach to interactive storytelling.

According to Laurel et al. 1991, a story is characterized by the following properties:

A story offers a context. Within the context, it offers activities and plots played by characters/actors. The narration and experience of the story creates a manipulation of space and time that produces cognitive processes within the mind of the reader/audience.

Certainly, the enjoyment of the audience is one major cognitive factor to be produced by a story.

Non-linear stories feature the possibility of the story's audience influencing the story. Audience interactions are of vital relevance for the process of narration. The following factors described by Mateas (1997) indicate the means of managing audience response:

- Locality of Control: the control of audience interactions can be local (for example, via actors) or global (like a chess program).
- Granularity of control: from very subtle control (like hypermedia, where every interaction possibility is predefined) to a course control (for example an

evaluation function that maps a couple of user interactions to a story manipulation).

– Generation of stories: from a completely predefined story (e.g. with only scene navigational interaction (change of viewpoints) to the generation of new plots and an open story end.

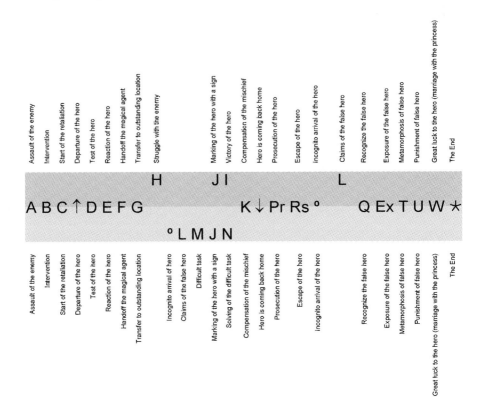

Figure 1. *The two general story structures of Russian fairy tales by Propp*

With these story structuring categories in mind, we define non linear storytelling as the telling of a story with an audience-impact on the storyline, but not on the story goal (the supposed end of the story); The story control should be global to enable a dramatic escalation to a climax of action; the interventions of the audience should take place within a story scene.

From a literary viewpoint, we define interactive stories with an integrated dramatic structure as the interactive presentation of Novella, (see Braun et al. 2002a)

The structure used to build suspense indicates a difference between a story and a game: A game creates suspense by offering the possibility of winning or losing - a story creates suspense in the dramatic play of escalating actions.

The Russian formalist Propp 1958 gives a detailed, plot and character-based, semiotic description of story structure for Russian folk tales, completely independent from the content of the story. He described the structure with morphological functions, relating to the several subsequences in a story and the actors of a story. It is possible to extend this approach to every possible story by changing the morphological functions.

Propp explored two typical structures of Russian fairy tails, described in figure 1; the dark block describing the *hero struggles with the villain* structure, the light block describing *the hero solves the difficult task* structure. The alphabetical characters within both blocks indicate the semiotic equivalent parts.

Propp showed, that this story description structure in fact can be manipulated by a story author to narrate variants of the appropriate described story, see figure 2.

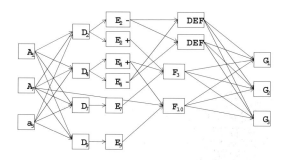

Figure 2. *Variations of a story by selecting morphological functions.*

As shown by the author (Braun, 2002a), it is possible to get a structure of interactive stories by the morphological rating of several narrative sequences and dramaturgical classification (so-called dramatis personae) of the story's characters. This way it is possible to narrate variants of a story, if the story is based on any morphological story model. The advantage of this model is the defined end of the story – the audience will always get to the end of the story within the scope of pre-defined conditions. By expanding the original story model to administrative structures for context management and by mapping morphological functions to concrete scenes (containing 'screenplay' for virtual characters), a coherent and conclusive story is warranted.

The resulting story engine application performs the story on two abstract sub-levels:

– by processing the collection of playable function sequences, a real time user adapted storyline is generated. Collection is done in regard to several factors like the morphology, actual user interaction, the overall playable scenes, the scenes already played out, possible nested storylines (so called moves) and other pre-defined constraints (e.g. limited playtime)
– by mapping the functions on scenes, the story is narrated.

As the story model is based on a morphological approach, it can be changed easily by changing the underlying morphology.

In conclusion, it is possible to achieve a short and middle-term cycle of enjoyment by mapping the story structures via the story engine to scenes, containing dramatic characters, with those characters performing a conversational interaction with the user/audience.

The following section gives a project example to explain the uses of the approach.

5.   THE 'GEIST' PROJECT

The storytelling & conversation approach has been used in several application fields; for example, its structures are used for an augmented reality cultural heritage system (mobile Augmented Reality information system in an urban environment enabling history as an immersive experience project; Geist, (see Kretschmer et al. 2001). 'Geist', the German word for 'spirit', is used as metaphor for the spirit of history;

Figure 3. *The Castle of Heidelberg*

Geist shows explicitly the correlation of humanlike communication/interaction story structures and the user's enjoyment and fun with the application. Within the Geist System, the history of an arbitrary city – within Geist the city of Heidelberg and the Thirty Years' War – is shown in such a way that the audience receives an immersive, dramatic and action-rich experience with a high factor of fun and enjoyment, see figures 3 - 5.

Figure 4. *User, enhanced with Augmented Reality equipment, watching a ghost.*

Figure 5. *The ghost 'Katharina' interacting with the user.*

The historical data are served via an interactive story that includes:
− the environment - buildings, parks, gates, fountains, etc.
− the historical image of the environment - buildings in their historical form, artefacts from the past that do not exist in the current time.
− Different dramatic characters of the historical age. Figure 5 shows an actor used to perform the dramatic characters.
− The user - involved as a dramatic entity of the story.
   The user is experiencing the Thirty Years' War first-hand and is interactively involved in the fate of the virtual characters.

The user is utilizing interfaces that offer an acoustic, graphic and haptic access to the story - via augmented reality seamlessly integrated into her own reality – to see with her own eyes and touch with her own hands - to interact with the historical characters and manipulate the storyline.

The suspense of the story is generated by the morphological story model. The story is stored in the form of dramatic scenes, containing virtual characters, virtual buildings, storyboards, etc. A story engine application is selecting the next scene to be played out, this in relation to the interaction of the user. (Simplified: if the user accomplishes a scene, she will get another scene that increases the drama and suspense for her.)

Within the scenes, conversational interaction is used to permit a humanlike communication with the actors. This means that the user is interacting with the virtual characters as if they were actors within an interactive theatre.

The system is tested with kids of the age 12-15. Those kids were engaged with the story and gave very positive feedback.

6. CONCLUSION

This chapter describes the impact of conversation and storytelling as short and medium period factors of user satisfaction, to be used in software applications. The author recommends an orientation of the user interface towards human needs to gain a short-period cycle of user satisfaction. This is achieved in regard to assistance and delegation with a conversational interaction metaphor, described as an explicit and symbolic top-down approach. For the medium-period satisfaction of the user, the author suggests the use of humanlike information structures like stories to access information in a way that is easily understandable for the user. The author suggests a morphological story engine as prototyped within the Geist project. The prototype implementation shows two general points:

First, the usage of literary approaches to interactive storytelling is generally possible. Suspense can be increased by using story models drawn from literary theory. Second, to involve the user in a dramatic story, one has to use humanlike interaction metaphors, like conversation, to focus the human on the story progress, rather than on the interface.

7. REFERENCES

Braun, N. (2002a). Automated Narration - the Path to Interactive Storytelling, *Workshop on Narrative and Interactive Learning Environments*, Edinburgh, Scotland.

Braun, N. (2002b). Symbolic Conversation Modeling Used as Abstract Part of the User Interface, *Proccedings of the International Conference in Central Europe on Computer Graphics, Visualization and Computer Vision*, WSCG, Czech.

Braun, N., Schneider, O. and Habinger, G. (2002). Literary Analytical Discussion of Digital Storytelling and Its Relation to Automated Narration, HCI Europe '2002, Workshop *Understanding User Experience: Literary Analysis meets HCI*, London, UK.

Cassell, J., Bickmore, T.W., Billinghurst, M., Campbell, L., Chang, K., Vilhjalmsson, H. and Yan, H. (1999). Embodiment in Conversational Interfaces: Rea, *Proceedings of the CHI'99 Conference on Human Factors in Computing*, ACM Press, New York, USA, pp. 520–527.

Crangle,C., Fagan, E., Lawrence, M.,Carlson, R. W., Erlbaum, M. S., Sherertz, D. D. and Tuttle, M.S. (1997). *Collaborative Conversational Interfaces*, Stanford University, USA.

Harris, M. D. (1985). *Introduction to Natural Language Processing*, Reston Publishing Co. Inc.

Kretschmer, U., Coors, V., Spierling, U., Grasbon, D., Schneider, K., Rojas, I. and Malaka, R. (2001). Meeting the Spirit of History, *Proceedings of the International Symposium on Virtual Reality, Archaeology and Cultural Heritage*, Greece, pp. 161-172.

Laurel, B., Bates, J., Strickland, R. and Abbe, D. (1991). Interface and Narrative Arts: Contributions from Narrative, Drama and Film, *Proceedings of CHI '91*, ACM Press, New York, USA, pp. 381 – 383.

Mateas, M. (1997). *An Oz-Centric Review of Interactive Drama and Believable Agents*, CMU-CS-97-156, Carnegie Mellon University, USA.

Propp, V. (1958). Morphology of the Folktale, in *International Journal of American Linguistic*s, Vol. 24, Nr. 4, Part III, Bloomington, IN.

JONATHAN SYKES AND RICHARD WISEMAN

CHAPTER 20

DECONSTRUCTING GHOSTS

1. FEAR IS FUN

Initially, you might not consider fear and fun as being emotionally related. However, by looking at some activities in which people participate, it is clear that fear can be fun. Rock climbing, bungee jumping, sky-diving, car racing, mountain biking, paint-balling, and white water rafting are all activities where fear is a significant factor in the enjoyment of the sport. It is the presence of adrenalin in the bloodstream, caused by fear, which attracts so many people to such activities.

If fear is to be used as the fun element upon which a video game is constructed, it is important that we choose the correct fear mechanism for exploitation. Gray (1971) assigns fears to one of two categories: learned or innate. Learned fears are those that we can attribute to a previous experience. A fear of hamsters, for example, may occur if bitten by a hamster during childhood. Because *learned* fears are directly linked to an individual's experience, they are not prevalent throughout society. In contrast, those fears which Gray argues to be 'innate' are found to affect a sizeable proportion of the population. Such phobias include fear of snakes, spiders, the dark, strangers, loud noises, falling, heights, death, imaginary creatures, etc. Because mass media, such as film and computer-games, attempt to appeal to the widest possible audience, it is 'innate' fears that are typically exploited.

The fear of ghosts and other supernatural entities is a widespread phenomenon. It is a fear already exploited as a means of having fun. Halloween is a celebration of all things that scare us. It is a time where people delight in both causing fear in others, and the experience of fear itself. Tales of the supernatural are common across all mediums of entertainment, including literature, cinema, theatre, television, and radio. This chapter looks at the possibility of enhancing the fun associated with 'horror' based computer-games by deconstructing paranormal experiences.

1.1 Deconstructing ghosts

As part of the Edinburgh Science Festival 2001, Wiseman, Watt, Stevens, Greening, & O'Keeffe (2002) investigated whether the reputably haunted rooms within

Mark A. Blythe, Andrew F. Monk, Kees Overbeeke and Peter C. Wright *(eds.)*,
Funology: From Usability to Enjoyment, 243—248.

Edinburgh's underground vaults are perceived to be more frightening than other rooms in the vaults (which do not have the same reputation for being haunted). In total, 220 volunteers spent approximately five minutes alone in one of ten vaults. They were then asked to record any unusual occurrences and rate how frightening the experience was. The participants were 'blind' to the reputation of the various vaults; i.e. they were not aware of which were thought to be haunted and which were not. Nonetheless, Wiseman et al.'s findings show a significantly strong correlation between rooms which were rated by participants as being 'more frightening', and rooms that have a reputation for being haunted.

Wiseman et al. comment on structural similarities between rooms that are reputably haunted. Room size was considered to be potential factors which may have led participants to feel unnerved. This is supported by Kaplan's evolutionary theory of environmental psychology, which argues that humans feel uncomfortable in environments where they feel exposed to the threat of attack – such as large open spaces, and dark, isolated environments (Kaplan, 1987). If this is the case, it would seem plausible that in extreme circumstances the human brain could perceive illusory, paranormal-like experiences which convince the agent to flee to a safer place.

If stimuli which induce feelings of a supernatural presence in the real world can be introduced into the virtual world, computer game players will have the chance to enjoy the experience in a safe and controlled environment.

2.   THE VIRTUAL VAULTS

To determine whether the visual properties of a reputably 'haunted' environment might induce fear, a computer generated representation of Edinburgh's underground vaults has been constructed. This study is a repeat of Wiseman et al.'s (2002) investigation. However, instead of visiting the 'real' vaults, participants report how they feel in the computer simulated environment.

2.1 Method

As part of the Edinburgh Science Festival 2002, members of the public were invited to tour the Virtual Vaults. In total, thirty-nine people agreed to participate in the pilot study. Their ages ranged from 12 to 59. Because of the educative nature of the festival, many of the participants were at the younger end of the scale, with the mean age being 27. Children under the age of 12 were not allowed to participate, and children between the ages of 12 and 16 required guardian permission before they could take part.

Each session would begin with an initial briefing, informing participants of the previous study by Wiseman et al (2002) and a short history of the hauntings associated with the vaults. The purpose of the briefing was to gain informed consent, and to increase anxiety in a way that mirrors the traditional ghost tour. To further increase anxiety, the tour of the virtual vaults was conducted on the stage of a local theatre, behind a heavy black curtain. Except for a narrow green spot light, the stage was in darkness. This maintained the 'creepy' context, and also enhanced the display image by increasing the contrast on the visual display unit.

When seated, participants were asked to wear a head-mounted display (HMD). Using the HMD the viewer can browse the simulated world in the same way you view the real world. As the head is moved, the screen updates the visual scene to represent the new perspective. This one-to-one mapping between head movement and screen display increases the level of presence, and can make the participant feel as though they are actually inside the virtual environment.

Movement around the virtual vaults was conducted by the experimenter. This was to allow the participant to concentrate on the visual experience, rather than on the control mechanism. The vault first experienced by participants alternated between participants, as did the direction of exposure. Therefore each trial would begin in a different vault to the last, and the tour would follow either a clockwise or anti-clockwise route through the environment. Participants were led to the centre of each vault where they were left to view their surroundings for approximately 30 seconds, at which point the experimenter would guide the participant through the virtual environment, into the next vault.

When viewing each vault the participant was asked to vocalise their experiences. They were asked to report whether they could see something, hear something, or feel something that might be considered unusual. The experiences were then recorded for later analysis.

2.2 Results

Of the thirty-nine participants who took part in the study, 64% reported an 'unusual' experience. Experiences ranged from apparitional sightings, a sudden chill on entering a virtual vault, feeling of another presence inside the vault, and the perception of breathing on the back of the neck, to the report of an itch, perceptions of levitation, feelings of discomfort and an increase in anxiety.

Table 1. *Distribution of participants and experiences by age group*

Age Group	No. of Participants	No. Reporting Experience	Percentage Reporting at Least One Experience
12 > 16	11	9	82 %
16 > 30	12	5	42 %
30 > 40	6	6	100 %
40 > 50	7	5	71 %
50 >	3	0	0 %

It may seem intuitive that younger participants would be more scared, and therefore more likely to report an experience. However, it can be seen in Table 1 that the ratio of experiences across age groups was largely consistent, with a slight drop (42%) for the 16–30 age group. There were no reported experiences by participants aged above fifty, but the number of participants within this age group was very low.

Table 2. *Distribution of experience across the real and the virtual vaults*

Vault Number	Mean Number of Experiences		Number of Experiences Reported in Virtual Vaults		
	Real World	Virtual World	Visual	Auditory	Somatic
1	1.000	0.077	2	0	1
2	0.440	0.103	2	0	2
3	0.913	0.103	3	0	1
4	1.200	0.128	2	0	3
5	0.625	0.179	3	1	3
6	0.330	0.103	2	0	1
7	0.647	0.026	0	0	1
8	0.632	0.230	6	0	3
9	1.130	0.310	9	1	2
10	0.750	0.231	4	1	4

It is clear from Table 2 that the distribution of experiences in the virtual vaults, and the type of experience reported is not consistent across the vaults. Vault nine has a higher frequency of experiences, and they are predominantly visual in nature. This is in keeping with the paranormal phenomena reported in the real vaults, where vault nine is renowned for its high number of reported experiences. However, Spearman's analyses of correlation found no significant correlation between the distribution of experiences in the real vaults, and the distribution of experiences reported in the virtual vaults.

2.3 Discussion

If the experiences reported in Wiseman's initial experiment were evoked entirely by the visual scene we would expect the distribution of experiences reported in the virtual vaults to map onto the distribution of experiences found in the real vaults. However, this was not the case. We can therefore conclude that either the current simulation fails to deliver the same visual complexity necessary to produce such a response, or that the visual structure is not the exclusive factor in the formation of such experiences. The latter of the two explanations is perhaps more appropriate given that paranormal-like responses were recorded during the study, and that visual experiences were dominant, rather than olfactory (of which there were none) or auditory (of which there were 3). There are many sensory cues in the real environment that are difficult to simulate in a virtual environment. In the real vaults there is an unusual scent and a taste created by the dust, the floor is uneven under foot, there are air pockets which flow through some rooms, and there is the occasional muffled noise which can be heard from the street, three storeys above.

Had such stimuli been included in the simulation, the distribution of reports in the virtual world may have better matched the distribution of responses in the real world.

Although there was no mapping between the real and virtual worlds, the study proved to be particularly successful in producing paranormal-like experiences. Even though participants were aware that the scene they had witnessed was merely a simulation, and therefore presumably free of supernatural forces, they would consistently report experiences normally associated with haunted environments. An explanation of this phenomenon might lie in the participant's anxiety level, and the context provided during the briefing session.

During the briefing session participants were provided with reading material that might build on anxieties already present in the reader. Additionally, participants were isolated behind a curtain and asked to wear the HMD (a piece of technology which is still largely surrounded in mystery), thus raising anxiety levels even further. It is possible that participants were interpreting their anxiety with respect to the context surrounding the experiment, which in turn affected their perception of the virtual environment (Schachter and Singer, 1962). If participants were aware of their own anxiety during the tour, through cognitive evaluation of their physical state they could conclude that they were feeling scared. What is particularly interesting is how the feeling of fear was so powerful that for many the result was a misinterpretation of the stimuli to the point of having paranormal experiences. The projection of anxiety onto ambiguous stimuli is supported by the finding that more visually based experiences occurred in room nine, a room that is visually complex, providing more opportunities to misinterpret an image.

It is clear that some environments can make us uneasy, and it is easy to see how we can frighten ourselves into seeing almost anything. The question is how this information might be used to build games that are scary and fun? If context is as important as suggested here, the building of plausible and involving narratives will help raise the player's level of anxiety and provide a framework to structure their experience. If a strong narrative is interwoven with an environment that builds an expectation of fear, and increases the player's anxiety, it seems that fear is a natural product.

3. ACKNOWLEDGMENTS

Mercat Tours (http://www.mercattours.com) for providing continued access to the underground vaults in Edinburgh

Ian Baker, Sarah Haywood, Rosie Pragnell and Caroline Parker for their participation on this project.

4. REFERENCES

Gray, J. (1971). *Psychology of Fear and Stress*. London: Weidenfeld & Nicolson.
Kaplan, S. (1987). Aesthetics, affect, and cognition. *Environment and Behavior, 19(1)*, 3-32.

Schachter, S. & Singer, J. (1962). Cognitive, social and physiological determinants of emotional state. *Psychological Review*, 63, 379-399.

Wiseman, R., Watt, C., Stevens, P., Greening, E., & O'Keeffe, C. (2002). An investigation into alleged hauntings. *British Journal of Psychology*, (accepted for publication).

JENNICA FALK

CHAPTER 21

INTERFACING THE NARRATIVE EXPERIENCE

1. INTRODUCTION

I have a research interest in interfaces to games that are played, not on computers, but in the physical environment and that ultimately transform the world into a game board for computer games. Of specific interest to this agenda are activities that are narrative and social in their nature, not only in the interaction between people, but also in people's interaction with the physical world. Having spent time role-playing in online environments, in awe of their mechanisms for story generation and interactive game worlds, I still have to argue their failure to provide convincing and truly interactive environments for narrative experiences. Put differently, the unmistakable division between character and player, and between character environment and player environment in online role-playing, characteristically fail to induce a desirable level of suspension of disbelief. In contrast, *live role-playing games* offer particularly relevant examples of games where the physical world is adapted as a mature interface to an engaging and creative immersion in an interactive, social, and narrative context. They support social and collective exercises in emergent narrative creation where every participant, is part of the design effort. These narratives take place in a magical and imaginary domain in the cross-section between physical reality and fantastic fiction offering the kind of immersion that most interactive narratives promise as a technical goal, but have yet to deliver, where there is no physical division between player, character, and narrative. Some might argue that this level of immersion is the holy grail of interactive fiction and indeed entertainment, where the narrative thread, or content if you will, is embedded in physical locations and in objects around us, creating a tangible, ubiquitous, and even context-sensitive interface for the participants or players to unleash at.

In this chapter, I share observations and analysis drawn from participating in live role-playing events, primarily in the *Lorien Trust* game system. By studying the use of artefacts and physical game locations in this process, and observing how stories emerge from the interaction between players I hope to inform design thinking about interfaces to *narrative experiences* and to provide insights relevant to the topic of this book – *design for enjoyment*.

Mark A. Blythe, Andrew F. Monk, Kees Overbeeke and Peter C. Wright *(eds.),*
Funology: From Usability to Enjoyment, 249—256.

2.   LIVE ROLE-PLAYING GAMES

To define live role-playing (LRP) games is a knotty task, but for the purposes of this text, a definition that puts forward its essence is that LRP is a *dramatic* and *narrative* game form in which players portray fictional characters that come to life in a *web of stories*. The narrative emerges in the interaction between *characters*, *objects*, and *physical locations*. By dramatic, it is implied that roles are assumed in person rather than through virtual or abstract means, and by narrative it is implied that a main product or goal of these games is of a story nature.

Figure 1. *Live Role-players at Lorien Trust's 'The Gathering' in 2002*

Almost exclusively fictitious, the purpose of LRP games is primarily the dramatization of a make-believe world. They are fiction adventures, and although governed by a body of rules and background information that frame both individual role-play and the progression of the overall storyline, they are predominantly improvisational. Characters with ambitions and professions, dreams and hopes, come together to interact, react, and impact the narrative outcome in an unrehearsed but still measured fashion. While games are not stories, the narrative element of LRP is nothing less than pervasive, and the stories that are generated in the role-play are interactive stories that are lived and experienced with all senses. LRP spawns a highly engaging and immersive narrative environment in which the story is read and written simultaneously, inviting participation and providing the guidance to allow players to perform and partake by putting their creative imagination to work.

2.1 *Live vs. online role-playing*

An important difference between online role-playing games (RPG) and LRP is clearly noticeable in how LRP players interact directly with the narrative, while online environments do not allow for the same sophisticated sensory engagement. This is primarily due to the fact that our means of interacting with the real world (our perception of and navigation in space, sensory input, how we organize and manipulate artefacts, and so on) are transformed into abstractions in online environments. This highlights the substantial difference in using the world as a *metaphor* for interaction, as in the case of online games, and using it as a *medium* for interaction, as in the case of LRP where the immediacy of the physical world is extremely relevant. The online role-player is a puppeteer while the LRP player is a person going through a transformation into a character. One of the reasons LRP worlds are so engaging is that the experiences a character is subjected to also happen to its player.

3. LRP CASE STUDY

Drawing from the understanding that the physical world is a powerful facilitator of LRP games, a compelling design challenge for digital narratives and games is to extend them into the physical domain. If we create game worlds where points of interaction are not confined to a virtual environment and a personal interface, but rather support distributed and tangible interaction qualities, we can make advances towards truly immersive narrative experiences. Some previous work within this agenda includes the *Tangible MUD* (Falk: 2002) project where computer game mechanisms were designed to reside in physical objects – a spell-book and a desk lamp – and the *Pirates!* project (Björk, *et al* 2001) in which physical locations were mapped to computer game locations. The key motivation in the Tangible MUD project was to unveil what kinds of sensory gratification tangible interaction points can add to computer gameplay. The key motivation with *Pirates!* was to restore the social dimension of play to computer games by bringing the players back to the physical environment. Integrating tangible game objects and locations, future entertainment and interactive narratives will provide a "sensory proof" of its reality that is in stark contrast to the reality the interaction space of graphical games offer. LRP games offer the opportunity to further this research in that they allow us to study how the richness of the physical world supports and enhances engagement and story creation within the game context.

3.1 *Players, costume, and character identity*

The nature of character interaction in LRP games typically causes them to depend on social structures that cannot be formalized under a rules system. LRP players bring their personal attributes and social skills to their characters, which become highly viable resources in their role-play. Additionally, a character concept typically evolves through the interaction with other characters. This suggests a strong dependence on active and interactive players, which in turn indicates that the challenge of the game is less technical, and more of an interpersonal nature.

Three aspects of how players transform into game personas are of particular relevance to this study. Firstly, attention to detail in costume and accessories and other personal props is typically great, to the point of a player using very different costumes when playing different characters. Costumes are important instruments for supporting a player's transformation into and identification with their character. Secondly, as costume is tailor-made for a character, it serves as an outward statement about the character, thus not only strengthening the individual role, but also the interaction with others. Thirdly, a lot of effort is spent on preparation; most players will have spent a significant amount of time making costumes, planning strategies, synchronising actions with other players, and so forth. The time and attention spent on taking on a role reflects the dedication to the player culture, which ultimately is highly appreciated by the community they are part of. Contrast this transformation with the graphical representation avatars provide players of computer games. Donning a costume and performing a role in person is a representation of character that has yet to be made possible in computer games.

Figure 2. *The narrative emerges in the interaction between players*

3.1.1   Objects and Locations

The physical environment is the game world, or the stage on which the narrative is performed. This integration of game space and physical space creates a graspable game environment that players have to literally navigate in order to reveal the narrative content. Physical structures may be erected to enhance the game world, serving as specific locations of importance to the narrative, and where location-dependant role-play takes place. The physicality of the game world contributes to creating a highly immersive and tangible experience, in which the narrative induces very real physical sensations such as fear and excitement.

LRP players frequently use physical artefacts as props and tools in their role-play, primarily to back up their character roles. Commonly referred to as *physical representations* (or *physreps*), they represent game objects with tangible presence and functionality in the game. Mechanisms named *lammies* (because they are laminated pieces of paper) formalize physreps' functionality in the game. Figure 3 shows an example, an amber talisman that protects its wearer from certain diseases. The numbers printed on the lammie are codes referring to properties of the artefact, such as its value, origin, if it is magical, and so forth, which players with the appropriate skills can check against so called lore-sheets. In this fashion, a lammie is something of a *plug-and-play* feature of the game world. It offers a way to sanctify and transform arbitrary objects into official game artefacts.

Figures 3 & 4. *Physical artefacts populate the game environment*

4.   PRINCIPLES FOR DESIGN

To computer game designers, the game engine is a piece of software that simulates and renders the game world. It deals with e.g. visual effects, such as the animation of characters and objects, the texture of surfaces and other details in the environment. In LRP games, what I refer to as the game engine, in a relaxed sense of the term, are mechanisms that render textures of a more cultural nature. Understanding these mechanisms may be an important step in understanding what factors make successful interactive or game narratives. Which factors make up more and which make up less enjoyable or engaging experiences are still subject for further research, but there are properties of LRP games that are instrumental to creating the conditions for engaging and creative role-playing, which suggests implications for design. They are primarily motivated by the ways in which LRP environments extend and transform the physical world into environments that nurture and encourage players' engagement.

4.1 A believable game world

Computer gaming environments are increasingly realistic in using the physical world as a model for their game worlds. Many games have as a feature next to photographic graphical representations of the game environment in their attention to detail in scenery. LRP environments are founded on a different attention to detail, where the game world is believable and convincing because there is no separation between the game world and the physical world. We can note that physreps, including the environment itself, rarely take token shapes or forms, but are instead carefully crafted to convey purpose through physical manifestation. If an amber pendant is needed to make an amulet – such as the one in figure 3 – players use an amber pendant, not a feather or a stone. Elaborately populating the environment with theatrical props and game artefacts, as exemplified by the old library filled witch books (figure 5), and an alchemy lab (figure 6), is one way to make the players believe in and agree with what happens to their characters. Allowing the game to extend into the physical world is key to fostering coherent and meaningful role-playing relationships between characters and the game world.

Figures 5 & 6. *Convincing game environments, populated with game artefacts*

4.2 Magical interfaces

While believability is important, at least on the level of physical form, LRP worlds are typically rendered fantastic rather than realistic in regards to functionality. Therefore, what you see may not necessarily be what you get, and if that message is encoded and reflected in the design of an artefact, it often sparks curiosity and beckons the player to interact with the object. As an example of magical objects, take the puzzle in figure 4, which when solved not only spells out a message, but also functions as a key that unlocks the vessel that contains a particularly nasty lich creature. In this example, the player will know what to do, or how to interact with the puzzle, but cannot be certain what the result of that interaction is. The fact that it begins to suggest its functionality – the word "Death" is being spelled out when the pieces are put together – is part of encoding this particular artefact's magical message. When the game world is designed with mystery and concealed facts in mind, it adds to creating an alluring, if not seductive, environment that strengthens players' interest and commitment to engage with the game world. Interestingly, players are habitually sensitive to the fact that game artefacts often have unexpected effects, and their interaction with them is reflected in their typically curious but very careful approach to them.

4.3 Tangible and aesthetic interfaces

Aesthetics play an important role in creating engagement and maintaining the appeal of the environment. It deals with the expressive identity of things, their form and shape and how we experience them with our senses, and is of great consequence in rendering the reality of the LRP game world and making it meaningful to the players. While aesthetics traditionally deals with what appeals to the senses in terms of e.g. shapes and colours, what is emphasised here are the aspects that aid the *elegance of make-believe*. They are part of making the unreal real and giving integrity to the game world. Tangible interfaces, props, and costume, play a significant role, not only in that they are physical details that support the extension and manifestation of the game world in the physical world, but also because humans are inherently good at relating to and manipulating such objects.

4.4 Dedicated vs. token representation

Most objects and locations are incorporated into game play with context of use in mind, which again is reflected in the design. It is noteworthy that important game artefacts are often highly dedicated, specialised, and articulated tools for role-play, as in the case of the puzzle in figure 4, which is a unique item created for one specific purpose. This tends to put emphasis on the design of interfaces that communicate contextual functionality, rather than being generic or universal in their physical appearance. When designed with their context of use in mind, they are powerful tools in transforming the physical world into a game world. The costumes players don and the accessories they choose to illustrate their characters' positions or professions are some examples of this principle, as suggested by figures 1 and 2.

5. CONCLUSION

Our knowledge of the physical world and the skills with which we engage with it are powerful facilitators to LRP games. The artefacts, costumes, game-specific locations and buildings transform the physical world into a magic place where fantastic narratives are spawned. The level of engagement such a game environment creates –

with no physical division between player, character, space, and narrative – is the kind of immersion many interactive narratives and computer games seek to achieve but where they also fail. By looking at the appropriation of artefacts and physical game locations in LRP games, and observing how the stories emerge from the interaction between all these components, we can inform the design process for interfaces to interactive narrative applications.

6. ACKNOWLEDGEMENTS

This research is carried out in the Story Networks group at Media Lab Europe in Dublin, MIT Media Laboratory's European Research Partner. I want to acknowledge the support from the member's of this group, particularly that of Glorianna Davenport who has offered invaluable comments and support. Mark Blythe and Peter Wright were instrumental to the process of writing. Lastly I want to acknowledge the passion of LRP gamers and organizers – wherever you are.

7. REFERENCES

Björk, S., Falk, J., Hansson, R., and Ljungstrand, P. (2001). Pirates!: Using the Physical World as a Game Board. In *Proceedings of Interact'01*, Tokyo, Japan.
Costikyan, G. *I Have No Words & I Must Design,* http://www.costik.com/nowords.html (2002-11-20)
Costikyan, G. *Where Stories End and Games Begin,* http://www.costik.com/gamnstry.html (2002-11-20)
Crawford, C. *The Art of Computer Game Design,* http://www.erasmatazz.com/Library.html (2002-11-20)
Falk, J. (2002). The World as Game Board. *Position Statement, Workshop on Funology at CHI 2002.*

ERIK BLANKINSHIP AND PILAPA ESARA

CHAPTER 22

WHOSE LINE IS IT ANYWAY?
ENABLING CREATIVE APPROPRIATION OF TELEVISION

1. INTRODUCTION

"Live long and prosper" and "beam me up" are popular quotes from the Star Trek
television series. Quoting television can be considered a form of media
appropriation. If people are given the ability to manipulate video clips of television
directly will they construct their own media works? A software tool called talkTV
provides this form of access by chunking television into video clips of dialogue that
can be re-sequenced. An evaluation of this software tool occurred with Star Trek
fans at an annual science fiction convention. The exploratory findings of this study
suggest that if given access and the ability to re-purpose television, people enjoy
constructing short fan films.

1.1 Television fans as producers

Television shows come as packaged entertainment: well-assembled stories,
professional actors, and soundtracks all fitted together. They are generally designed
as passive entertainment. The audience might discuss the show around the water
cooler or online, but for the most part the audience is intended to *consume*
television.

   Not content with just watching their favourite shows, television fans have a
history of *producing* their own fictional stories. Fans of the Star Trek television
series are the most well known for constructing original fictions derived from the
show (Jenkins, 1992). Some fans' short films involve appropriating soundtracks,
sound effects, costumes, and digital star ship models. Music videos are another
format for fan appropriation in which video clips from the show are re-edited to
music so as to create new meanings dictated by the chosen song (Jenkins, 1992).
These activities fall under the banner of "fan fiction", which is replete with its own
sub-genres such as slash fiction, erotic stories between two characters separated by a
/ in the title (such as Kirk/Spock romances) (Jenkins, 1992). Fans create meanings
separate from those intended by the producers of the television series. In this way,
they claim ownership of media by integrating it into their own creations.

257

Mark A. Blythe, Andrew F. Monk, Kees Overbeeke and Peter C. Wright *(eds.)*,
Funology: From Usability to Enjoyment, 257—263.
© 2003 *Kluwer Academic Publishers. Printed in the Netherlands.*

Not all fans have the time or skills to easily create their own films. How can people's media appropriation be facilitated? As a research problem, the construction of fan movies was conceptualised in terms of its component parts. Our intuition is that television dialogue is a well-established way of appropriating media – people quote television shows often – so that with access to source material, fans could easily construct films. talkTV is a software tool designed to search television clips via dialogue. Our testing of this application among a group of Star Trek fans reveals useful insights into how fans appropriate media. Our work is a contribution toward a future in which this activity might be commonplace (Davis, 1997) and possibly automated (Sack & Davis, 1994).

1.2 Engineering

Dialogue is encoded into most television broadcasts as subtitled Closed Captions (CC), providing a ready index into a television show from which to segment video clips. talkTV requires fans to enter a text query into a database of television programs that retrieves video clips in which the queried words are spoken. For example, a search for "warp factor" retrieves clips in which characters speak these words. talkTV's database consists of four seasons of *Star Trek: The Next Generation*, providing about 100 hours of searchable dialogue. The tool also allows fans to create title slides by superimposing text over selected background videos. The backgrounds were pre-selected to provide different establishing shots featuring the star ship.

Figure 1. *The talkTV user interface. On the left are the search results in the form of video thumbnails. Clips are dragged to the storyboard panel on the right.*

Video clips of dialogue and titles can be dragged into and sequenced in talkTV's storyboard panel. Once added to the storyboard, video clips can be previewed in sequence as a short film. For example, a title slide reading, "Alien Encounter!" could be followed by a video clip of a character saying, "Sensor report!" followed by a clip of another character saying "An enemy ship!" or "Weird energy signatures..." depending on the fan's story. Fans can also browse completed fan films and modify them, so that multiple endings can be generated from one initial film.

2.   TO BOLDLY GO...

To study if talkTV enables fan to be producers of television, we decided to make it available to science fiction fans at an annual convention. Each participant was given a few words of instruction and was seated at their own computer terminal. Observations were taken of the participant's keystrokes and mouse movements, their body language and their comments. Completed movies were queued to a display monitor which looped prior completed movies. Immediately after participants viewed their movie publicly, they were asked to be interviewed. The informal interview was brief using open-ended questions to elicit information regarding people's initial intents, experiences and opinions.

In total, seventeen men and women were observed and interviewed. None of the participants appeared distracted or annoyed by either our note-taking or the comments of those in the crowd regarding their editing. Participants varied in ages from early twenties to early fifties with the average age being 33. The majority of participants were male (88%). Seven participants (41%) returned to either finish their movies or to create new movies. Although session times varied, on average, participants spent approximately 50 minutes in total working on their movies. Participants had varying degrees of computer experience. Some people used computers occasionally for e-mail whereas others used computers as part of their jobs. Several participants were experienced with video-editing software whereas others found the concept of pull-down menus and key word searches to be unfamiliar.

2.1 Findings

In total, 21 fan movies were created. The majority of participants endeavoured to create "mini-episodes" where continuity was key. These mini-episodes attempted to emulate the stereotypical Star Trek episode by beginning with a Captain's log, followed by a semblance of plot and conclusion. A refinement of the "mini-episode" was structured around characters asking questions and varied responses repeated to humorous effect. Several participants created films centred upon a keyword (i.e. "Klingon") without any attempt to create a plot or to maintain continuity between locations or situations. This kind of film was prevalent among the earliest users implying a development in film construction, as later users were able to view other's movies.

Interviews and observations reveal aspects of the participants' motives, strategies and thoughts regarding their experiences. Initially, participants began their sessions with one of two intents: to explore and see what could be done, or to create a narrative based on a theme or situation. Once they started, they began to form secondary goals. For example, some users found that they were forced to create a serious story rather than a humorous one. Others endeavoured to achieve continuity in their film by establishing a flow between the visual images, the lines of dialogue, the story line, or all three together.

While participants approached their filmmaking in various ways, common strategies emerged. For instance, it became clear to most of the participants that the software was dialogue-driven. Since participants were given minimal instructions and a few were not familiar with key words searches, this characteristic of the software was not readily apparent. Thus the selection of keywords to query became in itself a particular strategy. Another strategy derived from the lack of space to store clips. Some participants used their storyboard area as a kind of "image bank" placing their selected clips in that area and arranging them into a sequence later. Others placed clips on the storyboard in a linear fashion often having to use one keyword or memorizing keywords, in order to bring up intended clips when they were needed.

All the participants stated that they enjoyed their experiences. Commonalities between the participant's responses highlight three aspects of the talkTV experience which participants found to be "fun." The technical possibilities facilitated by the software, the experience of the actual editing process and the end product are all aspects of what made talkTV enjoyable. Many participants stated how fun it was as a technical possibility to actually be able to "make a mini episode". This was particularly true for a couple of users, who said they had never seen anything like this.

In addition to what one could do with the software, people enjoyed editing the television clips:

– "[It's] fun to query clips and then you can cut and paste…my own editing lab at my fingertips." (I-10)
– "It was funny to select [clips] and make them fit. [And] taking them out of context." (I-11,12)

These quotes emphasize the high degree to which participants enjoyed the editing process.

To edit effectively it is important to be able to query for meaningful (i.e: usable) clips. Those persons with a comprehensive knowledge of the television series found that it was fun to test themselves. As one fan commented, "It's a good way of testing your knowledge of the show. It triggers recall of episodes" (I-8). Several of the users had memorized whole seasons of the television show. Their ability to remember the scripts of various scenes enabled them to query efficiently for specific characters or locales. Less familiar fans still found the query searches "fun" because they were able to re-watch the television clips.

Although enjoyable, the editing process required thought and was in varying degrees, challenging. As one user described it:

— "I couldn't be pro-active today. I had an idea for [the character] Wes, had to search for people by chance. I was lucky if I found [a clip of] Wes speaking" (I-6)

This participant's frustration with trying to query for clips with certain characters emphasizes part of the challenge of searching dialogue for visual images. He later described his experience as "fun" once he found a "rhythm." His comments reveal an additional aspect of what makes talkTV "fun" – being able to master the software. Be it "coming up with the idea" (I-17) or "finding a way to tie it together" (I-4), the participants were proud of their ability to effectively mine the dialogue to create an actual movie. One user (I-19) described it as a "problem-solving" challenge. Once they mastered the "challenge", it became "fun." The participants often described their sense of accomplishment in terms of feeling like an actual director or screenwriter, occupations which affirm their appropriation of the media.

A final aspect of talkTV's fun is the creation of an "end product." When asked, participants generally responded favourably to the public feedback from their movie:

— "It was flattering that [one of the co-authors] laughed…I could sit for hours and tweak [my movie]." (I-9)

— "Heck, I was a little embarrassed and a little proud. [It was] something I had sat down and I did." (I-13)

— "[It's] cool getting to hear people laugh. It was fun when finished." (I-17)

A couple of participants who were dissatisfied with their movies faulted their own inexperience rather than the software. Several users felt they needed to "play with it" more, and many felt that greater familiarity with the software would enable them to make better movies, in their eyes.

Although using talkTV was enjoyable, it could benefit from refinement. Common complaints about the software included the desire for a bigger clip library, the need for the interface to be more intuitive and the inability to search for characters or certain categories of clips. These complaints suggest that users would like to continue working with talkTV and to do more with it. Rather than criticizing the functionality of the application, the users were more concerned with how to improve its pre-existing interface and capabilities.

In summary, the participants of this study appeared to enjoy the use of talkTV. Not only were users able to make movies, but they described their experiences as "obviously fun". In this context, talkTV was fun because a) it enabled people to make "mini episodes" and to be "a director", b) the editing process was enjoyable and facilitated creativity, and c) their completed movie showed mastery of the software and was typically well received by their peers.

3.   DISCUSSION

We tested if talkTV utilizes the popular Star Trek series as its source material. In order to find suitable participants for the software's evaluation, we implemented our study at a convention based on the series. Although we cannot posit that talkTV *enabled* fans to make movies, we have gained insights about how it was used to make movies. While participants actively engaged the dialogue-search, there was a desire to be able to search for non-dialogue based items, such as explosions. This suggests that other forms of indexing video for repurposing may be useful complements to a dialogue-based search (Davis, 1995) (Bove, Dakss, Chalom, & Agamanolis, 2000) (Mills, Pye, Hollinghurst, & Wood, 2000).

In addition, we found support for the common-sense notion that if television re-editing is fun, television viewers will appropriate the media to make their own films. The various aspects of fun revealed in this study are related to the quality and popularity of the source material and the manner in which their access to this material is facilitated. For example, participants were able to make films out of the actual clips from a popular television series rather than pre-made facsimiles, thereby enabling users to make "authentic" mini-episodes. An insight gained from this study is that users find it enjoyable to have access to original source material.

Connected to this aspect of fun is the shared knowledge about Star Trek between the participant filmmaker and their audience. The filmmaker takes for granted that their audience will meet them half way in making sense of their efforts. A brief introduction of a character or reference can have large significance for the right audience. For example, among the fan films made, a few fans inserted the character "Q" without any apparent introduction or plot connection. This character would appear seemingly out-of-place to viewers unfamiliar with his established role as an unpredictable omni-powerful being. In this way, part of the fun of talkTV derives from creating well-produced pieces, which others can appreciate.

Given the effort people put into establishing a meaningful plot and maintaining continuity within their short films, we argue that talkTV provides "hard fun". That does not mean "it's fun in spite of being hard... [but rather] it's fun because it's hard" (Papert, 1998). It is an activity that engages the subjects and compels them to do their best work. This kind of fun motivates television viewers to actively re-appropriate their favourite show. In a broader sense, this study highlights the possibility that television production is not just for fans but also for the typical television viewer. A different television audience not known for media appropriation might enjoy using a tool like talkTV to author their own show of choice. If television is rendered malleable and accessible, a wave of fan films for other genres might begin to supplant what is already playing.

4. ACKNOWLEDGMENTS

Special thanks to AlmaMedia and the sponsors of the MIT Media Laboratory.

5. REFERENCES

Bove, M., Jr., Dakss, J., Chalom, E., & Agamanolis, S. (2000). Hyperlinked Video Research at the MIT Media Laboratory. *IBM Systems Journal, 39, no. 3-4.*

Davis, M. (1995). *Media Streams: Representing Video for Retrieval and Repurposing.* Massachusetts Institute of Technology, Cambridge.

Davis, M. (1997). Garage Cinema and the Future of Media Technology. *Communications of the ACM, 40*(2), 42-48.

Jenkins, H. (1992). *Textual poachers : television fans & participatory culture.* New York: Routledge.

Mills, T. J., Pye, D., Hollinghurst, N. J., & Wood, K. R. (2000). *AT&TV: Broadcast Television and Radio Retrieval.* Paper presented at the RIAO 2000 (Recherche d'Informations Assistée par Ordinateur; Computer Assisted Information Retrieval), Paris.

Papert, S. (1998). Does Easy Do It? Children, Games, and Learning. *Game Developer, 88.*

Sack, W., & Davis, M. (1994). *IDIC: Assembling Video Sequences from Story Plans and Content Annotations.* Paper presented at the Proceedings of IEEE International Conference on Multimedia Computing and Systems, Boston, Massachusetts.

CAROLINE HUMMELS, KEES OVERBEEKE AND
AADJAN VAN DER HELM

CHAPTER 23

*THE INTERACTIVE INSTALLATION ISH: IN SEARCH OF RESONANT
HUMAN PRODUCT INTERACTION*

1.   THE HUMAN AS A WHOLE

The history of HCI can, in many ways, be seen as an ongoing attempt to capitalize on
the full range of human skills and abilities. (Paul Dourish, 2001)

In the beginning, computer science and HCI manifested themselves through encoded
patterns (e.g. punch cards) and command lines, thus calling upon the cognitive skills
of users. The shift to visual computing with a desktop and a mouse that was tightly
coupled to an on-screen cursor, expanded the interaction range towards perceptual-
motor skills. If we look at the current developments within HCI, like tangible
interaction, affective and social computing, we see a refinement towards the use of
perceptual-motor skills and the urge to incorporate emotional skills. It seems that
respect for the human as a whole has come into vogue, at least within a part of the
HCI research community.

This emphasis on the human as a whole can also be seen in the shift of
contextual focus. The computer is leaving the sphere of the workplace, thus
widening the spectrum of efficiency, productivity and 'getting things done' with
values like curiosity, playfulness, intimacy and creativity (Caenepeel, 2002;
Overbeeke et al., 1999). The computer has entered our daily and social life. It is no
longer just a means to perform our work; it helps us to pursue our lives (Gaver,
2002). In this way, the world of HCI has united with the world of product design.

Although this is an interesting and challenging way to go, it isn't an easy one,
especially in our contemporary culture, which has lost its unifying ideology (Branzi,
1989). We do not only have to develop the next generation of digital products with
which we can pursue our lives, we also have to decide what kind of life and society
we want these products to support. Buchanan (1998), Marzano (1996), Borgmann

Mark A. Blythe, Andrew F. Monk, Kees Overbeeke and Peter C. Wright *(eds.)*,
Funology: From Usability to Enjoyment, 265—274.

(1987) and Saul (1997) all plead for respect and humanism; for 'real' individualism, in which the individual is part of society and takes responsibility for that society. This implies that we shouldn't design products for a universal audience, or "the consumer". Products should be personal pathways that allow individuals to find and create their own experiences (Hummels, 2000b).

'*Capitalizing on the full range of human skills and abilities*', as Dourish (2001) mentioned in light of the history of HCI, is a condition for designing 'contexts for experiences'. However, we would like to expand the focus from human skills to the concept of *resonance*. In the remaining part of this text, we will explain this concept and our reasons for advancing it. Moreover, we discuss on the basis of the interactive installation called *ISH*, how to find salient aspects of resonance.

2.   RESONANCE

Resonance stems from the theory of ecological or direct perception, which also engendered the term affordance; a term that Norman introduced to the HCI community. Gibson (1979) used the term in combination with a radio metaphor to clarify the directness of our perceptual system. A radio station broadcasts information, i.e. waves with a particular radio frequency that is used by that particular station. The detection of radio waves is based on the principle of resonance. Given that many frequencies (stations) reach a receiver from the antenna, proper tuning of the receiver causes a current in it to resonate in response to one of the incoming signals, and not others.

In case of e.g. visual perception, the radio waves in this metaphor stand for light that is reflected (broadcasted) by our environment (the radio station). Our eyes (the antenna) let the signals pass through, and we (the radio) must tune in to the information. For example, if we want to write a message, we are tuned in to information in our environment that affords us to write. Thus when a pencil comes into view, our perceptual system resonates to that information (Michaels and Carello, 1981).

However, resonance does not only relate to our perceptual-motor skills. It relates to our cognitive and emotional skills too. Moreover, it is not only a temporal response, e.g. we want to write, so we resonate with a pen. We also resonate with products because we are people with certain needs, desires and intentions, a social and cultural history and position etc. Consequently, we do not resonate to the same products. To elaborate on the writing example, one person might resonate with a cheap disposable pen, another person with that fountain pen he got from his grandpa and another person might resonate with the I-Mac that he bought with his savings. What's the *real* difference?

Figure 1. The first author's Sunbeam toaster

Let us explore the concept of resonance a bit further with an example. The first author resonates with a Sunbeam toaster that she bought approximately ten years ago at a jumble sale. She resonates with it, because it functions better than well. It has a small catch which causes the slices to be automatically transported downwards at a calm pace and upwards again when they have a nice tan. This calm pace enhances the feeling of luxury and Sunday morning relaxation, which she associates with toast. She considers the toaster to be visually and tactilely pleasant, simple and easy to clean. It expresses for her respect and friendliness, which triggers her vivid imagination. The slow transportation of slices gives the impression that the toaster is almost saying: *"Come, hand me your bread. I will take good care of it and produce the most delicious toast, specially for you."* Due to this invitation, she places the slices of bread with a gentle and elegant gesture into the toaster. Finally, she bought it relatively cheap after some haggling, which she experienced as an additional advantage, especially in the beginning.

This example shows, that it is not just about tuning a product to one's skills, which makes a person resonate with a product. A resonant interaction is the result of a mixture of different ingredients like usability, human skills (cognitive, perceptual-motor and emotional), richness of the senses, individual and social needs, desires and interests, personal history, ways of acquiring the product, context of use (situation, timing, environment, social setting), aesthetics of interaction, intimacy, engagement and openness to find and create one's own meaning, story and ritual.

This implies three things. Firstly, resonance can be a concept that provides respectful and humanistic HCI/products, which allow individuals to find and create their own experiences.

Secondly, resonance can only be found in the ensemble of ingredients, thus requiring a holistic design approach. For example, Norman (2002) argues that pleasant and attractive products actually work better, providing that they are not used in emergency situations. Thus the whole is greater than the sum of its parts. This implies that people involved in the development of HCI and product design, e.g. designers, computer scientists, engineers, psychologists, marketers, should work together, combine their knowledge and develop integral solutions, in order to attain resonant products and interaction.

Thirdly, because of the personal character of resonant interaction, HCI and product developers should involve people for whom they are developing products right from the start, for inspiration, information, discussion, evaluation, testing and validation of resonant interaction.

Resonance is rather an unexplored area due to its complexity. Why do some people resonate with a certain product, while others do not? Can one formulate guidelines for designing products that evoke resonance? Within our own research we study resonance by building and testing interactive installations and a variety of products with the same function. Let us discuss one of these installations called *ISH*.

3. A DESIGN EXAMPLE: THE INTERACTIVE INSTALLATION CALLED
ISH

Figure 2. *The interactive installation called ISH (Image and Sound Handling)*

ISH (Image and Sound Handling) is an interactive multi-media installation that allows a group of people to create together an atmosphere through visuals and music. It is a dynamic research environment which allows us to evaluate resonant interaction through loops of (re)designing, building and testing. At the moment *ISH* consists of eight tangible products and a projection screen. Every product has its own character with respect to feed forward, feed back, time-delay, temptation, clarity etc., which allows us to evaluate different aspects of resonance. For example, is it necessary that a product shows what the user can expect after he carries out an action? Should a product seduce a person to explore it? How devastating is time-delay for resonance? Should one pursue subtle interaction? What makes interaction engaging and beautiful?

Hitherto, *ISH* focuses on tangible interaction. This doesn't mean that this is the only way to interact with products. We will explore other forms of multi-modal interaction in the future through *ISH*. However, we started with tangible interaction, because you inescapably handle objects in an expressive way, thus linking two important aspects of resonance.

We describe shortly the different components, before evaluating the installation with respect to resonance.

Figure 3. *Gatherish*

A person selects audio samples and images by moving his hands above and through the sand of *Gatherish*. The position of the hands and the character of the movements determine the expression of the sounds and images.

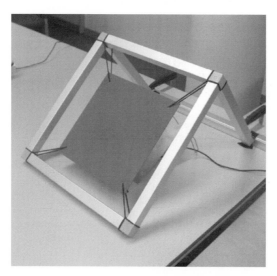

Figure 4. *Smallish*

Smallish alters the volume of the audio part and the size of the image in the active layer (which is selected through *Compositish*). The volume and the size increase by pushing the square plane.

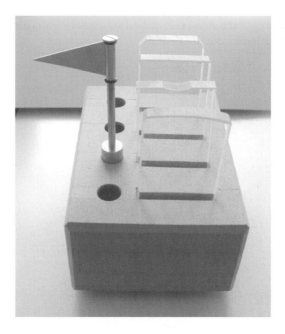

Figure 5. *Compositish*

Four sequentially placed images containing holes create the visual environment. A person determines with four tangible transparent cards the order of the four layers. Moreover, one of the layers can be made active by placing a banner next to it. One can manipulate the image in the active layer using *Gatherish*, *Smallish*, *Stirish* and *Jitterish*.

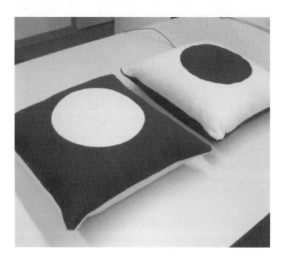

Figure 6. *Stirish*

The difference in force exerted to the pillows of *Stirish* alters the position and orientation of the selected image.

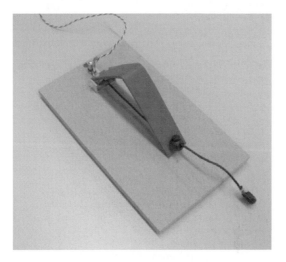

Figure 7. *Jitterish*

ISH has its own character, which means that the images have their own movements, depending on the mood of *ISH*. These movements are influenced by the kind and number of actions the users make on the eight products. Moreover, one can set the mood (tensed – relaxed) by increasing or decreasing the tension (curve) of *Jitterish*.

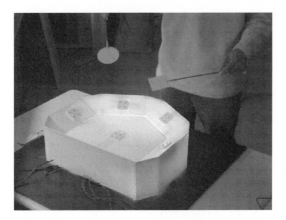

Figure 8. *Acoustish*

The audio part consists of sounds and rhythms, which can be interactively manipulated. The expression of the sounds and the rhythm can be altered with

Acoustish by making bridges between four infrared senders and receivers, using several reflectors.

Figure 9. *Rhythmish*

The expression of the visual pattern of tokens that is created with *Rhythmish* fits the expression of the rhythm section. For example, a low number of tokens placed in an orderly way, creates a simple and relaxed rhythm.

Figure 10. *Mixish*

Mixish determines the balance between *Acoustish* and *Rhythmish*. Shifting the cylinder towards *Acoustish* puts an emphasis on *Acoustish*, and shifting it towards *Rhythmish* fades *Acoustish* away.

4.   EVALUATION *ISH* AND CONCLUSIONS WITH RESPECT TO RESONANCE

ISH was primarily evaluated by observing people interacting with *ISH* and each other. During open days, demonstrations and conferences, we observed the behaviour and remarks of an audience that was unacquainted with our research.

Their behaviour and remarks showed that the overall installation, enabling people to generate visuals and music, resonate with most spectators during interaction. However, the social aspect of it, i.e. creating this atmosphere together, is still underexposed. This is partly the result of the set-up. All products faced towards a vertical screen, thus complicating natural interaction between people. The successor of the present set-up will arrange all products in a circle around a horizontal projection of the visuals.

The individual products show different reactions with respect to resonance. They can be divided into three groups.

For the vast majority *Smallish* (figure 4) and *Rhythmish* (figure 9) seem dead on target with respect to resonance. People considered them to be extremely clear and pleasurable. The mapping was considered natural in both cases: for *Smallish* between distance / force and size / volume and for *Rhythmish* between the visual pattern and the resulting rhythm. Moreover, the subtle flexibility when pushing the square of *Smallish*, caused by the elastic suspension was experienced as very pleasurable and resonant. The intimate and expectant moment of closing the box and hearing the created rhythm, seem to enhance the resonance with *Rhythmish*.

The feeling of sand through one's fingers, made *Gatherish* (figure 3) at least for a short period of time very attractive, similar to *Stirish* (figure 6) and *Acoustish* (figure 8). However, only a minority of the users experienced these three products as resonant over a longer period of time, because they require exploration. Cause and effect are not immediately clear. It appeared that exploration seekers - less goal-oriented and more imaginative people - find themselves attracted to this kind of interaction.

Most people experienced *Compositish* (figure 5), *Jitterish* (figure 7) and *Mixish* (figure 10) clear and simple to operate, with appropriate tactile and kinaesthetic feedback. They were considered pleasurable with respect to interaction, functionality and appearance. Nevertheless, they scarcely challenged extensive interaction, due to their simple and functional character. This made them less resonant for the exploration seekers in contrast with the goal seekers.

ISH shows the importance of pursuing diversity within product interaction; not all people resonate to the same things. In future work we will expand *ISH* with respect to diversity, by incorporating others forms of modality, like speech (intonation, volume) and gestures, and add / alter products.

ISH also revealed a major drawback: it is predominantly suited for short-term interaction. The example of the Sunbeam toaster showed that time has an important impact on resonance. Therefore, we are pursuing several other projects next to *ISH* to gather knowledge about resonance. For example, *Coppia Espressiva* offers digital musical instruments to individuals to create their own music (Hummels et al., submitted). Another project expands the idea of creating an atmosphere, but this time at home. How can a person create an atmosphere at home (music, lighting etc.) that fits his mood, through resonant interaction with a product? Our goal is to design and build several versions of an atmosphere controller, which people can experience at home over a period of time.

As stated before, resonance is not an easy goal to achieve, but it is certainly worth pursuing. The HCI and design community can help each other designing, building and testing experiential prototypes. After all, the proof of the pudding is in the eating.

5. ACKNOWLEDGEMENTS

We thank Rob Luxen, Philip Ross, Frans Levering, Rudolf Wormgoor and Joep Frens for their effort to prototype *ISH*.

6. REFERENCES

Borgmann, A. (1987). *Technology and the character of contemporary life*. Chicago: University of Chicago Press.
Branzi, A. (1989). We are the primitives. In: V. Margolin (Ed.). *Design Discourse: History theory criticism*. Chicago: University of Chicago Press.
Buchanan (1998). Branzi's dilemma: Design in contemporary culture. *Design Issues*, Vol. 14(1), pp. 3-20.
Caenepeel, M. (2002). Summer issue: Technology on the right side of the brain. *I³ magazine*, Nr. 12, June 2002, pp. 1.
Dourish, P. (2001). *Where the action is: the foundations of embodied interaction*. Boston: MA: MIT Press.
Gaver, B. (2002). Designing for Homo Ludens. *I³ magazine*, Nr. 12, June 2002, pp. 2-6.
Gibson, J.J. (1979). *An ecological approach to visual perception*. London: Lawrence Erlbaum Associates (reprinted in 1986).
Hummels, C.C.M. (2000). *Gestural design tools: prototypes, experiments and scenarios*. Unpublished doctoral dissertation, Delft University of Technology, Delft, The Netherlands.
Hummels, C.C.M., Overbeeke, C.J. and Ross, P.R. (submitted). In search for resonant human computer interaction: building aesthetic installation. Submitted to *Interact 2003*.
Marzano (1996). Introduction. In: Philips. *Vision of the Future*. Bussum: V+K Publishing.
Michaels, C.F. and Carello, C. (1981). *Direct perception*. Englewood Cliffs: Prentice-Hall.
Norman, D. A. (2002). Emotion & design: Attractive things work better. *Interactions*, Vol. IX(4), pp. 36-42
Overbeeke, C.J., Djajadiningrat, J.P., Wensveen, S.A.G, and Hummels, C.C.M. (1999). Experiential and respectful. *Proceedings of the international conference Useful and Critical: the position of research and design*, September 9-11 1999, U.I.A.H.
Saul, J.R. (1997). *The unconscious civilization*. New York: The Free Press.

STEPHAN WENSVEEN AND KEES OVERBEEKE

CHAPTER 24

*FUN WITH YOUR ALARM CLOCK: DESIGNING FOR ENGAGING
EXPERIENCES THROUGH EMOTIONALLY RICH INTERACTION*

Figure 1. *From the edge of her bed Sophie throws her high heels in the corner of the
room. It has been her first week at her first real job and she's not used to wearing
them every day. She's also not used to working such long hours. Getting up at six
and not being home before eight, is not her thing. Like today, that annoying Phil guy
had her work till nine, on a Friday! And then that terrible train ride. Tonight she
can get some real sleep and lie in. She still sets her alarm clock, because tomorrow
she arranged to meet with her Mum. They'll go shopping in the spring sale. While
one finger is pressing down the button that reads 'alarm', another is pushing the
'hour' button three times and then the 'minute' button another 30 times. The display
reads 9:31; she shrugs, releases the 'alarm' button and flicks the tiny switch to 'on'.
"Who designs these dumb products?" she mutters…*

To strive for the incorporation of fun in product use is to design for engaging
experiences. In order to do this we should respect all human skills in human-product
interaction. So while most current electronic products appeal to cognitive skills, we
believe that a person's perceptual-motor and emotional skills should be taken into
account as well. One way of opening up such an experience is to allow people to use
their natural expressive powers by permitting them to use their perceptual-motor

Mark A. Blythe, Andrew F. Monk, Kees Overbeeke and Peter C. Wright *(eds.),*
Funology: From Usability to Enjoyment, 275—281.

skills. Most current products do not tap into these skills because their functionality is accessible in just one way, and often a very poor way indeed. For example, to set Sophie's alarm clock, you have to push a tiny button several times, while holding another tiny button. Why not go one step further and try to design products that can adapt to a person's emotions and feelings to enrich the experience? If Sophie were able to express her feelings to the product, it could read these feelings and consider them when reacting to her.

Figure 2. *The sunny Saturday morning is rudely disturbed by an annoying sound. Tuut...tuut...tuut...tuut...tuut...tu.. Sophie smacks the alarm. With her stretched out hand still resting on the alarm clock she tries to regain her consciousness. Through the slits in her eyes she sees sunlight, startled, she sits up straight, but then remembers it's only Saturday. She smiles, shakes her head thinking: "I hate these stupid products!"*

For many people waking up and getting out of bed is not the most pleasant experience. The accompanying product, the alarm clock doesn't really help. Yes, it does wake you up, when you have set it properly, but it doesn't adapt at all to different situations. It is a perfect example of a product that should adapt to the diversity of emotional experiences. It is also a product with a simple functionality yet it has all the features of the current interface malaise, like a lack of politeness and nonsensical buttons (Cooper, 1999). That is why we chose the alarm clock as a vehicle for our research through design approach. In our research towards designing emotionally intelligent products we advocate designs that both allow for the recognition and expression of emotion while avoiding anthropomorphic design (talking heads) and physiological sensors. This product design-driven approach takes the interaction with the product as the starting point for the detection of emotion.

Figure 3. *Sophie slams the door behind her and stumbles into the bedroom. While fidgeting with the strap of her high heels she falls on her bed. At the cocktail party celebrating Phil's farewell she had behaved like a fool. At first she had ignored him, giving him the cold shoulder. But after a few drinks she confronted him and tried to tell him what she really thought of him. Phil just gave her a blank look and that made her angrier. Luckily, a colleague saw her behaving badly and took her away from the party just in time. She gave Sophie a lift home. But tomorrow she has to take that terrible train again. With one hand she reaches for her alarm. It looks like a purple disc with slider knobs. Her dad gave it to her a few weeks ago after she had wrecked her old one hitting it too hard out of frustration.*

The mood or emotional state you are in colours the way you interact with the world. For human-human communication this expression of emotion is essential. People express emotion through behaviour. In human-product communication people express their emotion as well, e.g., by slamming a door, shoving a chair away, or encouraging the printer with 'come on you can do it!'. Yet this behaviour does not enhance communication between user and product at all. On the contrary, if we fully express our negative emotion we might break the product.

In our product design-driven approach we take the interaction with the product as the starting point for the detection of emotion. While you interact with the product to communicate 'factual' information like the alarm time, the product senses your emotions from the way you handle it.

To make this possible we designed an alarm clock that meets the following three conditions:
1. It elicits rich emotional behaviour while the user communicates 'factual' information.
2. It has the ability to recognise this emotional behaviour.
3. It reflects and understands the expressed emotion.

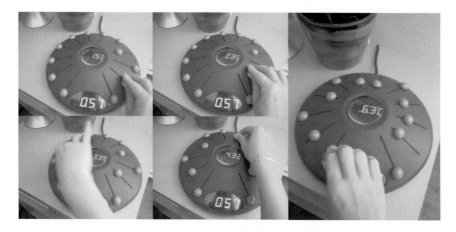

Figure 4. *She feels the round knobs and slides a couple of them towards the middle. At the party did she and Phil...? No?! She sits up and randomly starts to slide one or two sliders with each action. Using one hand she keeps sliding until she notices that the display shows 7:56. She pauses for a moment and thinks about tomorrow's 11 o'clock meeting with her new boss. She then slides the bottom two sliders all the way back to the outside. The display now shows 6:30. She waits and then firmly pushes the central button.*

Expressing emotions presupposes freedom of expression, and we therefore designed the alarm clock to allow for freedom in interaction. It offers a myriad of ways of setting the "factual" information i.e., the wake up time. People can choose to set it by displacing as many sliders as they can grasp or by sliding one slider at a time. This behavioural freedom affords emotions to influence and colour behaviour. The freedom of interaction is further enhanced by the fact that sliders can go back and forth. It stimulates playful interaction, as sliding actions are easily reversed and don't have serious consequences.

We demonstrated in an experiment the alarm clock's ability to recognise this behaviour and identify a person's mood from the interaction. We refer the interested reader to Wensveen, Overbeeke and Djajadiningrat (2002) as this goes beyond the scope of this chapter.

When expressing emotions it is important that the receiver gives some sort of feedback that the communication has succeeded. When Sophie expressed her feelings to Phil, his blank look only made her more angry. Just like people, products too should give some sort of reflection of the emotion, a sign of empathy, a sign of understanding. We therefore believe that different emotions should leave different behavioural traces on the product. A slap or a caress leaves a different trace on a face. Likewise, setting the time in a different mood leaves a different trace on the alarm clock. In our design the central display offers augmented feedback about the wake up time (factual information). But it is the successive patterns of the sliders that reflect the influence the emotion had on the setting behaviour leading to this wake up time. It is because of the richness of the inherent feedback that these traces can be perceived. Inherent feedback can be defined as "information provided as a natural consequence of making an action. It arises from the movement itself" (Laurillard, 1993).

Based on the interaction of setting the alarm in the late evening and the time-related aspects (alarm time, hours of sleep) the alarm clock makes a decision about what it believes is an appropriate sound. The next morning the alarm wakes you with this sound. The choice of this sound makes it clear that the alarm understood you. It shows its ability to adapt to the situation in an appropriate way.

Figure 5. *Rooooo… roo… Sophie hears the sound but it stopped before she realises what it is. She pulls the blanket a bit higher over her head. Roooo… rooo… roo… It seems to be more urgent this time. Rooo… roo… roo… By now she realises it's her alarm clock. She stretches her hand and touches the snooze button. The sound stops. When she looks at the alarm she sees the display showing 6:30. The pattern of sliders looks chaotic. She smiles, thinking that it looks a bit how it feels inside her head.*

It is important that the alarm clock knows the essential information, at what time you need to wake up. It is of less importance that the product exactly knows your emotions as long as you can teach the product how you function. In order for the product to learn about the decisions it took, whether they are appropriate or not, it needs feedback about these decisions. Again through a person's behaviour the product can receive this feedback by the way the snooze button is pressed by the user to turn off the alarm sound. The combination of the delay time (the time between starting and turning off the sound) and a person's behaviour of pressing or hitting the snooze button provides valuable information for the decision making system.

Next morning the inherent feedback in the form of the final slider pattern proves its importance again. Because the end pattern is still present and it is a reflection of last night's behaviour it provides feedback about the decision. It offers people the possibility of linking the alarm sound and the expression of the end pattern together.

This doesn't imply a one to one relationship between the expression of the sound and the expression of the end pattern. After all setting the alarm after a stressful night leading to a disorderly pattern should not result in a chaotic sounding alarm the next morning.

The slider pattern changes the appearance of the alarm clock and provides feedback for the user and insight into how decisions are made. Since it is the only perceivable change in the alarm clock it provides a reason for the user to believe there is causality between the slider pattern and the alarm sound.

Figure 6. Sophie draws the curtains from her balcony door. After she came home from work she drank some Italian rosé, watched the sunset and just enjoyed a warm autumn night. Setting her alarm she uses both hands and with gentle even actions makes a smooth and symmetrical pattern to set the alarm time to the usual 7:15.

The design of the alarm clock illustrates the importance of a tight coupling between action and appearance in interaction design. It distinguishes itself from current electronic products through traces and inherent feedback. Because of the inherent feedback the traces become visible, are made explicit for the user and guide her behaviour. For example, when using both hands on the sliders in an even and balanced way the resulting pattern is symmetrical and smooth. The way this pattern looks will push the user to either heighten the symmetry and smoothness or disrupt them depending on how she feels. Traces and inherent feedback thus work in synergy. Without inherent feedback using traces is meaningless, as the product cannot guide the user's behaviour: the trace is invisible and cannot invite the user to act in an emotionally rich manner. Next morning the inherent feedback also offers valuable information for the user and gives insight into the decision-making system of the alarm clock.

From our product design perspective, the appearance of interactive products can no longer be considered as arbitrary. Appearance and interaction need to be designed concurrently.

Figure 7. *Being a bit tipsy and feeling naughty she dents the smooth pattern with one swift move. The display shoots from 7:15 to 7:43. She adjusts one slider to set it to 7:25. "I wonder what that will do?"*

When you combine freedom of interaction, rich inherent feedback (slider patterns) loosely coupled with generated feedback (changing alarm sounds) and a system that tries to adapt to and can learn from specific situations you have a good recipe for an engaging experience. It invokes curiosity and playful interaction and maybe, maybe it offers us a recipe for having fun with our alarm clock too.

Twiiiiingwiiiiing... priit... twiiiiiiingwiiiiing ... priit... the soft sound reaches Sophie. When she hears the sound appear for a second time she gently strokes the snooze button. She pulls the blankets away, sits up straight and reaches for her alarm. She looks at the pattern while replaying the sound in her head. "Funny..." she thinks and pushes all the sliders to the outside to avoid the sound from playing again. "...at least we understand each other."
She steps over the empty bottle of rosé, giggles and walks to the shower.

REFERENCES

Cooper, A. (1999). *The inmates are running the asylum*. Indianapolis, SAMS McMillan.
Laurillard D. (1993*). Rethinking university teaching: A framework for the effective use of educational technology*. Routledge, London.
Wensveen, S.A.G., Overbeeke, C.J., & Djajadiningrat, J.P. (2002). Push me, shove me and I show you how you feel. Recognising mood from emotionally rich interaction. In: N. Macdonald (Ed.), *Proceedings of DIS2002,* London, 25-28 June 2002, pp. 335-340.

COMPILED BY HOKYOUNG RYU

INTEGRATED BIBLIOGRAPHY

This integrated bibliography is intended as a resource for the reader to find the more archival references from individual chapters. It includes journal papers, books and some of the more accessible conference proceedings. For urls and other sources the reader is referred to the reference section at the end of each individual chapter.

Adelsward, V., & Oberg, B. M. (1998). The function of laughter and joking in negotiation activities. *Humor-International Journal of Humor Research, 11*(4), 411-429.

Adorno, T., & Horkheimer, M. (1986). *Dialectic of Enlightenment*. London: Verso.

Agre, P. E. (1997). *Computation and Human Experience*. Cambridge: Cambridge University Press.

Alberg, C., & Shneiderman, B. (1994). Visual information seeking: tight coupling of dynamic query filters with starfield displays, pp. 313-317, *CHI '94 Proceedings*, Boston, Massachusetts.

Apter, M. J. (1989). *Reversal Theory: Motivation, Emotion and Personality*. London: Routledge.

Arnold, M. B. (1960). *Emotion and Personality: vol 1. Psychological Aspects*. New York: Colombia University Press.

Atkinson, J. M. (1982). Understanding formality: notes on the categorisation and production of 'Formal' interaction. *British Journal of Sociology, 33*, 86-117.

Attardo, S. (1993). Violation of conversational maxims and cooperation - the case of jokes. *Journal of Pragmatics, 19*(6), 537-558.

Bakhtin, M. M. (1981). *The Dialogic Imagination: Four Essays* (Emerson, C. Holquist, M., Trans.). Austin, TX: University of Texas Press.

Bakhtin, M. M. (1984). *Problems of Dostoevsky's Poetics* (Emerson, C., Trans.). Minneapolis: University of Minnesota Press.

Bakhtin, M. M. (1986). *Speech Genres and Other Late Essays*. Austin (McGee, V.W., Trans.). Austin, TX: University of Texas Press.

Bakhtin, M. M. (1993). *Toward a Philosophy of the Act*. Austin, TX: University of Texas Press.

Bandura, A. (1997). *Self-Efficacy: The Exercise of Control*. New York: W.H. Freeman.

Bates, J. (1992). Virtual reality, art, & entertainment. *Presence: Teleoperators and Virtual Environments, 1*(1), 133-138.

Bateson, G. (Ed.). (1972). *Steps To an Ecology of Mind*. New York: Ballantine Books.

Beach, W. A. (1990). Language as and in technology: facilitating topic organization in videotex focus group meeting. In M. J. Medhurst, A. Gonzalez, & T. R. Peterson (Eds.), *Communication and the Culture of Technology*. Pullman: Washington State University Press.

Bennett, J. (2001). *The Enchantment of Modern Life: Attachments, Crossings, and Ethics*. Princeton: Princeton University Press.

Bernson, P. J., & Perrett, D. I. (1991). Perception and recognition of photographic quality facial caricatures: implications for the recognition of natural images. *European Journal of Cognitive Psychology, 3*, 105-135.

Bickmore, T., & Cassell, J. (2001). Relational agents: a model and implementation of building user trust, pp. 396-403, *CHI 2001 Proceedings*, Seattle, WA.

Bolter, J. D., & Grusin, R. (2001). *Remediation: Understanding New Media*. Cambridge, MA: MIT Press.

Boorstin. (1995). *Making Movies Work: Thinking Like a Filmmaker*. Beverley Hills: Silman-James Press.

Borgmann, A. (1984). *Technology and the Character of Contemporary Life*. Chicago: University of Chicago Press.

Branzi, A. (1989). We are the primitives. In V. Margolin (Ed.), *Design Discourse: History, Theory, Criticism*. Chicago: University of Chicago Press.

Bruner, J. S. (1976). Nature and uses of immaturity. In J. S. Bruner, A. Jolly, & K. Sylva (Eds.), *Play: Its Role in Development and Evolution*. New York: Penguin books.

Bruner, J. S. (1996). *The Culture of Education*. Cambridge, MA: Harvard University Press.

Buchanan, R. (1998). Branzi's dilemma: design in contemporary culture. *Design Issues, 14*(1), 3-20.

Buchenau, M., & Fulton, J. (2000). Experience prototyping, pp. 424-433, *DIS 2000 Proceedings*, New York, NY.

Cacioppo, J. T., Berntson, G. G., Larsen, J. T., Poehlmann, K. M., & Ito, T. A. (2001). The psychophysiology of emotion. In M. L. J. M. Haviland-Jones (Ed.), *Handbook of Emotions* (Second ed.). New York: The Guilford Press.

Caillois, R. (1958). *Man, Play and Games*. Chicago: University of Illinois Press.

Calder, A. J., Young, A. W., Rowland, D., & Perrett, D. I. (1992). Micro-expressive facial actions as a function of affective stimuli: replication and extension. *Personality and Social Psychology Bulletin, 18*, 515-526.

Cann, A., Calhoun, L. G., & Banks, J. S. (1997). On the role of humor appreciation in interpersonal attraction: It's no joking matter. *Humor-International Journal of Humor Research, 10*(1), 77-89.

Card, S., Mackinlay, J., & Schneiderman, B. (1999). *Readings in Information Visualization Using Vision to Think*. San Francisco, California: Morgan Kaufmann Publishers.

Carroll, J. M., & Rosson, M. B. (2001). Better home shopping or new democracy? Evaluating community network outcomes, pp. 372-379, *CHI 2001 Proceedings*, Seattle, WA.

Carroll, J. M., & Thomas, J. C. (1988). Fun. *SIGCHI Bulletin, 19,* 21-24.

Cartwright, D., & Zander, A. (1960). *Group Dynamics. Research and Theory.* (Second ed.). Evamstone: Row, Peterson and Company.

Cassell, J., Bickmore, T. W., Billinghurst, M., Campbell, L., Chang, K., Vilhjalmsson, H., & Yan, H. (1999). Embodiment in conversational interfaces: Rea, pp. 520-527, *CHI '99 Proceedings*, Pittsburgh, Pennsylvania.

Channel, J. (1997). "I Just Called to Say I Love You": love and desire on the telephone. In K. Harvey & C. Shalom (Eds.), *Language and Desire*. London: Routledge.

Cheek, N. H., & Burch, W. R. (1976). *The Social Organization of Leisure in Human Society*. New York: Harper and Row.

Choi, D., Kim, H., & Kim, J. (1999). Toward the construction of fun computer games: differences in the views of developers and players. *Personal Technologies, 3*, 92-104.

Cohill, A. M., & Kavanaugh, A. L. (1997). *Community Networks: Lessons from Blacksburg, Virginia*. London: Artech House.

Cole, J. I. (2000). *Surveying the Digital Future*. Los Angeles, California: UCLA Center for Communication Policy.

Coleridge, S. T. (1817). *Biographia Literaria; or Biographical Sketches of my Literary Life and Opinions*. London: Rest Fenner.

Consalvo, C. M. (1989). Humor in management: no laughing matter. *Journal of Humor Research, 2*(3), 285-297.

Cooper, A. (1999). *The Inmates are Running the Asylum*. Indianapolis: Sams, McMillan.

Csikszentimihalyi, M. (1990). *Flow: The Psychology of Optimal Experience*. New York: Harper and Row.

Csikszentmihalyi, M. (1975). *Beyond Boredom and Anxiety: The Experience of Work and Play in Games*. San Fancisco: Jossey Bass Publishers.

Csikszentmihalyi, M. (1992). *Flow. The Psychology of Happiness*. London: Rider.

Davenport, G., Holmquist, L. E., Thomas, M., Bjork, S., Tallyn, E., Oldroyd, A., de Boer, P., Axelsson, A. S., Schroeder, E., Ljungberg, F., Gater, H., Hebert, C., Persson, P., Renstrom, J., Stintzing, L., Watson, T., Olsson, A., Beckestrom, B., Lindblom, A., Schroeder, R., Simon, K., Truve, S., Wistrand, E., Nitsche, M., Binsted, K., Rodatz, C., Thuresson, B., Walldius, A., Rankin, P., Rinman, M. L., Dormann, C., Hales, C., & Helander, M. (1998). Fun: a condition of creative research. *IEEE Multimedia, 5*(3), 10-15.

Davis, F. D., Bagozzi, R. P., & Warshaw, P. R. (1992). Extrinsic and intrinsic motivation to use computers in the workplace. *Journal of Applied Social Psychology, 22*(14), 1111-1132.

Davis, M. (1995). *Media Streams: Representing Video for Retrieval and Repurposing*. Cambridge, MA: MIT Press.

Davis, M. (1997). Garage Cinema and the Future of Media Technology. *Communications of the ACM, 40,* 42-48.

Debord, G. (1995). *The Society of the Spectacle*. New York: Zone Books.

December, J. (1996). Units of analysis for Internet communication. *Journal of Communication, 46*(1), 14-38.

DeCerteau, M. (1984). *The Practice of Everyday Life*. Berkeley, CA: University of California Press.

Deckers, L. (1993). On the validity of a weight-judging paradigm for the study of humor. *Humor-International Journal of Humor Research, 6*(1), 43-56.

Degen, H. (2000). Performance model for market-oriented design of software products. *International Journal of Human-Computer Interaction, 12*(3-4), 285-307

Desmet, P. M. A., & Hekkert, P. (1998). Emotional reactions elicited by car design: a measurement tool for designers. In D. Roller (Ed.), *Automotive Mechatronics Design and Engineering* (pp. 237-244). Dusseldorf, Germany: ISATA.

Desmet, P. M. A., & Hekkert, P. (2002). The basis of product emotions. In W. Green & P. Jordan (Eds.), *Pleasure with Products: Beyond Usability*. London: Taylor & Francis.

Desmet, P. M. A., Hekkert, P., & Jacobs, J. J. (2000). When a car makes you smile: development and application of an instrument to measure product emotions. In S. J. Hoch & R. J. Meyer (Eds.), *Advances in Consumer Research* (pp. 111-117). Provo, UT: Association for Consumer Research.

Desmet, P. M. A., Overbeeke, C. J., & Tax, S. J. E. T. (2001). Designing products with added emotional value; development and application of an approach for research through design. *The Design Journal, 4*(1), 32-47.

Dewey, J. (1925). *Experience and Nature*. LaSalle, Illinois: Open Court.

Dewey, J. (1934). *Art as Experience*. New York: Perigree.

Djajadiningrat, J. P., Gaver, W. W., & Frens, J. W. (2000). Interaction relabelling and extreme characters: methods for exploring aesthetic interactions, pp. 66-71, *DIS 2000 Proceedings*, New York, NY.

Djajadiningrat, J. P., Overbeeke, C. J., & Wensveen, S. A. G. (2002). But how, Donald, tell us *how?*, pp. 285-291, *DIS 2002 Proceedings*, London.

Dourish, P. (2001). *Where the Action is: The Foundations of Embodied Interaction*. Cambridge, MA: MIT Press.

Draper, S. W. (1999). Analysing fun as a candidate software requirement. *Personal Technologies, 3*, 117-122.

Drew, P. (1987). Po-faced receipts of teases. *Linguistics, 25*, 219-253.

Dreyfus, H. L., S.E., D., & Athanasiou. (1986). *Mind over Machine : The Power of Human Intuition and Expertise in the Era of the Computer*. Oxford: Basil Blackwell.

Druin, A. (2002). The role of children in the design of new technology. *Behaviour & Information Technology, 21*(1), 1-25.

Dunne, A. (1999). *Hertzian Tales: Electronic Products, Aesthetic Experience and Critical Design*. London: RCA CRD Research publications.

Ehn, P. (1998). Manifesto for a digital Bauhaus. *Digital Creativity, 9*(4), 207-216.

Ehn, P., & Lowgren, J. (1997). Design for quality-in-use: human-computer interaction meets information systems development. In M. Helander, T. K. Landauer, & P. Prabhu (Eds.), *Handbook of Human-Computer Interaction* (Second ed., pp. 299-313). Amsterdam, NL: Elsevier Science.

Ekman, P. (1985). *Telling Lies*. New York: Norton.

Ekman, P. (1993). Facial expression and emotion. *American Psychologist, 48*(4), 384-392.

Ekman, P. (1994). Strong evidence for universals in facial expressions: a reply to Russell's mistaken critique. *Psychological Bulletin, 115*(2), 268-287.

Ekman, P., & Friesen, W. V. (1975). *Unmasking the Face: A Guide to Recognizing Emotions from Facial Cues.* Englewood Cliffs, NJ: Prentice-Hall.

Ekman, P., & Friesen, W. V. (1978). *Facial Action Coding System: A Technique for the Measurement of Facial Movement.* Palo Alto, CA: Consulting Psychologists Press.

Ellis, J. B., & Bruckman, A. S. (2001). Designing palaver tree online: supporting social roles in a community of oral history, pp. 474-481, *CHI 2001 Proceedings,* Seattle, WA.

Etcoff, N. L., & Magee, J. J. (1992). Categorical perception of facial expressions. *Cognition, 44*(3), 227-240.

Fisher, P. (1998). *Wonder, the Rainbow, and the Aesthetics of Rare Experiences.* Boston, MA: Harvard University Press.

Frank, M. G., & Ekman, P. (1993). Not all smiles are created equal - the differences between enjoyment and nonenjoyment smiles. *Humor-International Journal of Humor Research, 6*(1), 9-26.

Freud, S. (1960). *Jokes and Their Relations to the Unconscious.* London: Routledge & Kegan Paul.

Friedman, B. (Ed.). (1997). *Human Values and the Design of Computer Technology.* Cambridge: Cambridge University Press.

Frijda, N. H. (1986). *The Emotions.* Cambridge: Cambridge University Press.

Fry, P. S. (1995). Perfectionism, humor, and optimism as moderators of health outcomes and determinants of coping styles of women executives. *Genetic Social and General Psychology Monographs, 121*(2), 211-245.

Gaver, B. (2002). Designing for homo ludens. *I3 magazine, 12,* 2-6.

Gaver, B., Dunne, T., & Pacenti, E. (1999). Cultural probes. *Interactions, 6,* 21-29.

Gaver, B., & Heather, M. (2000). Alternatives: exploring information appliances through conceptual design proposals, pp. 209-216, *CHI 2000 Proceedings,* The Hague, The Netherlands.

Geirland, J., & Sonesh-Kedar, E. (1999). *Digital Babylon: How the Geeks, the Suits, and the Ponytails Tried to Bring Hollywood to the Internet.* New York: Arcade Publishing.

Gell, A. (1992). The technology of enchantment and the enchantment of technology. In J. Coote & A. Shelton (Eds.), *Anthropology, Art, and Aesthetics* (pp. 40-63). Oxford: Clarendon Press.

Gentner, D., & Nielsen, J. (1996). The anti-Mac interface. *Communications of the ACM, 39,* 70-82.

Gibson, J. J. (1986). *The ecological approach to visual perception.* Hillsdale, NJ: Lawrence Erlbaum.

Glass, B. (1997). Swept away in a sea of evolution: new challenges and opportunities for usability professionals. In R. Liskowsky, B. M. Velichkovsky, & W. Wunschmann (Eds.), *Software-Ergonomie '97. Usability Engineering:*

Integration von Mensch-Computer-Interaktion und Software-Entwicklung (pp. 17-26). Stuttgart: B.G. Teubner.

Glenn, P. J., & Knapp, M. L. (1987). The interactive framing of play in adult conversation. *Communication Quarterly, 35*, 48-66.

Goffman, E. (1972). *Encounters: Two Studies in the Sociology of Interaction.* Harmondsworth: Penguin.

Goffman, E. (1974). *Frame Analysis: An Essay on the Organization of Experience.* Boston, MA: Northeastern University Press.

Gooding, M. (Ed.). (1995). *A Book of Surrealist Games.* Boston, MA: Shambhala Redstone Editions.

Gray, J. (1971). *Psychology of Fear and Stress.* London: Weidenfeld & Nicolson.

Hampes, W. P. (1999). The relationship between humor and trust. *Humor-International Journal of Humor Research, 12*(3), 253-259.

Harris, M. D. (1985). *Introduction to Natural Language Processing.* Reston, VA: Reston Publishing Co. Inc.

Hassenzahl, M. (2001). The effect of perceived hedonic quality on product appealingness. *International Journal of Human-Computer Interaction, 13*(4), 481-499.

Hassenzahl, M. (2002). Character grid: a simple repertory grid technique for web site analysis and evaluation. In J. Ratner (Ed.), *Human Factors and Web Development.* Mahwah, NJ: Lawrence Erlbaum.

Hassenzhal, M., Platz, A., Burmester, M., & Lehner, K. (2000). Hedonic and ergonomic quality aspects determine a software's appeal, pp. 201-208, *CHI 2000 Proceedings*, The Hague, The Netherlands.

Hay, J. (2001). The pragmatics of humor support. *Humor-International Journal of Humor Research, 14*(1), 55-82.

Hogg, M., & Abrams, D. (1993). Towards a single-process uncertainty-reduction model of social motivation in groups. In M. Hogg & D. Abrams (Eds.), *Group Motivation: Social Psychological Perspectives.* New York: Harvester Wheatsheaf.

Hopper, R. (1992). *Telephone Conversation.* Bloomington; Indianapolis: Indiana University Press.

Huizinga, J. (1950). *Homo Ludens: A Study of the Play Element in Culture.* Boston, MA: The Beacon Press.

Igbaria, M., Schiffman, S. J., & Wieckowski, T. J. (1994). The respective roles of perceived usefulness and perceived fun in the acceptance of microcomputer technology. *Behaviour & Information Technology, 13*(6), 349-361.

Izard, C. E. (1979). *The Maximally Discriminative Facial Movement Coding System (MAX).* Newark: Instructional Recourses Centre, University of Delaware.

Jackson, P. (1998). *John Dewey and the Lessons of Art.* New Haven, London: Yale University Press.

Jacques, R., Preece, J., & Carey, T. (1995). Engagement as a design concept for multimedia. *Canadian Journal of Educational Communication, 24*(1), 49-59.

Janlert, L. E., & Stolterman, E. (1997). The character of things. *Design Studies, 18*, 297-314.

Janson, H. W. (1977). *A History of Art: A Survey of the Visual Arts from the Dawn of History to the Present Day*. London: Thames and Hudson.

Jenkins, H. (1992). *Textual Poachers: Television Fans & Participatory Culture*. New York: Routledge.

Jensen, R. (1999). *Dream Society. The Coming Shift from Information to Imagination*. London: McGraw-Hill Book Company.

Johnstone, T., & Scherer, K. R. (2001). Vocal communication of emotion. In M. L. J. M. Haviland-Jones (Ed.), *Handbook of Emotions* (Second ed., pp. 220-235). New York: The Guilford Press.

Jordan, P. (2000). *Designing Pleasurable Products: An Introduction to the New Human Factors*. London: Taylor and Francis.

Kahneman, D. (1999). Objective happiness. In D. Kahneman, E. Diener, & N. Schwarz (Eds.), *Well-being: The Foundations of Hedonic Quality* (pp. 3-25). New York: Sage.

Kaplan, S. (1987). Aesthetics, affect, and cognition-environmental preference from an evolutionary perspective. *Environment and Behavior, 19*(1), 3-32.

Kappas, A., Hess, U., & Scherer, K. R. (1991). Voice and emotion. In R. S. Feldman & R. Bernard (Eds.), *Fundamentals of Nonverbal Behavior* (pp. 200-237). Cambridge: Cambridge University Press.

Karasek, R. (1979). Job demands, job decision latitude, and mental strain: Implications for job redesign. *Administrative Science Quarterly, 24*, 258-307.

Karasek, R., & Theorell, T. (1990). *Healthy Work: Stress, Productivity, and the Reconstruction of Working Life*. New York: Basic books.

Klein, J., Moon, Y., & Picard, R. W. (2002). This computer responds to user frustration: theory, design, and results. *Interacting With Computers, 14*(2), 119-140.

Klein, M. (2000). *No Logo, No Space, No Choice, No Jobs, Taking Aim at the Brand Bullies*. London: Flamingo.

Lang, P. J. (1985). *The Cognitive Psychophysiology of Emotion: Anxiety and the Anxiety Disorders*. Hillsdale, NJ: Lawrence Erlbaum.

Laurel, B. (1993). *Computer as Theatre*. Reading, MA: Addison-Wesley.

Laurel, B., Bates, J., Strickland, R., & Abbe, D. (1991). Interface and narrative arts: contributions from narrative, drama and film, pp. 381-383, *CHI '91 Proceedings*, New Orleans, Louisiana.

Laurillard, D. (1993). *Rethinking University Teaching: A Framework for the Effective Use of Educational Technology*. London: Routledge.

Lee, J., Kim, J., & Moon, J. Y. (2000). What makes internet users visit cyber stores again? key design factors for customer loyalty, pp. 305-312, *CHI 2000 Proceedings*, The Hague, The Netherlands.

Lemert, C., & Branaman, A. (1997). *The Goffman Reader*. Oxford, UK: Blackwell Publishers Ltd.

L'Engle, M. (1980). *Walking on Water*. Tring, U.K: Lion Publishing.

Lester, J. C., Converse, S. A., Kahler, S. E., Barlowe, S. T., Stone, B. A., & Bhogal, R. (1997). The persona effect: affective impact of animated pedagogical agents, pp. 359-366, *CHI '97 Proceedings*, Atlanta, Georgia.

Logan, R. J. (1994). Behavioral and emotional usability: Thomson consumer electronics. In M. Wiklund (Ed.), *Usability in Practice*. Cambridge, MA: Academic Press.

Mackenzie, C. (1997). Where are the motives? a problem with evidence in the work of Richard Thaler. *Journal of Economic Psychology, 18*, 123-135.

Makela, A., & Battarbee. (1999). It's fun to do things together: two cases of explorative user studies. *Personal Technologies, 3*, 137-140.

Makela, A., Giller, V., Tscheligi, V., & Sefelin, R. (2000). Joking, storytelling, artsharing, expressing affection: a field trial of how children and their social network communicate with digital images in leisure time, pp. 548-555, *CHI 2000 Proceedings*, The Hague, The Netherlands.

Malone, T. W. (1984). Heuristics for designing enjoyable user interfaces: lessons from computer games. In J. C. Thomas & M. L. Schneider (Eds.), *Human Factors in Computer Systems* (pp. 1-12). Norwood, NJ: Ablex.

Manning, P. (1992). *Erving Goffman and Modern Sociology*. Cambridge: Polity Press.

Michaels, C. F., & Carello, C. (1981). *Direct Perception*. Englewood Cliffs, NJ: Prentice-Hall.

Monk, A. F. (2000). User-centred design: the home use challenge. In A. Sloane & F. van Rijn (Eds.), *Home Informatics and Telematics: Information Technology and Society* (pp. 181-190). Boston, MA: Kluwer Academic Publishers.

Monk, A. F., Hassenzahl, M., Blythe, M., & Reed, D. (2002). Funology: designing enjoyment, pp. 924-925, *CHI 2002 Extended Abstracts*, Minneapolis, MN.

Mono, R. W. (1997). *Design for Product Understanding: The Aesthetics of Design from a Semiotic Approach*. Stockholm: Liber AB.

Murray, J. H. (1997). *Hamlet on the Holodeck: The Future of Narrative in Cyberspace*. New York, NY: The Free Press.

Nielsen, J. (1993). *Usability Engineering*. New York: Morgan.

Norman, D. A. (1998). *The Invisible Computer*. Cambridge, MA: MIT Press.

Ortony, A., Clore, G. L., & Collins, A. (1988). *The Cognitive Structure of Emotions*. Cambridge: Cambridge University Press.

Pagulayan, R. J., Keeker, K., Wixon, D., Romero, R. L., & Fuller, T. (2003). User-centered design in games. In J. Jacko & A. Sears (Eds.), *The Human-Computer Interaction Handbook: Fundamentals, Evolving Technologies and Emerging Applications* (pp. 883-906). Mahwah, NJ: Lawrence Erlbaum Associates.

Penny, S. (2000). Agents as artworks and agent design as artistic practice. In K. Dautenhahn (Ed.), *Human Cognition and Social Agent Technology*. Amsterdam: John Benjamins.

Peppers, D., & Rogers, M. (1993). *The One to One Future: Building Relationships One Customer at a Time*. New York: Currency/Doubleday.

Picard, R. W., & Klein, J. (2002). Computers that recognise and respond to user emotion: theoretical and practical implications. *Interacting With Computers, 14*(2), 141-169.

Prentice, D. A. (1987). Psychological correspondence of possessions, attitudes, and values. *Journal of Personality and Social Psychology, 53*(6), 993-1003.

Prigogine, I., & Stengers, I. (1984). *Order Out of Chaos*. London: Flamingo.

Pu, P., & Faltings, B. (2000). Enriching buyers' experiences: the smartclient approach, pp. 289-296, *CHI 2000 Proceedings*, The Hague, The Netherlands.

Putnam, R. (2000). *Bowling alone: The collapse and revival of American community*. New York: Simon & Schuster.

Rader, C., Brand, C., & Lewis, C. (1997). Degree of comprehension: Children understanding visual programming environment, pp. 351-358, *CHI '97 Proceedings*, Atlanta, Georgia.

Reeves, B., & Nass, C. (1996). *The Media Equation: How People Treat Computers, Televisions and New Media Like Real People and Places*. Cambridge: Cambridge University Press.

Roijec, C. (1985). *Capitalism and Leisure Theory*. London: Tavistock.

Rosson, M. B., Carroll, J. M., Seals, C. D., & Lewis, T. L. (2002). Community design of community simulations, pp. 74-83, *DIS 2002 Proceedings*, London.

Rozin, P. (1999). Preadaption and the puzzles and properties of pleasure. In D. Kahneman, E. Diener, & N. Schwarz (Eds.), *Well-being: The Foundations of Hedonic Psychology* (pp. 109-133). New York: Russell Sage Foundation.

Ruch, W. (1994). Extroversion, alcohol, and enjoyment. *Personality and Individual Differences, 16*(1), 89-102.

Ruch, W., & Ekman, P. (2001). The expressive pattern of laughter. In A. W. Kaszniak (Ed.), *Emotion, Qualia, and Consciousness* (pp. 426-443). Tokyo: Word Scientific Publisher.

Russell, J. A. (1980). A circumplex model of affect. *Journal of Personality and Social Psychology, 39*, 1161-1178.

Russell, R. E. (2000). Humor's close relatives. *Humor-International Journal of Humor Research, 13*(2), 219-233.

Rutter, J. (2000). The stand-up introduction sequence: comparing comedy comperes. *Journal of Pragmatics, 32*(4), 463-483.

Sacks, H. (1974). The analysis of the course of a joke's telling in conversation. In R. Bauman & J. Sherzer (Eds.), *Explorations in the Ethnography of Speaking* (pp. 337-353). Cambridge: Cambridge University Press.

Sacks, H. (1995). *Lectures on Conversation. Volume 1&2*. Cambridge, MA: Blackwell.

Sandweg, N., Hassenzahl, M., & Kuhn, K. (2000). Designing a telephone-based interface for a home automation system. *International Journal of Human-Computer Interaction, 12*(3-4), 401-414.

Saul, J. R. (1997). *The Unconscious Civilization*. New York: The Free Press.

Schachter, S., & Singer, J. (1962). Cognitive, social and physiological determinants of emotional state. *Psychological Review, 63*, 379-399.

Schmitt, B. H. (1999). *Experiential Marketing*. New York: The Free Press.

Schwartz, S. H., & Bilsky, W. (1987). Toward a Universal Psychological Structure of Human-Values. *Journal of Personality and Social Psychology, 53*(3), 550-562.

Schwartzman, H. (1978). *Transformations: The Anthropology of Children's Play*. New York: Plenum.

Seifert, K., Baumgarten, T., Kuhnt, T., & Hassenzahl, M. (2001). Multimodale mensch-computer-interaktion: tool oder gimmick? In K.-P. Timpe, R. Marzi, V.

Karavezyris, & H.-H. Erbe (Eds.), *Bedienen und Verstehen. 4. Berliner Werkstatt Mensch-Maschine Systeme* (pp. 275-291). Dusseldorf: VDI-Verlag.

Self, W. (1994). *My idea of fun.* London: Penguin books.

Seligman, M. E. P., & Csikszentmihalyi, M. (2000). Positive psychology: an introduction. *American Psychologist, 55,* 5-14.

Shneiderman, B. (1987). *Designing the User Interface: Strategies for Effective Human-Computer Interaction.* Reading, MA: Addison-Wesley.

Skynner, R., & Cleese, J. (1993). *Life And How To Survive It.* London: Methuen.

Slater, D. (1998). Work/leisure. In C. Jenks (Ed.), *Core Sociological Dichotomies* (pp. 391-404). London: Sage Publications Ltd.

Smith, D. C., & A., C. (1999). Making programming easier for children. In A. Druin (Ed.), *The Design of Children's Technology* (pp. 201-222). San Francisco: Morgan Kaufmann.

Solso, R. (1999). *Cognition and the Visual Arts.* Cambridge, MA: MIT Press.

Sonnentag, S. (1996). Work group factors and individual well-being. In M. A. West (Ed.), *Handbook of Work Group Psychology* (pp. 345-367). Chichester: John Wiley & Sons.

Springel, S. (1999). The new media paradigm: users as creators of content. *Personal Technologies, 3,* 153-159.

Stephenson, W. (1967). *The Play Theory of Mass Communication.* New Brunswick, NJ: Transaction Publishers.

Stone, M., Fishkin, K., & Bier, E. (1994). The movable filter as a user interface tool, pp. 306-312, *CHI '94 Proceedings,* Boston, Massachusetts.

Strasser, S. (1982). *Never Done: A History of American Housework.* New York: Pantheon Books.

Sutton-Smith, B. (1988). Introduction to the transaction edition. In W. Stephenson (Ed.), *The Play Theory of Mass Communication.* New Brunswick, NJ: Transaction Publisher.

Taylor, A., & Harper, R. (2002). Age-old Practices in the 'New World': a study of gift-giving between teenage mobile phone users, pp. 439-446, *CHI 2002 Proceedings,* Minneapolis, MN.

Thackara, J. (2000). Edge effect: the design challenge of pervasive interface, *CHI 2000 Plenary presentation,* Seattle, WA.

Thompson, E. P. (1963). *The Making Of The English Working Class.* London: Gollancz.

Tractinsky, N., Katz, A. S., & Ikar, D. (2000). What is beautiful is usable. *Interacting With Computers, 13*(2), 127-145.

Tufte, E. R. (1984). *The Visual Display of Quantitative Information.* Chesire, Conneticut: Graphics Press.

Turkle, S. (1995). *Life on the Screen: Identity in the Age of the Internet.* London: Phoenix.

Veatch, T. C. (1998). A theory of humor. *Humor-International Journal of Humor Research, 11*(2), 161-215.

Viegas, A., & Donath, C. (1999). Chat circles, pp. 306-312, *CHI '99 Proceedings,* Pittsburgh, Pennsylvania.

Vogel, H. L. (1998). *Entertainment Industry Economics*. (Fourth ed.). Cambridge: Cambridge University Press.

Vygotsky, L. S. (1998). Imagination and creativity in childhood. In R. W. Rieber (Ed.), *The Collected Works of L.S. Vygotsky*. New York: Plenum.

Webster, J., & Ho, H. (1997). Audience engagement in multimedia presentations. *Data Base For Advances in Information Systems, 28*(2), 63-77.

Wensveen, S. A. G., Overbeeke, C. J., & Djajadiningrat, J. P. (2002). Push me, shove me and I show you how you feel: recognising mood from emotionally rich interaction, pp. 335-340, *DIS 2002 Proceedings*, London.

Williams, R. (1998). Erving Goffman. In R. Stones (Ed.), *Key Sociological Thinkers* (pp. 151-162). London: Macmillan Press Ltd.

Willis, P. (1990). *Common Culture*: Open University Press.

Willis, P. (2000). *The Ethnographic Imagination*. Cambridge: Polity Press.

Wilson, S. (2002). *Information Arts: Intersections of Art, Science and Technology*. Cambridge, MA: MIT Press.

Winograd, T. (1986). *Understanding Computers and Cognition*. Norwood, NJ: Ablex.

Winograd, T. (1996). *Bringing Design to Software*. New York, NY: Addison-Wesley.

Zajonc, R. B. (1965). Social facilitation. *Science, 149*, 269-274.

Ziv, A. (1988). Teaching and learning with humor: experiment and replication. *Journal of Experimental Education, 57*(1), 5-15.

Zizek, S. (1999). The fantasy in cyberspace. In E. Wright (Ed.), *The Zizek Reader*. Oxford: Blackwell.

Zsambok, C. E. (1997). Naturalistic decision making: where are we now? In C. E. Zsambok & G. Klein (Eds.), *Naturalistic Decision Making*. Mahwah, NJ: Lawrence Erlbaum.

Human Computer Interaction Series

KLUWER ACADEMIC PUBLISHERS – DORDRECHT / BOSTON / LONDON